Courts and Criminal Justice in Contemporary China

Courts and Criminal Justice in Contemporary China

Susan Trevaskes

LEXINGTON BOOKS

A division of
ROWMAN & LITTLEFIELD PUBLISHERS, INC.
Lanham • Boulder • New York • Toronto • Plymouth, UK

LEXINGTON BOOKS

A division of Rowman & Littlefield Publishers, Inc.
A wholly owned subsidiary of The Rowman & Littlefield Publishing Group, Inc.
4501 Forbes Boulevard, Suite 200
Lanham, MD 20706

Estover Road
Plymouth PL6 7PY
United Kingdom

British Library Cataloguing in Publication Information Available

Library of Congress Cataloging-in-Publication Data

Trevaskes, Susan, 1964–
Courts and criminal justice in contemporary China / Susan Trevaskes.
p. cm.
Includes bibliographical references and index.
ISBN-13: 978-0-7391-1987-7 (cloth : alk. paper)
ISBN-10: 0-7391-1987-7 (cloth : alk. paper)
ISBN-13: 978-0-7391-1988-4 (pbk. : alk. paper)
ISBN-10: 0-7391-1988-5 (pbk. : alk. paper)
1. Criminal procedure—China. 2. Criminal justice, Administration of—China. I. Title.
KNQ4610.T74 2007
345.51'05—dc22 2007009274

Printed in the United States of America

™ The paper used in this publication meets the minimum requirements of American National Standard for Information Sciences—Permanence of Paper for Printed Library Materials, ANSI/NISO Z39.48–1992.

To Rosemary, Graham, Sang Ye, and Shen Yi.

Contents

Tables

Acknowledgements

This book has only been made possible with the support and generosity of my colleagues, friends and family. I owe a great debt to my colleagues Borge Bakken, Michael Dutton, Mary Farquhar, Nick Knight, Mark Finnane, and Maureen Todhunter, for their generous counsel. Their expertise was very much appreciated and their advice and comments on the drafts of this book were invaluable. Thank you to the Australian Research Council for funding part of this project and to the Griffith Asia Institute for providing editorial and travel assistance.

I would also like to express my sincere gratitude to former Baotou Court President Yun Guangqing for allowing me to visit the Baotou courts. I would especially like to thank judges at the Baotou Intermediate Court Office of Research and the Qingshan Basic Court for allowing me to interview them, for giving me the opportunity to observe everyday court life, and for the information I requested. I would also like to express my gratitude to former Beijing Intermediate Court President Ji Shuhan and his staff for allowing me to observe criminal trials. Thanks also to Wei Jianming, Zhao Ming, and Li Yuanzheng.

Finally, I would like to express my deep appreciation to my husband, daughter, mother, and father. Thank you Sang Ye for your intellectual support and advice, and for your help with translating strange names and places. Thank you Shen Yi for putting up with parents like us. Thank you Rosemary and Graham Trevaskes for all your loving kindness and for your proofreading assistance with the Baotou translations.

Introduction

More people are executed in China each year than in all other states in the world combined. China's execution rate increases dramatically during anti-crime campaigns. There have been three main "Strike Hard" (Yanda) campaigns since 1983. Three of Amnesty International's annual China reports for the first four years of the new millennium highlighted as central to their human rights concerns the Yanda anti-crime campaign conducted from April 2001 to April 2003. In the first three months of this campaign alone, from April to July, over three thousand criminals were sentenced to death.[1] Yanda was originally employed in the immediate post-Mao period in 1981 as a policy to deal with emerging social order crimes, particularly crimes committed by juveniles and "hooligans" (*liumang*), and in 1983, Yanda developed into a full-blown anti-crime campaign that lasted for three years. Murray Scot Tanner described the 1983 Yanda campaign as the "bloodiest chapter in post-Mao Chinese politics."[2] Some reports put the national figure of people sentenced to death over the three years at over thirty thousand (including those sentenced to death with a two-year reprieve).[3] Far from meeting the initial aims of the campaign—creating the conditions necessary for social stability and economic prosperity—the end results of the campaign created what Borge Bakken describes as a "brutalizing effect" in society. Here was a post-Cultural Revolution society where criminals were far more willing to use violence and revenge than ever before, partly in response to rampant state use of the death penalty.[4] While scholars in the field of Chinese law acknowledge accomplishments in civil and economic law over the last twenty years, it is widely accepted that the authorities have failed to deliver the promises of modernization and reformation to the criminal justice system.

This book is about two interrelated manifestations of judicial power in the People's Republic of China (PRC): law and order campaigns, and expressive punishment. It examines today's court practices and their antecedents in China by exploring "law on display" in local court trials, rallies, and campaigns. The accent is on 1980s justice, since it will be argued that criminal court practices in this period set the foundation for practices into the twenty-first century. The argument here is that, while other aspects of Chinese law—civil and economic law—have developed into modern systems of justice administration, criminal law has not. As a study of the public performance of criminal court work, this book examines how law and punishment is constructed and represented both in practice and in rhetoric. It explores the historical background of Yanda and other public displays of social control in courts, concluding with a look at today's criminal court work.

Background

There is an historical dimension that grounds contemporary Chinese crime control functions and practices in particular, and criminal court work in general, in a wider socio-legal context. Following the disaster of the Cultural Revolution, and as part of the reformist agenda of the early 1980s, the Deng leadership endeavored to transform a number of sites of public memory. The site of law in China was transfigured into the discourse of modernization (*xiandaihua*) and was given meta-narrative status as a linchpin of reformist rhetoric and practice. A new means of governance was promoted, one that relied not on Party policy but on law and regulation, thus distancing Party policy as the rhetorical mainframe of state power in the PRC. A new language of governance, privileging the rhetoric of law and promoting political legitimacy as residing in notions of order and progress, signaled the end of an era of Maoist political legitimacy based on class struggle, chaos, and disorder.

The promotion of a new political legitimacy and authority became a pressing issue for legal institutions in the late 1970s and into the 1980s. Courts and other legal institutions faced the imperative of creating a new modernist institutional culture by modifying both their image of authority and their authority relations with other government and Party agencies and the community at large to fit into the new ethos of reform. This required courts to pursue a "fast-track"[5] shift in practices and appearance to reflect a change from Maoist popular justice culture to Dengist political culture. The fast-track approach to law reform in the post-1978 period led Chinese criminal justice institutions to rely heavily on rhetorical and symbolic displays of reformist governance in order to develop their image as authoritative and credible. For example, law was sensationalized in the trial of Jiang Qing and the Gang of Four in the late 1970s. In the early 1980s, criminal justice policy in China shifted from privileging political crime to focusing on social and economic crimes. These crimes became the focus of law on display in various anti-crime campaigns from 1980 to 1986. The Tiananmen massacre marked a re-emphasis on political crimes on display in the late 1980s. More recently, criminal justice agencies have again set their key agendas on crime control through "Strike Hard" (Yanda) anti-crime drives. In fact, the notion of "Yanda" itself is a public performance of the law.

Another crucial part of developing institutional authority in China during the reform period was to promote criminal law not simply as a set of abstract rules but as "collective social order." The collectivity of public responses to law and order therefore became paramount. Through "displaying law," criminal justice institutions inscribed the abstract citizen in China into the punitive process. This is a locus of the criminal law/society nexus in China. Hence the performative aspect of criminal justice operations is crucial to our understanding of law's empire in contemporary China. In this book I situate an examination of criminal court work within a socio-legal context that informs my approach to the performative nature of law in the PRC. The performative nature of court practices is reflected in the projection of images and messages delivered to a community of onlookers, spectators, and participants through public trials, sentencing rallies, and other programs where courts publicly display their authority. The chapters that follow are an applied study of the concerns raised in this chapter and in Chapter One.

Nowadays criminal justice studies outside the field of Chinese law recognize the importance of understanding both the instrumental and the symbolic aspects of judicial and penal practices, especially in relation to expressive punishment.[6] Moreover, socio-legal studies outside the field of Chinese law now recognize the importance of understanding the positive value of law as a constitutive phenomenon.[7] Writers in the field of criminal justice studies not related to China have long acknowledged law's symbolic potential in framing social understandings of appropriate conduct, values, and beliefs.[8] Law regulates "not only by coercing those who create disorder and by empowering those who sustain and reproduce order, but also by helping to fix and maintain 'common sense' understandings of the nature of society and social relationships in general."[9]

Underlying this discussion of the symbolics of law is a more basic concern of the question of order: how legal ideologies and practices help to shape and sustain dominant visions of "the order of things" in society. Relating this symbolic dimension of law to Chinese criminal court work, this study examines how criminal justice agencies seek to manage not only the conduct of individuals who commit crime, but also the social attitudes and expectations of a wider social audience. In short, this book examines the operational and the representational functions of law in criminal justice work in terms of the processes through which law operates to regulate social relations.

Rather than discuss court practices in general, this study examines criminal court work mainly through the window of the court records of one particular local court system in the city of Baotou in Inner Mongolia. This study moves from the micro to the macro (the national scene) and back and, while focusing mainly on one court, tells a bigger story about Chinese criminal court work via reference to dozens of other case studies of courts. Like the Baotou experience, these studies were documented by judges and published (mainly) internally as "restricted-circulation documents." Some of the other studies include provinces such as Yunnan, Guizhou, Hebei, Ningxia, and Liaoning, municipal courts in Tianjin, Xining (Qinghai), and Yulin (Shaanxi), and county courts in Miyang (Henan), Luoding (Guangdong), and Qingxu (Shanxi). As will be discussed in detail below, the historical court records from Baotou dating back to 1949 were compiled by criminal justice officials in the 1990s in order to help future generations of court officials to learn through the experiences of the past. It is in this respect that the objective of this book intersects with the rationale of contemporary official history writing in the PRC: that is, the idea of "summarizing experiences" (*zongjie jingyan*) to give context to the present.

The Baotou Courts

The idea of "summarizing experiences" has been a mainstay of communist politico-legal rhetoric since the establishment of the PRC. First touted as a way of presenting politico-legal policy in the form of judicial narrative, *zongjie jingyan* was employed as a method of bringing together disparate practices into a unified national approach to court work at a time when no substantive or procedural laws existed. The first project of summarizing the experience of criminal court work was initiated in response to a rash of child rape cases in 1953. Courts across the country were asked to summarize their experiences in handling such cases. At a national judicial symposium a year later, the Supreme People's Court (SPC) issued a report on "Some Opinions on Summarizing the Experiences of Handling of Female Child Rape Cases and Sentencing Practices" (*Guanyu chuli jianyin younu de zongjie yingyan he chuxing yijian*), which served as a guide in lieu of an existing law. The Communist Party Central Committee's ratification of the findings and opinions of this report paved the way for a new rhetorical and operational means of approaching the management of judicial work under the auspices of "summarizing experiences." In May 1954 a SPC symposium convened to summarize judicial experiences issued instructions for all local courts throughout the country to follow suit, summarizing all their experiences "which support the function of adjudication work as a means of guaranteeing national economic construction; the experiences of sorting out long-pending cases and reexamining and redressing incorrectly tried cases; the experiences of adjudicating narcotics related cases; the experiences of notarization work; and the experiences related to the general system of adjudication."[10] In short, these were experiences that would benefit the development of a more systematized and efficient bureaucracy to support economic construction of the nation. The practice of summarizing experiences, therefore, became a basis upon which a standardization of court work in general, and judicial procedure in particular, could be formulated in the absence of detailed stipulations and procedural guidelines.[11]

In 1986, thirty-six years after the establishment of the people's courts in the PRC, a research unit attached to the Central Party Committee (CPC) of the Chinese Communist Party (CCP) commissioned a summary of the experiences of trial work (*shenpan gongzuo*) in the PRC. To give the history of law and legal institutions an empirical foundation, and to function as a basic record of the institutional history of courts, a decision was made to write a comprehensive history of one particular local court system. The intention was that this case history would serve as a model for subsequent case histories. The rationale of this case history is based on a number of concepts from the lexicon of socialist folklore, firstly and most importantly, the notion of "summarizing experiences" in the judicial realm as a means of connecting substantive law with socialist reality. The Baotou text follows this tradition of summarizing experiences as a way of standardizing judicial practice. In this era, it is intended as a supplementary guide to how court work is done and how courts want to been seen to be administering justice.

The local court system chosen as the first detailed case history of a court in the PRC was Baotou Intermediate Court and the eight basic courts under its supervision and guidance. The basic people's courts in Baotou are courts situated at district or county level under the "guidance" of the Baotou Intermediate Court. They hear ordinary criminal and civil cases and are closely tied to their superior court, the Baotou Intermediate Court, through a system of organizational supervision that is built into the structure of the courts. The supervisory role of the Baotou Intermediate Court over the basic courts involves direct "guidance" in most decisionmaking and policymaking in both judicial and administrative matters. The Baotou Intermediate Court and each of the basic people's courts under its supervision are administrated separately. These basic courts are: Kundulun Court, Qingshan Court, Donghe Court, Shiguai Court, Baiyun Court, Outer Suburbs Court, Tumote Court, and Guyang Court.

Staff from the Baotou Intermediate Court and the local municipal archives office were commissioned to collate and write what became *Baotou fayuanzhi* (*The Annals of the Baotou Courts*). The courts in Baotou, the largest city in Inner Mongolia, were chosen as an exemplar for institutional history writing of individual courts in the PRC and as a source of data for a more general history of the court system.[12] The Baotou history was intended as a representative history of all local courts in the PRC. *The Annals* personalizes the law, giving it a concrete reality, and provides historical markers that make the story of law and justice in one city a national story. Produced as a modernist text explicating its recent past and legitimating its present reality, *The Annals* gives Dengist law and justice a meta-narrative status.

The Annals is a restricted-circulation publication (*neibu faxing*) written by judicial officials for judicial officials. The compilers of the book at the time of writing all held professional status in the Baotou Intermediate Court. The main writer of the document was Ma Weigang, a Baotou Intermediate Court vice-president; other members of the team included Huang Peifu and Cao Bin, both judges in Baotou. *The Annals* is not an isolated history, but is part of a larger national project constructing a comprehensive history of the public and social institutions and people of the People's Republic of China. The book was written under the auspices of the Contemporary Chinese History Editorial Committee, which has compiled a massive series of case studies and biographies on contemporary China titled "Series on Contemporary China" (*Dangdai Zhongguo congshu*).[13] It is one of the two hundred or so volumes commissioned by the Contemporary Chinese History Editorial Committee covering a vast array of institutional, Party, and governmental histories and biographies.

The document's significance lies not only in the rich and textured data detailing the machinations of justice administration in a local court, but also in its role as a model of court work and as an exemplar of court institutional history writing. Commissioned as a reference resource on institutional practice, *The Annals* was designed as a guide for present judicial practice, and as such, it presents itself as a faithful account of local history played out in the shadow of a broader Chinese history. In this sense, as a local history it is set against the backdrop of a broader historical context and is therefore fashioned on the basis of the dictum that history is a "mirror to the present" (*yigu weijing*). The compilers based this on the traditional idea of "using the past as a mirror" to record the rise and fall of events. As the compilers explain: "[h]istory is a mirror and the present reality must be seen as a continuation of the past."[14] The text therefore provides the working judicial professional with a framework and model for interpretation of the role of courts in history and the role of court workers in the everyday routines of court work.

The Annals was compiled as a conscientious effort to "seek truth from facts" and to reflect all of the various aspects of change and development in the thirty-six-year history of court work in the basic and intermediate courts.[15] It was written in order to preserve history, provide resources, and instruct and educate (*cunshi, zizheng, jiaohua*),[16] incorporating "the failures as well as successes, bad as well as good experiences and it contains the agony and the ecstasy of court life."[17] As a history of the official trials and tribulations of court life, *The Annals* is presented in the form of narrative summaries, diary-style recording, and statistical data. The 200-page, 150,000-word document is divided into the following parts: "The Evolution of Court Structure" (*Jiegou yange*), "Summary of Criminal Trial Work" (*Xingshi shenpan*), "Summary of Civil Trial Work" (*Minshi shenpan*), "Summary of Economic Trial Work" (*Jingji shenpan*), "Synopsis of Personnel" (*Renwu jianjie*), "Chronicle of Events" (*Dashiji*), and "Appendix" (*Fulu*).

As noted above, while the case study of PRC criminal court life in the body of this book is based mainly on the Baotou experience, this study also includes contributions from courts all over China. In this sense, *The Annals* is the flagship study while the other texts employed lend further depth of evidence to that provided in Baotou.

Organization of this Book

Chapter One explores two central issues: politics and authority-building in criminal court work. It also outlines the main argument of the book, which concerns the often contradictory ways in which courts in China since 1979 have struggled to publicly represent themselves in order to maintain their social authority to administer justice.

In Chapter Two, I consider how the judicial authorities activate the creative and educative potential of the law through the projection of judicial authority in trials. The construction of a professional persona in the Baotou in the 1980s courts involved a process whereby authorities exercised their claim to office by projecting the expectations and aspirations of procedural propriety through public trials. Developing judicial authority in Baotou depended on a claim to validity and credibility, and not merely on the existence of people who fill an authority role and perform duties. We find in Baotou, then, that judicial authority depended on the ability of court officials to make convincing claims to their legitimacy as administrators of justice. The courts attempted to establish and cultivate their belief in their own legitimacy by means of securing particular constitutions of order in judicial procedure. The open trial embodied a clear message that, in the post-1978 period, the means for securing justice no longer lay in the unmediated will of the masses which characterized the "lost" years of court work from 1958 to 1976; it was portrayed, rather, as increasingly institutionalized in the procedural and bureaucratic processes of trial work. So, while the moral authority of socialist legality continued to be represented as a reflection of the will of the masses (as the legitimizing force of punishment), the conditions under which this new vision of judicial authority was constructed in the 1980s were nevertheless more closely connected to the larger institutional and political project of reform. In this respect, within the discursive boundaries of reformist ideologies, the conceptual goalposts of authority moved from unmediated revolutionary popular justice to reincorporate the institutionally-based claims of legitimacy that were first promulgated in the period of institution building of the 1950s. In the final section I look at some of the institutional constraints on the development of an authoritative persona in criminal trial work.

Chapter Three examines expressive punishment in the context of the public sentencing rally. According to the president of the Supreme People's Court, in his annual address to the National People's Congress in 2002, ninety-eight million members of the public in China attended trials and rallies in the previous year. Most people in China who experience a taste of PRC justice do so in their attendance as the cheering public at a sentencing rally. The public sentencing rally is a degradation ceremony in which the judgment and sentence of a convicted criminal, already determined in court, is announced in a public forum, in a venue such as a market place, stadium, community hall, at the site of the crime, or the criminal's workplace. The audience can range from a few dozen to over one hundred thousand. Even today, the theatrics of the rally include the parading of criminals in trucks throughout the streets of a town on their way to prison or to an execution ground. An examination in Chapter Three of the act of expressive punishment in sentencing rallies shows that, despite the push to effect a new modernist legal culture based on professionalism, regularity, and bureaucratic rationality, criminal justice practices have continued to rely on the theatrics of expressive punishment.

Chapter Four examines the rationales, targets, and implementation of three anti-crime campaigns in Baotou from 1980 to 1983. These campaigns, which dominated criminal court work in the first three years of the new decade, reveal the cooperative nature of interagency relations between the three organs of criminal justice. These campaigns are explored in relation to the socialist criminological principles and rhetoric of "social harm" and "flexibility." This study suggests that moves to change court practices as a means to accelerate wider social and economic transformation were made all the more challenging in a political system whose institutional culture and rhetoric of "socialist transformation" dominated work practices well beyond its use-by-date of 1976.

"Yanda" (Strike Hard) is a policy for "striking heavy blows" at "enemies" of China's modernization drive. It is essentially a policy of employing the principle of "severity and swiftness" to deal with criminal cases considered a major threat to social order. "Severity" is applied as a sentencing rationale and involves meting out the heaviest punishment possible under law. For more than seventy types of criminal offences in China this means the death penalty. "Swiftness" is the speeding up of criminal procedure to deal with targeted criminals in a timely manner, often within two weeks of arrest. Yanda policy was originally employed in the immediate post-Mao period in 1981 as a means of dealing with emerging social order crimes, particularly crimes committed by juveniles and "hooligans" (*liumang*). It developed into a full-blown anti-crime campaign in 1983 that lasted three years. Chapters Five and Six provide the first detailed examination of Yanda at the grassroots level. Chapter Five looks at Yanda from the political perspective of its implementation, and Chapter Six examines the impact of meting out justice "severely and swiftly" through an examination of case studies provided by provincial courts, a outline of the problem of "courts without courtrooms," and an examination of the "flexibility and principle" debate.

In the final chapter, I project my evaluation of 1980s criminal court work into criminal court work in twenty-first century China through an analysis of China's latest Yanda campaign from 2001 to 2003. This study reveals that courts today continue to grapple with the tension between the political imperative to protect social order and the economic imperative to develop a credible, professional, and legitimate judiciary.

Notes

1. Amnesty International Annual Report 2002 at <www.amnesty.org>.

2. Murray Scot Tanner, "State Coercion and the Balance of Awe: The 1983–1986 'Stern Blows' Anti-Crime Campaign," *The China Journal* 44 (2000): 93.

3. See Murray Scot Tanner, "Campaign-style Policing in China and its Critics," in *Crime, Punishment, and Policing in China*, ed. Borge Bakken (Lanham, MD: Rowman & Littlefield, 2005), 175.

4. Borge Bakken, *The Exemplary Society: Human Improvement, Social Control and the Dangers of Modernity in China* (New York: Oxford University Press, 2000), 394.

5. Ronald C. Keith, *China's Struggle for the Rule of Law* (London: St. Martin's Press, 1994).

6. David Garland, "Punishment and Culture: The Symbolic Dimensions of Criminal Justice," Studies in *Law, Politics and Society* 11 (1991): 191–222; David Garland and Peter Young eds., *The Power to Punish; Pat Carlen, Magistrate's Justice* (Martin Robertson and Co., London, 1976); David Garland, *Punishment and Modern Society: A Study in Social Theory* (Chicago: University of Chicago Press and Oxford University Press, 1990); David Garland, *The Culture of Control: Crime and Social Order in Contemporary Society* (Chicago: University of Chicago Press, 2001).

7. For example, see Susan Silbey, "Making a Place for Cultural Analysis of Law," *Law and Social Inquiry* 17 (1992): 39–62; Austin Sarat and Thomas R. Kearns eds., *Law in the Domains of Culture* (Ann Arbour: The University of Michigan Press, 1998); Austin Sarat and Thomas R. Kearns eds., *Law in Everyday Life* (Ann Arbour: University of Michigan Press, 1993).

8. See Richard V. Ericson, "Why Law is Like News," in *Law as Communication*, ed. David Nelken (Aldershot: Dartmouth, 1996), 195–230 and Garland, *Punishment and Modern Society.*

9. Roger Cotterrell, *Law's Community: Legal Theory in Sociological Perspective* (Oxford: Clarendon Press, 1995), 8.

10. "Summary of Criminal Trial Work," in *Baotou fayuanzhi: Baotou shi difangzhi congshu* (The Annals of the Baotou People's Courts) Baotou fayuanzhi bianxuan weiyuanhui eds. (Neimenggu: Neimenggu Chubanshe, 1990), 14.

11. Dangdai Zhongguo lishi weiyuanhui eds., *Dangdai Zhongguo de shenpan gongzuo* (Court Work in Contemporary China) (Beijing, Dangdai zhongguo chubanshe, 1993), 71.

12. "Fanlie" (Introductory Notes) In *Baotou fayuanzhi*. Hereafter, I refer to this as *The Annals*, and all reference to this book will be cited in English under their chapter headings. All translations in this book unless otherwise stated are those of the author.

13. This includes the publication on contemporary Chinese court work, *Dangdai Zhongguo de shenpan gongzuo*.

14. "Preface," *The Annals*, ii.

15. "Introductory Notes," and "Preface," *The Annals*, ii.

16. "Preface," *The Annals*, ii.

17. "Preface," *The Annals*, ii.

Chapter One

Politics and Authority-Building in Criminal Court Work

> It was almost 6 a.m. when dozens of judicial police vans and sedans entered the gates of the lockup . . . the soon-to-be sentenced prisoners emerge . . . timidly and with heads bowed, they are forced into the waiting vans as their names are called. Their foot shackles clang on the floor of the van. Some have a resigned look of dread on their face, some in a trance-like state. . . . It's 7 a.m. and the motorcade of nearly 100 vehicles leaves the lock-up, with police lights blazing but with sirens silent. The motorcade follows the main road to the location of today's rally, the People's Sports Stadium, just as people on the street emerge on their way to work. More than ten thousand workers in transit see the passing motorcade. Soon after 8 a.m., the audience at today's rally arrive just as the vehicles reach the stadium. . . . At 9 a.m. precisely, the rally officially begins. On the raised podium located on the field at the center of the stadium stand the judges who pronounce sentencing. Surrounding them on all sides are more than four thousand members of the masses who sit silently in anticipation. . . . The announcement of the start of the rally brings spontaneous applause from the crowd. The first batch of criminals to be sentenced are brought out onto the stage, their foot shackles clanging as they step onto the podium. Today's judges are wearing their judicial robes. One judge [at a time] faces the audience and begins reading out the written judgments, each judgment notice detailing the criminal act, the criminal charge and the sentence.[1]

The above is a description of a mass sentencing rally in Tianjin in 2001. Why is it that in the new millennium in China, in an era of unprecedented judicial reform, courts continue to rely on the rhetoric and practices of shame punishment to express their authority and legitimacy? This book is an attempt to describe and explain this paradox by reference to the immediate past, the post-1978 period in China, and its aftermath. The contemporary scene within which key issues of crime and punishment play out in China today is set against a backdrop of judicial reforms that were implemented in the 1990s, the latest being in 1999, in the form of a five-year reform plan that promised sweeping changes to the judicial system. One set of reforms in particular, announced by Judge Xiao Yang, President of the Supreme People's Court (SPC), aimed to improve the internal organizational structure of courts, the recruitment of judges, and the trial process, including improvements to the standards of burden of proof, cross-examination, and rules of evidence. This proclamation of a new commitment to judicial reform and professionalism was based on the premise that economic modernization demanded an authoritative judiciary with enough teeth to settle disputes and enforce judgments. The recent adoption of black judicial gowns in China provides the visual accompaniment to this reformist rhetoric. Juxtapose this professionalization drive with the brutality of the Yanda campaigns and we find an anomaly in the development of a rule of law in today's China.

The situation in this new millennium for criminal justice agencies is that now, more than ever, they are caught up between two conflicting expectations and demands—the promises of economic prosperity and the threat of social instability. So, in an era when there has been an unprecedented push to professionalize the ranks of the Chinese criminal justice system and to bestow an air of authority and credibility on their work, criminal justice workers have found themselves caught up in a nationwide war against crime that requires them to apply the law "severely and swiftly" and to adjudicate cases at record speed. This situation suggests that, while there is ample evidence that the courts, procuratorate, and police have become much more bureaucratically effective and reliable as a result of policies that have encouraged procedural propriety and professionalism and the strict application of the law, we find also that these programs coexist with the morally-charged and emotive practices of crime control that have molded court work since its revolutionary days. This present-day tension between the aspirations of "rule of law" and the political imperatives of crime control has historical antecedents, and it is these antecedents that are central concerns of this book.

In September 1949, the People's Liberation Army (PLA) "peacefully liberated" the eighty thousand residents of Baotou city. The Guomindang's (KMT) Six Codes and its legal system were abolished almost immediately after the takeover as part of the plan to effect a system of revolutionary socialism. The revolutionary code of justice brought to Baotou from the Communist Party's revolutionary struggles in Jingganshan, Ruijin, and later Yan'an, was made the foundation of a new system of law based on class struggle and revolutionary justice. The first people's court in Baotou was set up in the local temple where authorities began to establish a judicial system without criminal codes. The first Baotou court president appointed by the incoming government was Wu Qinghe, a former People's Liberation Army (PLA) soldier with only six years of formal primary schooling.

Almost thirty years later, in the wake of atrocious failures of the Maoist reforms and the Cultural Revolution, the Baotou Intermediate Court and the eight basic courts under its guidance embarked on another revolution in organization and operation in response to the CCP's Third Plenum call for a new approach to socialist legality.[2] The intended metamorphosis was to involve a significant shift nationwide in the courts' approach to justice administration in the wake of far-reaching political, economic, and social changes inspired by the reform policies under Deng Xiaoping to open up the Chinese nation. In Baotou, the changes in court work were intended to be multifaceted. In January 1979, for example, in line with the introduction of the first criminal code in the PRC, a decision was made to shift in focus from closed trials to public trials, and for the first time the Baotou Intermediate Court set up a second criminal division to deal specifically with appellate criminal cases. Soon after, it was decided to set up a separate political section and an administration section in the court. These developments gave a strong indication of a more professional approach to justice administration, with specialized functions at all levels in the courts. Table 1.1 shows the extent of the organizational changes.

Each of the eight basic courts and the intermediate court had a general administration office (*bangongshi*) and separate judicial divisions (*ting*) in 1986. In 1957, there were only two judicial divisions in the Intermediate Court: the criminal and the civil division. By 1986, there were six specialized judicial divisions, detailed as follows:

Table 1.1. Number of Personnel and Structure of Internal Court Organization of the Baotou Intermediate Court Judicial Divisions and Administrative Sections, 1986

Judicial Divisions		Administrative Divisions	
No. 1 Criminal Division:	13	Office of Research and Investigation:	5
No. 2 Criminal Division:	11	Correspondence and Visits Section:	5
Civil Division:	16	Political Work Section:	5
Economic Division:	10	Internal Discipline and Investigation Group:	2
Case Division:	14	Administration Office:	27
Enforcement Division:	12	National Judicial Cadres University, Baotou Branch:	2

Source: Information collated by the author from information in the "Appendix," *The Annals*: 159.

Baotou's superior court, the Inner Mongolia Autonomous Region Higher Court, also took steps at that time. It opened discussions on trial procedure and the structure of trials, and to its subaltern courts, including in Baotou, announced the basic tasks of court work for that period. The following month, the Baotou courts embarked on the first of the basic tasks of criminal court work in the post-1978 era: a three-year program of redressing cases and rehabilitating victims of the Cultural Revolution and the Anti-Rightist campaign. In 1980, as a symbol of its newfound legality, the first public criminal trial since the 1950s was conducted in Baotou. The courtroom portrait of Mao was removed from its central position on the wall behind the judges' bench and replaced with the national emblem to symbolize a new public image of court professionalism, based on the ethos of procedural propriety (*chengxuhua*) and nation rather than on revolutionary justice.

If the job of understanding and interpreting the events and practices of criminal court work were simply a matter of categorizing them in terms of their formal-legal definitions, then the task would not be difficult. We could refer to laws such as the Organic Law of the People's Courts (1979), which sets out court duties and organization, to access a formal description of the courts' authority, jurisdiction, and characterization of the courts' tasks.[3] However, as sociologists David Garland and Peter Young note in their examination of legal penalty, analysis very quickly moves beyond formally describing the object of study to evaluating its origins, its functions, or its social significance.[4] The researcher then needs to "rethink" the object of study not in terms of formal legal description but in terms of recognized sociological, philosophical, or political categorizations.[5]

My rethinking of criminal court work was sparked by curiosity about the minutiae of criminal court work. An initial wondering about what criminal courts in China actually do on a day-to-day basis evolved into questioning how they operate, how these courts rationalize their actions, and how they exercise this power. The search for answers to these questions necessarily opens the window on how the courts have changed their operations in response to the nationwide open door economic and political reforms from the late 1970s. If we compare the revised Organic Law of the People's Courts, adopted in 1979, to the first Organic Law of 1954, we find that the jurisdictions, structures, and basic tasks of court work as set out in these laws do not fundamentally differ. Yet even a cursory comparison of pre-reform and post-reform court work suggests a significant change, both in how court workers do their work and how the courts present themselves publicly as legitimate administrators of justice. Whereas from the late 1950s to the late 1970s the courts adopted the policy agendas and rhetoric of Maoist "popular justice," in the 1980s, the new policy agendas and rhetoric of open reform compelled a different conceptualizing of the role of courts in Chinese society. The public image of criminal court work was made more rational, professional, and bureaucratic, even though courts continued with authoritarian "law and order" campaigns. "Rethinking" initial questions about the basic agendas and practices of criminal court work therefore compels their incorporation into a broader sociological inquiry about the development of judicial authority and social significance of courts during the first stage of the reform era.

The criminal courts in China therefore gained new purpose and status post-1978, resting on the tenet that a regulated, stable, and professionalized bureaucratic apparatus would avert future political disaster like the Cultural Revolution, and help secure the conditions of social and economic stability necessary for the smooth progress of socialist economic reform. Here it was expected that legal reform would provide an institutional and practical solution to the immediate social problems of crime and the long-term regulation of social and economic order. But the nature, scale, and force of post-Mao change exceeded expectations. The momentous economic and social changes that open door reform induced included exponential growth in crime. The social upheaval from economic reform—greater unemployment, mobility, and financial concerns in response to burgeoning inflation—inspired political authorities to change both the political rhetoric of criminality and the targets of regulation. This caused a shift from regulating political offences to regulating the social offences that reform and rapid change had induced.

On the one hand, then, we see aspiration toward a publicly credible and respected court system, with new affirmation of commitment to "professionalism," "rule of law," and "the independent administration of justice." However, in practice, the judicial organs' response to the threat of social instability in the early 1980s, under instruction from the national authorities, was to instigate a more authoritarian approach to crime control through law and order crime campaigns cast under the rubric of comprehensive management of public order (*shehui zhi'an zonghe zhili*). Therefore, while the call to a socialist rule of law heralded a new public presentation of law within a stable, professional, and increasingly autonomous court environment, this presentation coexisted with some aspects of court practice that were the ideological antithesis of this call.

Under these conditions, two distinct public representations of law developed concomitantly in official discourse. One characterized law as a professional apparatus legitimized by new procedural codes and adjudication through the "scientific" calculation of the written law; the other characterized law as an authoritarian style of justice administration manifest in the coercive strategies of crime control campaigns. This dissonance in practice and in representation highlights the difficulty of articulating and implementing a clearly delineated set of legal practices to conform with the new rhetoric of a revitalized socialist rule of law in the post-1978 period. A major problem with this dissonance between representation and practice is that criminal court work is commonly portrayed in official discourse as the "materialization" of mass will and hence the materialization of the power of the state and Party. But it is just as likely to be depicted as deriving from the emerging position of the court as an increasingly "autonomous" and rational administrator of justice whose practices are grounded in legal reason rather than in Maoist political logic.

The aspects of 1980s court work in Baotou mentioned earlier in this chapter highlight the ambiguity of official representations. They also present court practices as a hybrid of institutional and judicial activities with highly complex political and social determinants, functions, and effects. We see in the 1980s "internal differentiation"[6] in the range of judicial policy agendas, their objectives, and techniques of judicial administration. Details chronicled in *The Annals* indicate the varied and sometimes incongruous aims of court programs. Politico-legal policies aimed at increasing court professionalism and autonomy and the strict adherence to law sit rather uncomfortably alongside policies and programs aimed to encourage close coordination between the courts and other criminal justice agencies under the rubrics of "mutual coordination" and "comprehensive management of public order."

Legal and ideological discourses and the political rhetoric of law and order programs also mirror this "internal differentiation." In the anti-crime campaigns from 1982 to 1986, the morally charged and emotive law and order catchphrases such as "severity and swiftness" (*congzhong congkuai*) parallel seemingly incompatible rhetoric such as "independent administration of justice" (*sifa duli*), "trying cases in accordance with the law" (*yifa ban'an*), and "equality before the law" (*zai falu mianqian renren pingdeng*). Thus, although moves toward procedural propriety, professionalism, and the strict application of the law may have made courts more reliable and their administration more efficient, coercive practices of crime control that evolved from revolutionary days continued to mold criminal court work in the reform period.

This disjuncture complicates our interpretations of judicial institutions in China. To consider carefully what courts do, and the socio-legal outcomes of this, we need to examine not only how courts operate but also how they present the authority of the law and their own authority to the community. And as the above discussion has indicated, we need to recognize and account for the rhetorical and practical inconsistencies. As John Brigham argued in his account of the history of the U.S. Supreme Court, courts are not simply "there"; they are constructed on the basis of both political and social expectations and on social understandings of the value of that institution and on the back of past practice.[7] We therefore need to explore the intersections between the internal deeds and doings of the courts and their external environment in the context of the courts' history. In this study of Chinese courts from 1979 to 2003, we need to locate and examine the junctures at which public, political, and professional expectations and understandings of criminal court work have developed as a result of the 1978 Third Plenum decision to "strengthen the socialist legal system."

Some who study Western criminal justice systems and rationalities have long been interested in developing new ways of understanding the social significance of judicial and penal institutions through their operation and representation.[8] David Garland, for example, has examined the instrumental and symbolic functions of penal practices and has observed that people in their community "look to such procedures not just as instrumental mechanisms which will process the single offender in question, but as symbolic reassertions of order and authority which help to deal with the feelings of helplessness, disorder and insecurity which crime introduces into their lives."[9] For Garland, judicial and penal practices therefore provide "moral guidance, patterns of discernment and languages of condemnation which have wider social effects in organizing conduct in all walks of life, as well as their role in feeding back more directly their support for the established institutions of punishment."[10]

The Annals presents as a warts-and-all history of the courts purporting to be objective and factual, but it does so as part of a broader quest for those working in the courts for legitimation of the reformist judicial practices. Despite the fact that it was not written for a mass readership—indeed, perhaps, because it was written expressly for politico-legal authorities influential in decisionmaking—it is replete with the usual "Dengisms" expected in an officially-sanctioned history written in the 1980s and 1990s. Yet it presents court work at a level of detail to rival any history of local courts outside China, with an abundance of data, records of events, and stories of the Baotou courts' experience. How to interpret this information is thus another concern for the analytical framework of this study.

Two particularly interesting aspects of *The Annals* are the way in which its writers attempt persuasively to "present" the authority of the Baotou courts to the reader and the importance the writers attach to the public displays of justice, that is, the symbolic properties of trials and sentencing practices in the day-to-day functioning of courts. These representional aspects of criminal court work are significant for various reasons, not the least being that the narrative of the Baotou document is itself part of a conscious effort to develop a new public identity for the courts based on judicial authority.

Literature on jurisprudence and criminal justice in China contains little on "authority" as a concept for understanding the social significance of courts. Yet much of the rhetoric of socialist justice in Baotou is aimed at promoting an authoritative persona of the courts. John Brigham's *The Cult of the Court* argues that, "because institutions give action authority," researchers need to think about how authority works.[11] He argues that the authoritative significance of the U.S. Supreme Court revolves around the institutional practices, the discourses, and the ideological frameworks of action that constitute the court as a legitimate political institution.[12] Court practices as "socially constructed ways of acting" give and are given significance in the community in which they operate.[13] In other words, the practices of the courts are the very means through which the authority of the courts is construed by the courts' social audience. Professionals in the judiciary take account of the form and procedure involved in the rituals of court actions that develop over time in response to particular historical circumstances and that social audiences therefore come to expect of courts.[14] For Brigham, institutions of authority such as courts are constructed within the particular communities in which they are accepted as legitimate, and these communities therefore comprise not just participants and professionals in the legal community but the entire society under their jurisdiction.[15] He argues that conventional studies have neglected the social foundations of the court as a regulatory institution—foundations that account very much for the courts' authority—and his study seeks to address this oversight by tracing the processes through which ideological qualities of doctrine and office are imbued with social significance.

A crucial factor in constructing and conferring institutional authority is public perception. Brigham observes that the effectiveness of a legitimate institution of authority in securing widespread obedience to its decisions is a function of the institution having made these decisions through appropriate and socially sanctioned institutional procedures.[16] Hence, the significance of practices is not simply that they are performed as institutionally defined procedures, but, as Rawls suggests, that they are *seen* to be done in such a way. As Rawls claimed:

> The web of meaning that gives an institution its appearance of permanence stems from the fact that an individual knows the rules, but he also knows that "others know this and that they know that he knows this, and so on."[17]

Brigham's study of courts is based on one of the most influential concepts in the general field of socio-cultural studies of Western legal systems. This is the concept of law as an ideological and constitutive phenomenon. Susan Silbey's position is typical of contemporary socio-legal scholars who use this approach:

> The ideals and principles that legal institutions announce, even though they fail to support them, are part of how legal institutions create their power and authority. The ideals of law, such as open and accessible processes, rule-governed decision making, or similar cases being decided similarly—despite their inaccuracy as a description of how law works—are nonetheless part of shared understandings of what law is. Although the ideals are not accurate empirical descriptions, they serve as aspirations that help shape and mobilize support for legal institutions. The term "ideology" has been adopted to specifically name this representational and constitutive power attached to legal language, concepts, and practices.[18]

The modest settings of the intermediate and basic courts in China are not those of the upper echelons of power examined in Brigham's study on the U.S. Supreme Court. And what Chinese authorities refer to as China's socialist rule of law operates on principles different from those undergirding rule of law in nations where the dominant ethos, if not practice, is democratic process. Brigham's observations offer a useful springboard for analyzing court practices and their role in constructing court authority. However, the cultural and historical specificity of court life in China requires a more detailed emphasis on the particular form and scope of judicial power in a socialist society at a crucial period of change.

Authority became a pressing issue for courts in the immediate post-1978 period. Courts faced the imperative of creating a new court culture by modifying both their image of authority and their authority relations with other government and Party agencies and the community at large. As noted previously, this required courts to pursue a fast-track shift in practices and appearance to reflect a change from the Maoist culture of popular justice to Dengist political culture. We see in this strategy how, as Brigham argues, the authority and public identity of courts as legitimate administrators of justice are not simply a political "given." Court authority is developed through public and political expectations. It is constantly negotiated and renegotiated, constructed and reconstructed in the everyday judicial and administrative tasks that bring courts into contact with their social audience, the ultimate conferrers of court authority. Unlike in the United States, where the constitutive authority of the Supreme Court was developed over a long period of time in close connection with development of the authority of the U.S. Constitution, post-1978 courts in China have been required to fast-track the construction of court authority in accordance with the rhetoric of governance in the new China: procedural regularity and bureaucratic rationality. We see this, and the consequences, in Baotou and other court case studies included in this book.

Brigham's argument that there is "politics" not only in the U.S. Supreme Court, but also in the way that the Court is generally observed, is particularly instructive for this study of the Chinese court system in the reform period. He explains that both conventional commentary and policy assessment of the U.S. Supreme Court use a specific form of jurisprudential discourse that narrowly explains the Court's authority in terms of a perceived dichotomy between law and politics.[19] Over the past few decades, a number of socio-legal scholars have recognized the shortcomings of categorizing legal phenomena into a neat dichotomy between law and politics. One of sociology's most critical legal scholars, Alan Hunt, argues that studies as diverse as the Marxist ideology of law, and those of Weber and Unger have all sought to explain law to some degree in terms of a paradox between law as a consensual mechanism of shared societal values and law as a coercive arm of state power. In Unger's approach, for instance, this dualism is articulated as a dichotomy between "interactive" and "bureaucratic" law and for Weber, it is between formal and substantive justice.[20]

Hunt warns of the danger in employing dualistic explanatory frameworks, since these approaches necessarily assume that the concrete materialization of legal practices is the direct outcome of what is assumed to be binary characteristics of law's internal dynamic. Further, presuming a duality perpetuates a commonly held but false assumption that law's teleological progression is fixed: evolving from a base of coercive state power to a consensual, moral-ethical base. As Hunt argues, the danger in employing a teleological treatment of law to interpret its concrete operation runs the risk of reducing these operations, or explaining them away as the outcome of the progression/retreat of coercive/consensual modes of law that move along a supposed conceptual continuum. Conceiving law in this manner casts it as a "single paradigm lying between the polarities of ethics and power, and its progress is marked by an increase in its ethical base and a decline in its reliance on power."[21] Setting up such dichotomies therefore tends to result in "an unstable analysis that lurches between the polarities set up. They produce an 'either-or' effect in emphasizing 'either' the element of consent 'or' the element of coercion."[22] Consequently such analyses fail to articulate a clearly defined concept of law "which is not reducible to a choice between opposites or to a fluctuation between them."[23]

Hunt's critique offers a useful lesson for the present study. In examining the Baotou courts we need to steer clear of a scenario that assumes inevitability; that the post-1978 criminal justice system can only be explained as either "advancement" of law (towards a "rule of law") or "regression" into politics (a return to dominant Party politics and Communist ideology). Such an assumption fails to acknowledge or explain the complex relationship between past and present criminal court work that is at the heart of court work in the 1980s, a relationship that demands explanation if we are to avoid a one-dimensional or monochrome view of contemporary Chinese courts. Further, using narrow definitions of the political/ideological and the legal as the extremities or "bookends" of a conceptual continuum, or using their conventional conception as the sole explanatory device for interpreting Chinese criminal court work, will restrict the scope of inquiry and most likely muddy its findings. Instead, I suggest an alternative approach to address the anomalies of Chinese criminal court work without creating theoretical dichotomies within the internal nature of law or between law and politics/ideology, and without entirely reducing examination of the social functions and significance of judicial practices to the "surface" politics of Communist Party rule. I believe that an appropriate point of departure in interpreting criminal court work in Baotou is to rethink the "political" in courts. As Chapter Five indicates, I certainly do not discount the importance of examining Party politics and conventional Communist ideology in criminal court work. Nevertheless, I want to consider criminal court work within a larger analytical framework that accounts for a *variety* of power and authority relations. My main point here is that, while courts are indeed "political," there is more than one type of "politicking" in operation. Party politics surely pervades court organization and practice. However, to understand the social significance of courts, it is important to acknowledge the intrinsically political nature of adjudicating and sentencing. In any legal system, socialist or not, these acts are mechanisms used to regulate human conduct. Adjudicating and sentencing are thus deeply political practices since they are always forms of social control. But in an era such as the post-1978 period, when authority-building relied so heavily on the public performance of adjudication and sentencing, these practices take on an even more significant role in expressing court work as one of society's key regulators of social relations in a post-Mao, post-revolutionary world.

From this perspective, criminal court work both in the 1980s and today can be conceived as a medium for fulfilling programmatic objectives of crime control and for embodying a particular type of socialist bureaucratic rationality. At the same time, criminal court activities are shaped by a number of competing and often incompatible political and social forces that affect courts' response to the central tasks of adjudication and their agenda for crime control. Criminal court work is shaped by mundane considerations such as resources, administrative arrangements, personnel, and organizational ties with other judicial organs. Courts are also open to the wider social, economic, political, and historical factors that help to determine the direction of court tasks and agendas. Courts, like all social institutions, are therefore:

> affected by the forces of economics, politics, culture and technology . . . each one is situated within an ensemble of social forces and is structured by the values and social arrangements which form its effective environment. Social institutions thus live a complex life of their own, but they are also constitutive elements within a larger social structure. Each one forms a kind of junction point in the social field upon which a range of forces converge, as well as being a setting for its own particular norms and practices.[24]

Courts, like all social institutions, develop over time a particular means of managing and addressing the complexity of social life under their sphere of regulation. This includes the conflicts within their area of regulation. Because institutions develop a culture based around the regulation of social relations, they carry *internal* to their make-up, "traces of the contradictions and pluralities of interests which they seek to regulate" and are thus "scenes of particular conflicts" for a variety of social relations and disparate political aims and social objectives.[25]

> [I]nstitutions are the scenes of particular conflicts as well as being means to a variety of ends, so it is no surprise to find that each particular institution combines a number of often incompatible objectives and organizes the relations of often antagonistic interest groups.[26]

Here, David Garland refers to the often competing policies, aims, and ambitions that affect the functioning of institutions. Criminal court practices therefore embody a plethora of competing objectives from often rival agendas that do not always fit into some unified pattern of a uniform set of measurable principles.[27]

> In the shaping of any penal event—whether it be a sentencing decision, the formation of a regime, or the legislative enactment of a penal policy—a large number of conflicting forces are at work. Broad ideological ambitions may run up against immediate financial constraints, political expediency may conflict with established sensibilities, the perceived requirements of security may differ from those of morality . . . and the pursuit of one value will generally involve the violation of several others.[28]

Courts are in essence both a melting pot of societal tensions and conflicts and a mechanism for regulating these tensions and conflicts. Given the disparity of their agendas and the areas of social regulation under their management, courts necessarily contain within their institutional culture competing objectives from rival agendas that do not always fit into a neat and easily discernible "doctrine" of judicial management. In this study of the Chinese courts, I pursue this idea, arguing that the courts in the 1980s and today are at once melting pots of societal tensions and mechanisms created to deal with these tensions. Such is the central idea running through this book: that in the 1980s, criminal court work in Baotou and nationwide was caught between the promises of economic prosperity and the threat of instability. This required the criminal courts to be "all things to all people": an increasingly autonomous and thus increasingly legitimate bastion of "rule of law" values; a simultaneous expression of institutional procedural propriety and a raw expression of state power; and a simultaneous embodiment of the virtues of "socialist spiritual civilization" and a protector of "socialist material civilization."

The tensions and incongruities we explore in this book are the result of what occurs when social institutions are required, almost overnight, to simultaneously change their rhetoric and their authorative persona to fit the ethos of economic reform and modernization. In the immediate post-1978 period, courts and other legal institutions in China faced the imperative of creating a new modernist institutional culture by modifying both their image of authority and their authority relations with other government and Party agencies and the community at large to fit into the new ethos of "reform." A "fast-track"[29] approach to law reform was encouraged. This fast-track approach, encapsulated in Deng Xiaoping's dictum that "law is better than no law, faster [law-making] is better than slower [law-making],"[30] meant that Chinese legal institutions were predisposed to a process of relying heavily on rhetorical and symbolic displays of reformist governance as a key means of developing their image as authoritative and credible.

Monumental legal reforms announced at the CCP's Third Plenum of the Eleventh Central Party Committee in December 1978 were envisaged as part of the benefits that the wider political economic reform process would bring to developing a new legitimacy and authority for the post-1978 regime. This regime sought a path to legitimacy through promises of maintaining political stability and promoting economic development. To develop the economy through restructuring and privatization, and to promote democratic political structures and processes, the development of reformed judicial systems was recognized as a necessary accompaniment. However, efforts in all these areas were frustrated by the failure of government to first anticipate and then to effectively address the massive social changes engendered by reform. Social dislocation caused by unemployment and rapid economic adjustment was exacerbated by the continual refusal of political leaders to accept the inevitability of social instability. As Michael Dutton noted, this meant that the democratic reform program met a series of limitations at each turn in its development.[31] The limitations engendered by simultaneous demands of stability and reform impacted significantly on the institutions of social control in the reform era.[32]

This tension between reform and stability, which is reflected powerfully in Baotou criminal court work, is the unifying thread that runs through this book. The tension is between the commission of government to ensure greater levels of autonomy and professionalism for courts, and the simultaneous requirements by the Party/state that courts play a coercive role in the domain of social control under the leadership and tight direction of the Party. The strains evident in court work (and in court relations with government) tie in directly to the very limitations of the reform and democratization agenda, to the extent that the call for social and political stability has repeatedly been expounded as a precursor to reform and democratization.[33]

The courts, like all institutions of social control in China, attempted to accommodate this tension by organizing their central tasks around the dual programs of promoting reform and initiating hard-line agendas of social control. In the post-1978 period, courts structured their practices around the broad themes of socialist reform. They modified the format of their operations and sought to structure a new organizational identity based largely on an external image of professionalism. The courts made these moves in response to the social, political, and economic expectations of reform. But while the courts responded to the call to reform—through the implementation of criminal codes, restructuring and specialization of resources and activities, and the promotion of professional training—they had to negotiate a path to legitimacy through the structural, organizational, social, and political constraints facing all agencies of social control in

China. In short, the courts attempted to develop an authoritative persona of professionalism by portraying the locus of their authority to administer justice as residing in their legitimate institutional capacity to judge in a *bona fide* and professional manner in accordance with the newly promulgated criminal codes. The courts also attempted simultaneously to preserve their revolutionary persona of authority from the Mao period, manifest in hard-line and draconian law and order practices, by relying on images of mass-line justice to legitimize their moral imperative to punish. Therefore, while attempting to secure one representational form of authority based on the moral and punitive requirements of social order, courts also sought to depict their source of authority as residing in their legitimate institutional capacity as professionalized administrators of justice.

The tensions of criminal court work—both contradictions and pluralities of interests—can be grouped into two distinct areas. The first area can be traced to the internal, *operational* make-up of criminal court work. This includes incongruities at the technical level of adjudication and sentencing, such as the constraints on courts as a result of the limitations of court workers' professional knowledge and experience. It also includes tensions at both the bureaucratic and political levels, such as an unwillingness to change the entrenched internal structures of officialdom, the hierarchical structure of the court system, and the political constraints on courts from their ties with local government, Party committees, and the people's congress, in particular the problems of dependence for funding and resources. A number of studies have explored this tension as it is reflected in the operation of criminal justice. Works by Borge Bakken, Jianfu Chen, Donald Clarke, Susan Finder, Ronald Keith, Stanley Lubman, Randall Peerenboom, Murray Scott Tanner, and Harold Tanner are particularly insightful in this regard.[34]

The second area of tensions in criminal court work, which is the focus of this book, concerns the often contradictory ways in which courts struggle to *present* themselves to the wider community. The approach I take in this book to analyze the operation of criminal justice in China is novel to the field as it highlights the performative function of Chinese criminal law. Courts in contemporary China have had to mediate between disparate and often contradictory public presentations of law and justice—some punitive and moral in character, others rationalized and bureaucratic. The foregrounding of an ideology of professionalism as a required *modus operandi* for courts has compelled courts to reorganize public images and discourses of court authority while trying to address most effectively the explosion of new, unanticipated crime and administer justice in a professional and rational manner. Courts sought to portray the basis of their authority as both a means and an end. The ideology of procedural propriety was projected as a *means* to attain justice, while images and discourses of law's moral imperative to protect social order and to punish were projected as its *ends*.

Courts therefore publicly represented their authority to administer justice at once, based on the institutional legitimacy of courts to adopt codes of procedural propriety and on the inherently moral authority of the law to punish offenders and maintain social order. This style of representation generated profound dilemmas for courts because the discourses and ideologies courts have used to represent and justify some programs of reform compete against the quite incompatible ideologies and discourses that courts have used to represent other programs of reform. Courts had to adapt continually to try to satisfy rapidly changing social and political expectations and to convincingly deliver contradictory representations of their role in social order, modernization, and reform. Criminal court work thus became a continuous juggling act to accommodate deep disparities between the operational imperatives of crime control, the moral imperatives of punishment, the bureaucratic imperatives of efficiency, and the procedural imperatives of due process. In this book, these tensions are explored in the often contradictory way that courts portray their authority through public performances in trials, sentencing, and, in particular, in anti-crime campaigns.

Conclusion

In the general field of Chinese law studies outside China, there is a rich body of positivist literature that traces legislative developments in criminal court practice. However, it appears that little critical energy has been directed toward exploring the sociology of court life in China in relation to established literature on socio-legal studies outside the Chinese law field. I take up this challenge in this book.

Some Western scholars in the field of Chinese law evaluate contemporary Chinese law issues in relation to how far (or not) China has advanced in terms of adhering to Western legal principles such as presumption of innocence, judicial independence, and equality before the law. These concepts certainly appear in this study, but not as yardsticks to measure how far China has come in terms of a "rule of law" or in comparison with other systems. Rather than uncritically treating the defining principles of rule of law, socialist legality, and the ideologies and discourses of socialist law in policy documents and media reports as either meaningless political rhetoric or, alternatively, as a "given" political explanation of the reality of criminal process, this book seeks to understand their social significance as instances of "law on display." Rather than assuming that to comprehend and evaluate criminal court work in China we must work with the notions of rule of law that underpin Western legal systems, a more useful approach is proffered. This approach favors turning to consider what the courts say about *themselves* in terms of their operations and their aspirations. Focusing on what courts convey about themselves widens our viewing lens to take in the political, ideological, organizational, and social rationalities that traverse "Maoism" and "Dengism," rationalities that elude liberal or purely instrumentalist conceptions of rule of law as the framework. This vantage point enables us to examine the connections between past and contemporary court practice in relation to the "political" and the "ideological," without imposing an alien-liberal ideology on this analysis. In this book I do not seek to uncover a flawed conceptualization or an unrealized rule of law in China. To the contrary, my position is premised on the recognition that we need to consider the historical contingencies of economic, social, political, and legal development in the PRC.

In the body of this study, we see how courts are shaped by competing and often incompatible forces, and courts have their own way of dealing with the multifaceted nature of what is put under their regulatory control. We explore the culture of criminal court work, recognizing that as social institutions courts have in their "make-up" "traces of the contradictions and pluralities of interests which they seek to regulate" and are thus "scenes of particular conflicts" for a variety of social relations and disparate political aims and social objectives.[35] In the PRC, these contradictions and pluralities of interest in court life constitute the uneasy coupling of pre-1978 rationales and strategies of criminal justice and post-1978 anticipations and expectations of legal, political, economic, and social reform. They are the product of the interplay between the operation and presentation of criminal court work, the connection between past and present judicial practice, and the impact of national politics and reform agendas on the local conditions under which law operates in the courts.

In the following chapters we explore the "contradictions and pluralities of interest" in the operation of Chinese courts. We turn to the courts' key tasks and agendas in the post-1978 period and their key public sites of law on display in criminal court work—court propaganda work, court trials, the rehabilitation drive, and court anti-crime campaigns.

Notes

1. Ajuan Wu, "E you e'bao: gongpan dahui ceji," (Evil Reaps What Evil Sows: Sidelight on a Public Sentencing Rally) *Tianjin Ribao* (Tianjin Daily), April 23, 2001, 1.

2. The communiqué of the Third Plenary Session of the 11th Central Committee of the Communist Party stated: "In order to safeguard the people's democracy, it is imperative to strengthen the socialist legal system so that democracy is systematized and written into law in such a way as to ensure the stability, continuity and full authority of this democratic system and these laws; there must be laws for the people to follow, these laws must be observed, their enforcement must be strict and law breakers must be dealt with. From now on, legislative work should have an important place on the agenda of the National People's Congress and its Standing Committee. Procuratorial and judicial organizations must maintain their independence as is appropriate; they must faithfully abide by the laws, rules and regulations, serve the people's interests, keep to the facts, guarantee the equality of all people before the people's laws and deny anyone the privilege of being above the law." See, "Communiqué of the Third Plenary Session of the 11th Central Committee of the Communist Party of China," *Peking Review* 21, no. 52 (December 1978): 14.

3. Articles 1, 2, and 4 of the "Organic Law of the People's Courts" (1979) state that the people's courts of the People's Republic of China are the judicial organs of the state, that judicial authority of the People's Republic of China is exercised by local people's courts at various levels, military courts and other special people's courts, and the

Supreme People's Courts. And that the people's courts "shall exercise judicial power independently, in accordance with the provision of the law, and shall not be subject to interference by any administrative organ, public organization or individual." The Organic Law of the People's Courts of the People's Republic of China, in *The Laws of the People's Republic of China 1983–1986*, 71–72, Beijing: Foreign Language Press, 1987. (Hereafter, unless otherwise stated, all references to the laws of the PRC are cited from *The Laws of the People's Republic of China.*)

4. David Garland and Peter Young, "Towards a Social Analysis of Penality," in *The Power to Punish: Contemporary Penalty and Social Analysis*, eds. David Garland and Peter Young (New Jersey: Humanities Press, 1983), 9.

5. Garland and Young make this point and describe this process as it applies to the allied field of penal studies. Garland and Young, "Towards a Social Analysis of Penality," 9.

6. Garland and Young argue that any sociological study of penal institutions first requires recognition of the degree of internal differentiation within the policies and aims and organization of penal practices: "The penal realm is not a singular, coherent unit. It is a complex network composed of a variety of different institutions, practices and relations supported by a number of agencies, capacities and discourses." Garland and Young, "Towards a Social Analysis of Penality," 15.

7. John Brigham, *The Cult of the Court* (Philadelphia: Temple University Press, 1987).

8. See, for example, Richard V. Ericson, "Why Law is Like News," in *Law as Communication*, ed. David Nelken (Aldershot: Dartmouth, 1996), 195–230; David Garland, "Punishment and Culture: The Symbolic Dimensions of Criminal Justice," *Studies in Law, Politics and Society* 11 (1991): 191–222; David Garland and Peter Young eds., *The Power to Punish*; Pat Carlen, *Magistrate's Justice* (London: Martin Robertson and Co., 1976); Peter Manning, *Police Work: The Social Organization of Policing* (Cambridge, MA: MIT Press, 1977); Nicola Lacey, Celia Wells, and Dick Meure, eds., *Reconstructing Criminal Law: Critical Perspectives on Crime and the Criminal Process* (London: Weidenfeld and Nicolson, 1998); Stuart Henry and Dragon Milovanovic, *Beyond Postmodernism*. London: Sage Publications, 1996.

9. David Garland, *Punishment and Modern Society: A Study in Social Theory* (Chicago/Oxford: University of Chicago Press and Oxford University Press, 1990), 68.

10. Garland, *Punishment and Modern Society*, 68.

11. John Brigham, *The Cult of the Court* (Philadelphia: Temple University Press, 1987), 3.

12. Brigham, *The Cult of the Court*, 3 (my emphasis).

13. Brigham, *The Cult of the Court*, 24.

14. Brigham, *The Cult of the Court*, 24–25.

15. Brigham, *The Cult of the Court*, 25.

16. Robert Grafstein, "Legitimacy of Political Institutions," *Polity* 14 (1981): 58, cited in Brigham, *The Cult of the Court*, 30.

17. J. Rawls, *A Theory of Justice*, 55–56, cited in Brigham, *The Cult of the Court*, 30.

18. Susan Silbey, "Ideology, Power, and Justice," in *Justice and Power in Sociolegal Studies*, eds. Bryant G. Garth and Austin Sarat (Illinois: Northwestern University Press, 1998), 274.

19. Brigham, *The Cult of the Court*, 5.

20. Alan Hunt, "Dichotomy and Contradiction in the Sociology of Law," in *Marxism and Law*, eds. Piers Beirne and Richard Quinney (New York: John Wiley & Sons, 1982), 80.

21. Hunt, "Dichotomy and Contradiction," 77.

22. Hunt, "Dichotomy and Contradiction," 78.

23. Hunt, "Dichotomy and Contradiction," 78.

24. Garland, *Punishment and Modern Society*, 283.

25. Garland, *Punishment and Modern Society*, 282.

26. David Garland, *Punishment and Modern Society*, 282.

27. As David Garland and Peter Young argue, penal practices involve a particular institutional site which "relays and condenses a whole series of social relations within the specific terms of its practices." Garland and Young, "Towards a Social Analysis of Penalty," p. 21. They describe the fusion of social relations in the context of punishment: "An offender who is sentenced to imprisonment becomes the object of a relation of *force* . . . which is at one and the same time *legal* (it is an authoritative order of the court, the prison is a legally authorized place of detention, its officers have legal powers at their disposal . . .); *political* (the basis and limits of that authority and that force are ultimately political, as is the definition and enforcement of the criminal law . . .); *ideological* (the prison carries specific symbolic connotations which mark the prisoner, his act and his family; prison architecture and practices carry particular signifiers—isolation, work, reward, discipline, obedience, etc); and *economic* . . ." (p. 21).

28. Garland, *Punishment and Modern Society*, 285.

29. Ronald C. Keith, *China's Struggle for the Rule of Law* (London: St. Martin's Press, 1994), 21.

30. Deng Xiaoping cited in Keith, *China's Struggle for a Rule of Law*, 20.

31. Michael R. Dutton, *Policing and Punishment in China: From Patriarchy to the People* (Cambridge: Cambridge University Press, 1992), 325.

32. Dutton, *Policing and Punishment in China*, 325.

33. Dutton, *Policing and Punishment in China*, 325.

34. Borge Bakken, *The Exemplary Society: Human Improvement, Social Control and the Dangers of Modernity in China* (Oxford University Press, New York, 2000); Jianfu Chen et al., eds., *Implementation of Law in the People's Republic of China* (The Hague/Boston: Kluwer Law International, 2002); Keith, *China's Struggle for the Rule of Law*; Murray Scot Tanner, *The Politics of Lawmaking in Post-Mao China: Institutions, Processes and Democratic Prospects* (Oxford: Clarendon Press, 1999); Murray Scot Tanner, "State Coercion and the Balance of Awe: The 1983–1986 'Stern Blows' Anti-Crime Campaign," *The China Journal* 44 (2000): 93–125; Harold M. Tanner, *Strike Hard!: Anti-Crime Campaigns and Chinese Criminal Justice 1979–1985* (New York: East Asia Program, Cornell University, 1999); Randall Peerenboom, *China's Long March Toward Rule of Law* (Cambridge: Cambridge University Press, 2002); Ronald Brown, *Understanding Chinese Courts and Legal Process* (The Hague/Boston: Kluwer Law International 1997); Donald C. Clarke, "People's Court Execution Rules," *Columbia Journal of Asian Law* 10 (1996): 93–126; Susan Finder, "The Supreme People's Court of the People's Republic of China," *Journal of Chinese Law* 7 (1993): 145–224.

35. Garland, *Punishment and Modern Society*, 282.

Chapter Two

Courts on Trial[1]

Baotou Intermediate Court has two criminal divisions. The No. 1 Criminal Division (*xingyiting*) handles in the first instance any crimes that are punishable by life imprisonment or the death penalty. Apart from its adjudication functions, the No. 1 Criminal Division also has the task of "guidance work" (*zhidao gongzuo*), instructing and directing the business of the criminal court division of the lower basic courts. It is also charged with the responsibility of conducting investigation and research into cases pending, writing reports on the work of the division, exploring avenues for judicial reform in the criminal divisions in terms of productivity and quality of work, preparing court statistics, preserving stolen or illicit money and property, and collating case files.[2] Another key task of the No. 1 Criminal Division that it shares with the No. 2 Criminal Division (the appellate division) is the subject of this chapter. That is to "broaden the scope of the social effects of criminal court work" by, firstly, conducting open trials, secondly, conducting law propaganda sessions, and thirdly, selecting socially or politically important cases to propagate through street posters and media outlets. The criminal divisions of courts are expected to "use open trials to explain to the public the basic facts surrounding a crime, the reasons for the crime, the social harm caused by the crime and the punishment for the crime . . . in order for the defendant to accept responsibility for the crime and to allow the masses to understand the true nature and circumstances of the crime."[3] The criminal divisions also conduct law propaganda by selecting cases that demonstrate one or more aspects of the law and, in important cases, to convene public sentencing rallies in order to "frighten criminals and educate the masses."[4] They are also expected to select cases to publicize via posters, billboards, media releases, and radio and television broadcasts. Judges in criminal divisions are also required to conduct law information sessions in schools, enterprises, organizations, and work units.[5]

This chapter is about "law on display" in courts. Part of the thrust of the "fast-track" approach to legal construction and reform in the post-1978 period was the promotion of an ethos of court work based on procedural propriety in trials. Here, legitimacy and procedural propriety are intimately linked in the quest to develop an authoritative persona. Although some observers claim that promotion of procedural propriety is a general quest for all developing institutions in the modern state,[6] it appears to have particular relevance in the "fast-track" effort of courts to build legitimacy in the wake of the atrocities of the Cultural Revolution. The Baotou text reveals the importance that the courts attached to the symbolic potential of the open trial (*gongkai shenli*) as a means of projecting symbolic and educative messages about law, order, and authority in the new era of socialist legality. Using Baotou as the main exemplar, this chapter explores how courts symbolized and projected an authoritative persona in the post-1978 era and the impact of this on criminal court work today.

In the context of the post-1978 reforms, catchcries such as "judicial independence," "equality before the law" and "handling cases in accordance with the law" were all part of a wider claim to a new model of institutional authority based not on revolutionary justice but on organizational reform and institutionalization and regularization of government processes. Deng Xiaoping's oft-quoted December 13, 1978, vision that democracy would be "institutionalized" and "written into law" revealed the importance of institutionalized law as a source of authority in this new era. This vision was the basis for the development of four main aspirations for a law-governed order: "'to perfect the law' . . . 'to observe the law, and to act according to law,' to 'ensure equality before the law' and to strengthen the 'supreme authority of the law' in the life of the state."[7] Perhaps the speech that best encapsulates the aspiration of post-Mao legal and political reform to make the law a source of "supreme authority" is Zhao Ziyang's 1987 report to the Thirteenth National Party Congress, where he claimed:

> We should try to define, in terms of law or rules, what should be encouraged and what should be rejected. Only in this way can we bring about a new standard for political, economic, and social activities. And only in this way can we institutionalize various aspects of the society. . . . In short, through reform we should gradually establish a legal framework for our socialist democracy and institutionalize it. This is a fundamental guarantee against a recurrence of the "cultural revolution" and for lasting political stability in our country.[8]

The push to institutionalize democracy had two main implications for the promotion of a new culture of court work where the locus of authority was based on the promises of a socialist rule of law. First, it required the courts to actively encourage a conscious understanding of the necessity of a rule of law—a new moral and legal consciousness—among the citizenry, and to imbue a social morality of a rule of law into public consciousness through lively and speedy means in the form of "propaganda work" (*xuanchuan gongzuo*). Second, the push to institutionalize democracy meant that development of an authoritative persona for courts would reflect the new-found ethos of procedural propriety and procedural regularity, two rhetorical mainframes of a "rule-governed" order.

The importance that the state attaches to courts' propaganda work says much about the role intended for them in shaping the values and legal consciousness of the Chinese citizenry under a socialist rule of law. This emphasis indicates the dominance of understanding within the PRC Party/state that citizens' values and understandings of law and justice, and consequently their behavior, are open and can be fashioned by explicit education and deterrence programs. A reading of propaganda activities in Baotou prompts questioning of how judicial events help to construct a system of meaning within which judicial authority is represented and constituted. In the following discussion of propaganda work, I consider how courts construct a persona of authority using propaganda media, and the use of symbolic rituals of trials to help define and project court authority. Here I explore this area of criminal court work beginning with the general (propaganda work) and moving to the particular (Baotou trials as sites of judicial authority-building). This chapter also examines the self-conscious attempt by institutional authorities in the post-1978 period to develop a new court culture based on a professionalized system of justice administration that conforms with the expectations of the national open reform agenda. The legitimate institutional capacities of courts in China in the post-1978 period reflect a broad vision of political, social, and economic change. The Baotou courts, we find, have attempted to project a vision of their place in the new political order by identifying their judicial authority with changing political and community expectations about the necessity of procedural propriety.

In accordance with the national reform agenda, courts were compelled to establish a new court culture by reshaping their authoritative persona and adjusting their authority relations with other government and Party agencies. As argued previously, this required courts to pursue a "fast-track" turnaround in appearances, shifting from a strictly popular justice culture to Dengist political culture. Below, I explore the ways in which this fast-track to the development of a new image of judicial authority are negotiated and renegotiated, constructed and reconstructed in the everyday judicial and administrative practices of China's courts.

Rationales and Strategies of Law Propaganda Work

In the years following the Third Plenum in 1978, the Chinese government embarked on a nationwide legal education campaign to educate what some officials described as a legally illiterate citizenry (*falu wenmang*). Work units across the country engaged in legal education programs that the Party/state hoped would foster among citizens a basic understanding and "internalizing" of the moral and legal principles and values inherent in the government's reformist "rule of law," in the Constitution, and in the newly promulgated Criminal Law. In the early 1980s, local courts embarked on publicity programs under the rubric of propaganda work (*xuanchuan gongzuo*). Propaganda work for the courts involved both educative and deterrence functions. Local courts conducted "open trials" in accordance with newly promulgated criminal codes as the symbolic reassurance of a new post-Mao form of socialist legality. The courts invited work units to participate as audiences in mass sentencing rallies where procedural propriety was promoted as a new vehicle of justice in a new, open China. Ideologically, the local courts' propaganda work is located within a wider law propaganda program conducted by the Ministry of Justice under the ideological guidance of the CCP. So while local courts administer propaganda work independently of the Ministry of Justice propaganda programs, the aims and strategies of this propaganda work complement a wider strategy of "glorious social engineering."[9] Socialist law theory perceives that the law and legal institutions have the potential to impart social knowledge and understanding to create the new "socialist man," which implies both an educative and creative capacity of law to achieve perfectibility of humanity. As Phillip Chen explained:

> socialist legality makes it the duty of the whole people not only to scrupulously observe the law but also to cooperate actively in creating socialist law, whose function it is to give citizens a precise understanding of these "objective natural processes" of social evolution in order that they may organize all their essential individual activities in a "positive socialist society."[10]

Criminal court work is thus perceived as an interpreter and conduit of public morality and social conduct, as well as a facilitator of change in the social and moral nature of the individual.

Law propaganda work (*fazhi xuanchuan*) is, on the whole, part of an endeavor to effect the social transformation of the individual and society. It has been a component of the broader agenda of Communist Party propaganda strategies since the founding of the PRC.[11] In the post-1978 period, courts in China participated in a wider government program of socialization and reshaping citizens' ethics and values to prepare the citizenry ideologically, morally, and socially for the complexities of a planned socialist commodity economy. The new citizen of China was promoted as someone who needs to be cognizant of and compliant with the social values necessary to function in a civilized and economically developed society. On this basis, in accordance with the Constitution (Article 24) to promote education in "high ideals, ethics, general knowledge, discipline and legality, and by promoting the formulation and observance of rules of conduct," *fazhi xuanchuan* was made an important element of a wider plan to develop "spiritual civilization" in Chinese society.

The government introduced the policy of socialist spiritual civilization (*shehuizhuyi jingshen wenming*) in the early 1980s as an ideology to bridge the gap between the values represented in the "model citizen" of the Mao era and those represented as modern entrepreneurial values. As Wu Lei explains, the role of socialist spiritual civilization in the big picture of reform is to help fulfill the requirements of socialist modernization, to promote citizens who are "idealistic, moral, cultured and disciplined" and to help to advance the "quality of the ideology and morality of the Chinese people." The courts' role in propagating this ideology was to provide positive models of procedural propriety, professionalism, regularity, uniformity of practice, and strict observance of the law. This was to help citizens understand the content of the law and that post-1978 law is located in the formal institutions of justice and not in the revolutionary justice of class struggle.[12]

Like all socialization drives and campaigns since 1949, *fazhi xuanchuan* has been a conscious effort on the part of government to guide how Chinese people behave and think. It is a product of governmental philosophy that human behavior can be manipulated by conscious acts of persuasion and ideological education presented in ways that project both positive and negative models as guides to behavioral change. *Fazhi xuanchuan*, like all politico-educational drives, requires individuals to make a conscious effort to transcend the material limitations of their social and economic environment in order to fulfill the more grandiose vision of a civilized socialist society. *Fazhi xuanchuan* is therefore promoted as a valuable link in developing a social environment that will support the socialist legal system, as a means of cultivating legal consciousness (*falu yishi*), obedience of and respect for the law, and as an important medium for accomplishing comprehensive long-term public order.[13] In 1985, the Minister of Justice, Zou Yu, explained the importance of *fazhi xuanchuan* as a necessary response to a "weak sense of law" that pervades the public and private realm. He claimed that, because Chinese society is handicapped by a low level of education after several thousand years of feudal autocracy, "some citizens are not aware of the law and do not abide by it." He also pointed to the mindless complicity of some government functionaries who, "through the long years of revolutionary wars, fostered the habit of acting upon Party policies alone."[14]

Law education and propaganda work is based on the premise that a legally literate citizenry is an essential component of economic modernization. Hence, educating citizens through the work of *fazhi xuanchuan* is a means, not an end. It is a move considered necessary to ensure the success of an economic reform agenda, it requires positive participation of citizens who have a new consciousness of how social and economic disputes and social relations are to be regulated, and must be adjudicated formally through the nation's legal institutions. A new consciousness of the new socialist law is thus considered a necessary ingredient of national reform. Cultivating a more advanced social character in individuals requires that they be accustomed to the environment of change, and be active participants in that change. *Fazhi xuanchuan* drives followed the promulgation of all major laws in the PRC in the early 1980s, including the Constitution and the criminal codes. The Ministry of Justice organized campaigns under the ideological guidance of the Communist Party and in allegiance with the judicial organs. From 1982, primary schools, secondary schools, and universities began to conduct legal education classes.[15] At the same time, legal education classes were conducted in all government work units across the country.

The Symbolic Potential of Trials

At a National Seminar on Law Education in 1988, a vice-president of the Supreme Court, Zhu Mingshan, offered a number of opinions on the necessity and functions of the propaganda work of the court. In identifying its "unique nature," Zhu distinguished court propaganda work from the wider body of legal education programs. He defined it as an ideologically associated, yet organizationally separate, part of the government's wider call to educate citizens in the law. According to Zhu, the courts perform propaganda and education work in direct response to stipulations of the Organic Law of the People's Court that identifies the important educative role of courts. And, as he observed, it is a discrete type of propaganda work. Speaking for courts across the nation, Zhu specified that:

> We are not to be considered simply a part of the Communist Party's Propaganda Department as we are not concerned with all aspects of propaganda work. Neither are we to be considered simply a part of propaganda work of the Ministry of Justice as we do not conduct ordinary law education classes. We are not concerned with the most common forms of law propaganda work; we are concerned with the propaganda work specific to the people's courts.[16]

Vice-President Zhu explained the two key aspects of education work in courts, one relating to the courts' own propaganda work that is undertaken independent of other state organs, and the other relating to propaganda work addressed in coordination with the mass media.[17] In a speech on the Development of Comprehensive Public Order presented at a National Conference for Court Work, Lin Zhun, another vice-president of the Supreme People's Court, outlined a variety of measures open to courts in their role as propagators of law and justice. Courts could use newspapers, radio, television, and local court bulletins and could also assist in the presentation of law education classes (*xuexi ban*) held by the Justice Ministry and Bureau of Justice.[18] Court workers were also encouraged to visit work units, companies, and farms to give information sessions (*falu zixun*).[19] Showcase displays set up outside courts, police stations, and procuratorate offices displaying illustration of laws and cases were also frequent during the height of the legal publicity drives in the 1980s. Also during the 1980s, "blackboard newspapers" displayed on public notice boards in urban areas and various exhibitions held in public arenas and public address systems in rural areas provided a means of basic legal education. The staging of these educative events usually coincided with the promulgation of particular laws or during anti-crime campaigns to promote crime prevention.[20]

Media such as newspapers, television, and radio provide a significant avenue for communication and play an integral role in disseminating messages about the courts, the law, punishment, and justice. However, the most important communication media available to judicial institutions are the public trial and the sentencing rally.[21] Legal and penal practices have the symbolic potential to organize, classify, and construct images and messages about law, justice, and authority, and this is well-established in the contemporary literature on socio-legal studies. As David Garland notes:

> In its own way, penal practice provides an organizing cultural framework whose declarations and actions serve as an interpretative grid through which people evaluate conduct and make moral sense of their experience. The penal system thus acts as a regulatory social mechanism in two distinct respects: it regulates conduct through the physical medium of social action, but it also regulates meaning, thought, attitude—and hence conduct—through the rather different medium of signification.[22]

Like penal practices in general, court practices have the symbolic potential to organize social understanding of the court's own authority and its identity as a legitimate administrator of justice. Court practices, while performing an immediate instrumental goal, are also symbolic reassurances of the capacity of the state both to protect its citizens and to reflect the prevailing moral order. As symbolic "messages," the courts' adjudication and sentencing practices help to establish judicial legitimacy in the eyes of the public by convening the courts' institutional authority and by presenting court strategies and attitudes toward crime as the legitimate social and moral norm. The courts' capacity to affect their social environment therefore extends beyond their most immediate function of determining guilt and sentencing individual offenders. Adjudicative and sentencing practices are not merely a practical legal means to a particular social end (crime control), they are also practices performed in the public gaze, purporting to embody the morality of the public.[23]

We need to consider the significance of Chinese courts deliberately conducting trials in the public gaze in this light. *The Encyclopedia of Public Security in China* describes the public trial, or open proceedings (*gongkai shenli*), as a trial held in public where both the time and the location of the trial are publicized before the event. This allows for the public to attend trials, for the media to conduct interviews, and for the verdict of cases to be announced publicly. The public trial is seen as a means of attracting the participation and enabling the supervision of the masses, and is considered an important expression of socialist democratic justice.[24]

Historically, the CCP has promulgated the public trial as the legitimate format of adjudication in periods when the Party has promoted socialist construction and regularization of industry and government as the central political tasks of that stage of social development. During these periods, the scientific nature of socialist legality is promoted as a guiding light for economic reform and construction, while the hard-core propaganda of "mass line" and "popular justice" is backstaged. In the 1950s, for example, in periods when the imperative of economic construction and the necessity of a more systematized and efficient bureaucracy were the focus of national attention, procedural regulations in courts were tightened and focus was placed on procedural propriety. In late 1978, again with the imperative of economic reform, a reworking of the 1950s themes of socialist legality to accentuate the values of "equality before the law" and "independent administration" brought a return in 1978 to the legitimization of open trials as a regularized, organized, and institutionalized means of justice administration.

The open trial is an important representation of the main message of legal reform—the idea of openness, standardization of procedure, fairness, and due process. The courtroom provides both the content and the symbolic arrangements necessary for the dissemination of messages about procedural propriety. As SPC Vice-President Zhu Mingshan explains:

> The content of all propaganda must be directly related to trial work [adjudication and sentencing]. . . . Courts should avoid any form of propaganda that is empty of content and any kind of legal speech-making which is dull or dry. We should jointly present cases that make for a vivid, lively and concrete propaganda display. First and foremost, we must employ concrete trials to the full, and bring into full play the use of the courtroom as a stage for propaganda. It is well documented that if trials are conducted properly, their educational effects will be great. On the other hand, if trials are not conducted well, it may result in a loss of confidence in court work and in the legal system in general, on the part of those who attend trials.[25]

The salient point here is that, in adjudicating in the courtroom, judicial authorities seek to actively construct, extend, and reinforce social understandings of law and justice through the very conduct of their courtroom tasks. An internal judicial publication outlining judicial procedures in the reform period describes the benefits of trials in a similar light. First, it identifies trials as the most appropriate medium to embody, promote, and express the democratic and just spirit of court work. The publication says that, in giving the defendant the right to freely state his/her opinions, to be represented by counsel and to participate in the case debate, the system of open trials demonstrates to the public that trial work is just, open, and operates to protect the interests of the people. Second, the publication claims that open trials provide an opportunity for supervision of court work by the masses, thus enhancing the quality of court work. Conducting trials under the supervision of the masses helps to ensure that cases are tried justly and objectively, that the defendant's and the prosecution's arguments are reasonable, that the evidence submitted is sufficient, and that judgment is correct and in accordance with the law.

Third, the publication claims that open trials are beneficial for maintaining a close link between judicial organs and the masses, and as a vivid and lively method of presenting legal education to the public. Because open trials entail the processes of determining guilt and exposing crime, those who attend open trials learn to distinguish what types of behavior constitute a crime, what rights are protected under the law, and the extent of harm that criminals inflict on society. Trials demonstrate that "criminal cunning cannot succeed in escaping the arm of the law." In exposing criminal activities to the masses, open trials also serve to "educate the masses in improving their vigilance and unconscious respect for the law." These trials serve as a useful warning to any unstable elements, making them think twice about defying the law and, in so doing, help to achieve the objective of crime prevention.[26] The process of the open trial demonstrates that justice is attained through procedural propriety "in accordance with the law." The format of the open trial provides onlookers with a language and classification of social concepts to determine what is deviant, what is illegal, and what is just.

SPC Vice-President Lin Zhun, in an address to court officials, captured the importance of trial work as an integral part of law education. He maintained that, because all court activities can be said to revolve around the central tasks of trial work, the propaganda work of the courts needs to promote the legal system by employing appropriate model trials as exemplars of justice.[27]

> The basic medium in which propaganda and education work is conducted by the people's courts takes the form of open trials. Every case that in accordance with the law should be tried openly, must be tried openly. But must we therefore assume that once a trial is conducted openly, it fulfils the propaganda and education work of courts? The Shanghai Higher Court has an opinion on this: "Conducting trials openly in accordance with the law is *only half the task*. A second aspect of trial work is to carry out legal education through open trials. It is to conduct legal education with the motive being to present a warning [to potential criminals], to assist in reducing disputes and to bring into full play, the social effects of trials."[28]

In calling for the courtroom to be "a classroom for law propaganda," Lin places trials as the centerpiece of the educative tasks of court work: in demonstrating the law through concrete examples of trials, trials provide "a *direct* means of educating the masses to obey the law."[29] We find, therefore, that the operative elements of the fabric of instrumental practices of courts are the very symbolic activities that courts employ as a mechanism for organizing and communicating to the public key messages about crime, law, deviance, justice, and authority. The assumed capacity of judicial authorities to regulate public understanding of these notions through trials makes trials signifying practices.

The actual format, procedure, and actors in the trial are integral components in the message since the format of the trial prefigures any message that is communicated.[30] In this sense, the symbolic arrangements of trials can be understood as rituals that operate within the mundane routines of adjudication, guilt determination, and sentencing. The symbolic quality of the actions performed gives the ritual its defining characteristics. Particular judicial acts such as delivering summarizing statements, adjudicating court debates, and declaring the verdict and sentencing are messages that are part of the ritual of the trial.[31] In providing a framework within which regulative rules operate, the ritual of the trial establishes purposeful associations between the social participants and the rules applied to particular behavior. As such, the processes and actions of judicial actors in trials do not simply express a certain point, but create the reality of the particular event and the meanings attached to the event.[32]

Furniture, fittings, and other spatial arrangements of trials carry both legal and presentational significance. Spatial arrangements, modes of dress and address, procedure, props, and actors in the trial process also act as "carriers of meaning" in the trial. In particular, they carry meanings about authority relations in the trial process. The rules on spacing in the courtroom of the intermediate court in China convey particular meanings about the authority roles and relationships of participants.[33] An excerpt from a circular issued by the SPC in 1982 demonstrates the importance placed on the overall presentational design of courtrooms as a physical setting designed to accentuate the legitimacy and authority of the court.

> Courtrooms are the sites in which people's courts exercise their judicial authority in trying cases. . . . Courtroom design must be practical and must look stately, dignified and tasteful. The courtroom design must embody the unique characteristics attributed to trial work and its design must therefore be distinctly different from common auditoriums, theatres and other buildings. Architectural standards of courtrooms must exceed those of normal buildings.[34]

This symbolic importance of courtroom design to the development of an authoritative persona is nowhere more evident than in official recommendations for courtroom design and architecture. A key politico-legal circular produced by judicial authorities notes that, ideally, the external design of court buildings should embody a sense of stability and practicality, and the ideal court house should be built with at least a dozen stairs leading up to the main entrance. The interior design of the courtroom should reflect the delineation of activities: the main arena of trial activity should take up at least two-thirds of the room, the area in which the trial process itself takes place should be kept separate from the public gallery by a rail or banister, and judges should have access to entrances and exits separate from those for the general public and other participants. Walls and furnishing should be in darker colors such as tan or dark red to reflect the somber atmosphere of the courtroom and there should be no adornments on walls. If at all possible, natural lighting should be used. If not, recessed lighting is preferable and there should be no pendulous lights or lighting attached to walls. Courtrooms should be designed with an incline up to the gallery so that the audience in the public gallery is able to view proceedings clearly. However, no seating position in the courtroom should exceed the judge's bench in height. An impression should be created that the collegiate bench is the exclusive area of the judiciary. Hence, there should be no direct access from the public gallery to the bench.[35] The spatial arrangements of the courtroom allow the judge to be positioned, as Michael Dutton observes, "at the epicenter of power."[36] The defendant, on the other hand, is seated at the center of the judge's line of vision, and the defense and prosecution, seated at the judge's side, "are offered only a partial view of the accused, for they will offer only partial statements of his crime."[37]

Judicial authority is represented not only in spatial arrangements, but also in the procedural transactions between the judge, prosecution, and defense. From the moment the collegiate panel enters the courtroom, it is the presiding judge who is the center of legal and presentational significance. The presiding judge controls the timing of each stage of the trial. All activity, from handling documents to questioning witnesses, is via the presiding judge, and each stage of the trial proceeds only with the prior consent of the judge. Judges are thus the center of communicative activity as well as the center of ceremonious presentation.[38] Below we briefly examine the organization of courts and the judicial process in the PRC in order to understand what kind of judicial authority is projected in criminal trials.

The Organization of Justice

Mirjin Damaska's *The Faces of Justice and State Authority* offers a typology of modern legal systems based on the idea that there exists a strong connection between the wider political culture of a social system and authority relations within the system of justice administration[39] He explores both the character of judicial authority and the functional attributes of justice administration as a way of distinguishing characteristics of legal processes in modern states. Beginning with the assumption that there is a linkage between the general character of political authority and the character of procedural design, he argues that there are a number of common characteristics related to those systems of justice administration, which are primarily marked by a hierarchically organized system of judicial authority. He contrasts these characteristics with those pertaining to "coordinate" systems of judicial authority which feature a less integrated, more horizontal distribution of authority (common law systems, for example, which rely on lay officials, Party control over proceedings, oral testimony, and limited review). In "activist" states such as the PRC, criminal law is, in essence, an instrument for the implementation and realization of state policy. It follows from there that the judicial format in judicial institutions in an activist state is one that reflects a "policy-implementing" disposition rather than a "conflict-resolving" disposition.

Law in this context "springs from the state and expresses its policies."[40] In China, the programmatic nature of the law and judicial activity is brought out in the political arrangements of state power and in the ideological frameworks of socialist law and social development that support these arrangements. "Policy-implementation" is a defining rationale for the format of procedure in courts in an activist state. The hierarchical forms of authority (favored mostly in inquisitorial systems such as in China) are distinguished by the use of a permanent career bureaucracy whose duties are performed in specialized stages controlled by strict adherence to technical and bureaucratic standards. Justice administration in hierarchical systems relies mainly on written records of proceedings, and testimony is usually organized in case files which follow the case up the procedural ladder.[41]

The judicial-executive relationship in the PRC can be conceived of as a form of "corporatism": a structure of state power that promotes "a certain conception of the good and implies a highly managed and regulated civil society, organically linked to the state."[42] The judicial-executive relationship is therefore characterized by "a *division* of power rather than a separation of power."[43] There is close consultation between the judiciary and other executive agencies, and strong tendencies "for the judiciary to yield to other agencies where these agencies are thought to have greater competence," and for the corporatist elements of judicial-executive relations to "draw sustenance from organic conceptions of the state."[44] The political arrangements of state power in the PRC compel the programmatic, policy-implementing nature of judicial activity in the ideological frameworks of socialist law. *Division* of power rather than *separation* of power between state legislative bodies and other politico-legal agencies is reflected in the judiciary's relationship with the legislature (the people's congresses at each corresponding level) and with other agencies including the procuratorate (public prosecution) and the public security organs (the police).[45] These relationships are organized to maximize the successful achievement of state objectives and to accommodate the smooth implementation of Party and government policy. Courts "are seen as part of the bureaucracy rather than as an entity constituted outside of the executive. Within this framework, the task of the Chinese judiciary is to consult and co-operate with other agencies."[46]

This tightly integrated organization of officialdom involves a multilayered structure of supervision and superior review.[47] Supervision and superior review—or what Mark Findlay calls "structures of dependence"[48]—operate on a number of levels. These encompass a wide range of roles and responsibilities of judicial, political, and Party organs including governmental and Party organs at both higher and corresponding levels. Regular review and audit by superiors is not confined to the judicial practice of appeal and is instead an integral component of the routine responsibilities of Party, judicial, and state organs. Review provides a system of mutual cooperation and mutual checks and balances between corresponding politico-legal organs (the courts, procuratorate, and police), between organs of state power (the people's congress) at the corresponding level, between the courts and Party organs at corresponding and higher levels, within the hierarchy of the court system (courts at higher levels), and in the internal organization of courts.

The Organic Law of the People's Courts (1979) and the Constitution (1982) (and now the Judges Law of 1995 and the new Criminal Procedure Law (CPL) 1996) provide for this multilayered system of supervision and superior review by subjecting the people's courts at each level to dual leadership by its superior court and by the people's congress at its corresponding level.[49] The foundation of state organization, the National People's Congress (NPC) and its Standing Committee, "merges legislative with executive power."[50] State power is "unitary instead of plural" and is characterized by a "division of labor and responsibilities for sectors of government under the unified guidance of state power."[51] The people's court is responsible to the people's congress at each corresponding level. The people's congress elects presidents of courts at the corresponding level and appoints and removes vice-presidents, chief judges, and associate chief judges of court divisions.[52] Courts are part of the administrative structure of the state and are like other administrative organs. They rely on the Ministry of Finance of the State Council and its local departments at each corresponding level of government for all funding including capital, resources, and salaries.[53]

Court hierarchy facilitates supervision over lower courts by higher courts. The court system is organized on a "four levels and two trials" basis with the highest judicial institution of the state, the Supreme People's Court (SPC), at the top of a four-tiered structure comprising also local people's courts at provincial, municipal, and county level and special courts.[54] The local people's courts comprise higher people's courts (*gaoji renmin fayuan*) at the level of province or autonomous region, intermediate courts (*zhongji renmin fayuan*) at the level of municipality or prefecture, and basic people's courts (*jiceng renmin fayuan*) at the level of county or district. In some basic courts, mainly in rural townships and outlying areas, there are branch courts known as people's tribunals (*renmin fating*) that hear cases on behalf of the basic people's courts. The SPC "supervises"[55] the administration of justice at lower levels of the judicial system through a number of adjudicatory and administrative means, including issuing judicial interpretations, circulars, and conference summaries, conducting "adjudication supervision," reviewing and approving some capital sentences of lower courts, and hearing appellate cases of second instance.[56]

Judicial Procedure

One common thread that runs through 1950s and 1980s Baotou court history is that judicial procedure is depicted and legitimated as an essential tool of policy implementation. The trial is organized essentially as an investigation, an inquiry in which the process of "fact-finding" in the courtroom is controlled by judicial authorities. In the policy-implementing mode of procedure, the trial is primarily a matter of tailoring the outcome of a dispute to fit the contours of existing governmental or judicial policies and is not presented as a judicial contest played out between equal parties. Damaska explains case selection in a "policy-implementing" format of judicial procedure in the following way:

> In the legal process of the reactive state, decisions are justified more in terms of the fairness of procedures employed than the accuracy of results obtained. In contrast, procedural rules and regulation in an activist state occupy a much less important and independent position: procedure is basically a handmaiden of substantive law. If the purpose of the legal process is to realize state policy in contingent cases, decisions are legitimated primarily in terms of the correct outcomes they embody. A proper procedure is one that increases the probability—or maximizes the likelihood—of achieving a substantively accurate result rather than one that successfully effects notions of fairness or protects some collateral substantive value.[57]

Five characteristics of Damaska's policy-implementing style of judicial procedure stand out as the most appropriate characteristics of the policy implementing style of criminal procedure in the PRC Criminal Procedure Law (1979) and in subsequent subsidiary regulations on procedure. They are that:

- case selection is a means of controlling court outcomes; there is official monopolization of trial process, and decisionmaking controls court outcomes;
- the trial is essentially conceived as an inquiry and the object of inquiry (the defendant) is primarily a supplier of information;
- the status and role of parties in court debate is largely determined by the "policy-implementing" goal of trial;
- the central position of the decisionmaker is highlighted in the judgment and conclusion process.[58]

In China, the criminal trial is an investigation by civil servants comprising a collegiate panel (three judges) or, in minor criminal cases, a single panel with one presiding judge. The defendant is the object of procedural action and is, in essence, "an information source."[59] The independent bench (comprising a single judge) and the collegiate panel are the two basic organizational formats for trial hearings. The independent bench comprises a single judge for simple civil and criminal cases and the collegiate panel comprises one judge and two people's assessors or three judges. In appellate cases, the panel comprises three or five judges.[60] The presiding judge in each case is appointed by the court president, and the chief judge of a division and the panel make collective decisions on the principle of "the minority giving in to the majority."[61] A collegial panel is not a permanent entity; it is formed and disbanded for each trial. For each case that is accepted by the court that requires a collegial panel, the chief judge of the particular division of the court selects one or more judges to form a collegial panel.[62]

A judge (*shenpanyuan*) has the task of representing the court in exercising the judicial authority given by the state, by adjudicating trials in the first and second instance and providing recommendations and opinions in their area of jurisdiction and expertise. The responsibility of a criminal division judge in a single-judge trial is to examine the case file, investigate the details in the file, make notes on cases, analyze and decide which evidence is to be admitted, and write a draft of the intended sequence of the proceedings. The responsibility of a presiding judge in a collegial panel is to perform the above functions of a single-trial judge as well as to guide (*zhihui*) all judicial activity and to organize members of the collegial panel. Other judges in the collegial panel are required to assist in fulfilling judicial tasks and must take part in judicial decisionmaking during deliberation. It is the responsibility of a judge during a trial to ascertain the time, location, motive, intent, method, and consequence of a crime and to clarify the facts of the case. It is the judge's responsibility to determine criminality, guilt, or innocence and, in cases in which an offender is convicted of a crime, to determine the object (*zhuti*) infringed, the social harm caused, and the specific relationship between the criminal act and consequence of the criminal act.[63] Table 2.1 sets out the number and divisional positions of judges and assistant judges in the Baotou Intermediate Court in 1986.

Table 2.1. Judges and Assistant Judges in Baotou Intermediate Court in 1986

Division	Personnel
No. 1 Criminal Division	4 Judges 2 Assistant Judges
No. 2 Criminal Division	6 Judges
Civil Division	4 Judges 1 Assistant Judge
Economic Division	1 Judge 1 Assistant Judge
Case Petitions Division	6 Judges 1 Assistant Judge
Enforcement Division	1 Judge 1 Assistant Judge

Source: Information from "Appendix," *The Annals*: 177–82.

The first and most important stage of a criminal trial is the *inquiry* stage (*diaocha*), in which the judge interrogates the defendant and witnesses and where material evidence is presented to the court. The judge must be seen to be "seeking truth from facts" (*shishi qiushi*) through a process of fact-finding. As part of the judge's inquiry, the defendant is expected to give a full statement. The defense and the procuratorate have the right to question the defendant during this process. The victim or their representative has the right to question the defendant after the judge has completed the questioning.[64]

Most cases rely on written witness statements, not cross-examination. If witnesses are available to attend trial they are called to provide testimony at the inquiry stage of the trial. When the witness is seated, the presiding judge will first confirm his/her identity and relevance to the case, other parties, or victim. If the procuratorate or defense asks to cross-examine the witness, the presiding judge allows questions to proceed. Expert witnesses may read out their findings and the presiding judge allows the procuratorate to question the witness.[65] During the inquiry stage of the trial, the collegial panel (or single judge) should allow for the presentation of all material and documentary evidence given by the procuratorate, defendant, or defenders, whether harmful or beneficial to the defendant. Documentary evidence includes any statements or written words that are presented as proof. Material evidence includes physical goods and trails such as tools, footprints, or blood.[66]

The *debate* stage of the trial (*bianlun*) is when the defense has the opportunity to put its case forward (usually to argue for mitigated punishment) and to present an alternate view of the facts brought out in the inquiry stage. The main aim of the debate is to ensure that all facts supporting the prosecution or defense of the accused can be presented to the court. The arguments brought out in the debate supplement the facts and evidence presented in the most important part of the trial, the inquiry. If the arguments in the debate seriously bring into question the validity of the facts presented in the inquiry stage, the panel may require that the facts be reinvestigated. In this case, the presiding judge can announce a suspension of the debate and a return to the inquiry stage of the trial. When the inquiry is complete, the judge will announce the recommencement of the debate. After at least one round of debating, the presiding judge may announce a time limitation on the second round, or announce the conclusion of the debate. After the conclusion is announced, the defendant has the right to present a final statement.[67] If the defendant's final statement contains facts or new evidence that will influence the criminal charge or sentence determination, the collegial panel declares a return to the inquiry stage of the trial.

Using the explanatory value of the above discussion of trials as a means of conveying messages about judicial authority, let us turn to explore authority-building through trials and procedure in the Baotou criminal court.

Representing Authority in Baotou Trials and Procedures

A reading of the chapter in the Baotou document "Putting into Effect the Structure of Criminal Procedure" reveals the importance of dramatizing routine judicial procedures in the development of judicial authority. The Baotou chapter on criminal procedure summarizes the evolution of the system of criminal procedure and procedural rules in the 1950s and presents an account of the first public trial in Baotou in the post-1978 period. As the text makes clear, the public display of socialist justice at work in trials serves as an important means for judicial authorities to seek validity and credibility as administrators of justice in the reform era. Depictions of the professionalism and authority of court workers are part of a new court culture promoted in the post-1978 period. The Baotou text portrays the authority of judicial decisionmaking in court trials as deriving from strict adherence to the written law. Hence, the rhetorical catchcries of "procedural propriety—independent administration of justice," "equality before the law," and "trying cases in accordance with the law"—firmly anchor the actions of the Baotou courts in the broader rhetorical settings of economic and political reformist ideologies. Through trials, the criminal courts in Baotou have sought to educate the public by propagating messages about law and order, crime, and crime control.

Although the propaganda messages of trials are largely about law and order—about how the state responds to crime and how crime does not pay—the messages are also about the court itself. Trials provide an arena from where the claim to the court's authority is articulated to the larger community. This process of constructing and reinforcing judicial authority is based on two characteristics: one grounded in the aspirational rhetoric of reform (the ethos of judicial professionalism and a strict adherence to the new procedural law) and the other based on a form of nostalgic reference to mid-1950s socialist justice. Since the development of institutional authority is put forward as an important complement to the post-1978 reforms, it is useful to consider how institutional authority fits within the aspirations and expectations of reformist ideologies. Here we will explore the format and narratives of trials and court procedure in the 1980s as described in the Baotou document to identify the link between the development of court authority and the aspiration of reformist ideologies.

From the Baotou text we learn that, in constructing a professional persona in the Baotou courts, authorities exercised their claim to office by projecting the expectations and aspirations of the procedural propriety of past and present court work. The development of judicial authority in Baotou has depended not merely on the existence of people who fill an authority role and perform duties, but also on the claim of court workers to the validity and credibility of their roles. We find that in Baotou judicial authority has depended on the ability of court workers to make convincing claims to the public about their legitimacy as administrators of justice. The courts have attempted to establish and cultivate their belief in their own legitimacy by means of securing particular constitutions of *order* in judicial procedure.

The Baotou text does not provide a detailed description of judicial procedure in Baotou in the 1980s. Instead, it describes Baotou's first open trial in twenty-two years held in September 1979, a trial that showcases the Criminal Procedure Law enacted only months earlier. The 1979 Criminal Procedure Law of the People's Republic of China (CPL) was implemented in Baotou with all the fanfare expected of a crucial and long-awaited turning point in the development of a professionalized and authoritative judiciary. The CPL's significance is further enhanced by a reminder of the credibility that the Baotou courts lost in the years of leftist chaos from 1957 to 1976:

> In 1957, during the Anti-rightist campaign, a number of comrades in the court were denounced as rightist because they offered positive criticisms of the system in order to help the Party make improvements. These were criticisms about legal concepts that were completely in keeping with the laws of the time, for example, the concept of equality before the law, the concept of courts being independent, being subject only to the law and so on. Procedural propriety was denounced as being "pedantic and overly-literal about the law," and there was criticism of the court for "using law in isolation" and "sentencing lightly." From this time on, key aspects of court work, such as the system of people's assessors, the collegial panel, and the process of appeal, were quashed, being replaced with a system whereby all cases had to be examined and approved by Party members; a situation whereby Party policy took the place of the law. This situation persisted until the promulgation of the Criminal Procedure Law in 1979.[68]

The CPL was the first complete law on criminal procedure promulgated in the thirty-year history of the PRC. Based on the "concrete experiences of the people in carrying out the people's democratic dictatorship," its aim was to punish criminals, to ensure procedural regularity and accuracy in order to protect citizens' rights, to educate citizens, to uphold the socialist legal system, and to "guarantee the cause of the socialist revolution and socialist construction."[69] As "The Summary of Criminal Trial Work" suggests, the implementation of the CPL in Baotou is described as a test of the courts' authority to administer justice.

> The passing of the Criminal Law and the Criminal Procedure Law along with five other important laws in the Second Session of the Fifth National People's Congress in July 1979 heralded a new stage in the construction of the socialist legal system. From this time on, the courts had rules to follow and laws to abide by. Because of the state of legal nihilism that had ensued for a long period, the idea of the Party taking the place of government and the idea of Party policy taking the place of law, had become the norm in the minds of some personnel. So, when the "Two Codes" were implemented, all eyes were on the courts to see whether the courts really would handle cases "in accordance with the law." The masses' anxiety was both a kind of pressure and a challenge for the courts. The masses supervised the courts in handling matters strictly according to the law. In accordance with the Party Central Committee Document No. 64 (1979), in the second half of 1979 the two tiers of the Baotou courts began on the one hand to wage an attack on criminals and on the other hand to initiate "on the job training" to implement the Two Codes.[70]

The CPL was implemented at a time when there were no large courtrooms, few amenities, few trained judicial staff, and a severe shortage of funds in Baotou. Training, staff, funding, courtrooms, and other resources are elements essential to running courts effectively. They are also the very props required for courts to develop and promote their authority to administer justice. That the Baotou courts forged ahead in their goal of creating a new post-1978 court culture by promoting institutional legitimacy and authority despite these limitations speaks of how court workers recognized the significance of procedural propriety as a key symbol of reform. This came at a time when the courts' image of credibility and authority in other areas was severely hamstrung by thirty years of neglect of government funding and judicial training. Hence, the Baotou text explains that procedural rules are based on the "fine traditions" of procedural propriety in the 1950s—not the unattainable well-furnished courtrooms, silk judges' robes, and highly educated staff—a practicable claim to support judicial authority in the post-1978 period. The importance of the "fine traditions" of the mid-1950s to be continued post-1978 can be discerned in the emphasis on the courts "relying on concrete experiences" of the masses and the Party. Here, the pedigree of 1980s procedure is made directly dependent on the legitimacy endowed upon mid-1950s procedure, and the source of this legitimacy is that in both periods the courts "rely on the masses," "proceed from present reality," and "seek truth from facts."

In this explication we find multiple reasons for the significance of court procedure as a framework for building judicial authority. It is not just that the performance of court work "proceeds from present reality" and "seeks truth from facts," or that it is based on the fine traditions of past practices and procedures. Crucial to this conceptualizing is that court work is *seen* to be performed in such a way. In other words, public perception is recognized as crucial to establishing and legitimizing court authority.

As noted above, the Baotou document reveals how the conceptualization of court procedure as a symbol of judicial authority in the 1980s relies heavily on a detailed background of legal processes in the mid-1950s. This is because 1950s court work is used to provide a legal tradition to legitimize reformist procedures and practices of the 1980s. The procedural details in the Baotou chapter on judicial procedure are essentially the details of procedural rules from the earlier period to accentuate this ideal. In turn, the basis of 1950s court work is explained as the "concrete experience" of the (pre-1949) socialist revolution. Here, one interpretation of history is legitimizing another:

> From the end of 1954 to 1955, the Municipal People's Court made all efforts to apply the "Organic Law of the People's Courts" to court work and there was a vast improvement compared to the period before the Organic Law. The court put into effect the system of public trials, people's assessors and collegiate panels, in its entirety. After a period of implementation of the Organic Law, the

> courts developed in more detail . . . [a] . . . framework of court procedure based on concrete experience.[71]

A model trial held on September 28, 1978 was organized as a public event to provide an exemplar of procedural propriety. The trial was to demonstrate publicly that the court was performing in accordance with both the traditions of good socialist practice and in accordance with the expectations of the post-1978 reform agendas. Criminal justice workers and more than six hundred of the "masses" attended the trial. The vice-president of the Baotou Intermediate Court, Li Wenkao, one of the only judicial staff members who had hands-on experience as a trial judge, convened the first public trial-cum-training session for judicial staff in a hired auditorium. The Baotou text described spatial arrangements of this hired courtroom:

> The auditorium was brightly lit, the national emblem was hung up on the wall above the judicial bench and two judicial police stood at either side of the bench. At the center of the courtroom were the key judicial officers and the court clerk. The dock was positioned in front of the bench. To the right of the bench was the prosecution's table and to the left was the defendant's table.[72]

Until then, a portrait of Mao was usually hung on the wall of the courtroom, not the national coat of arms. The hanging of the national emblem was a symbol of a renewed sense of procedural propriety: rule of law, not rule of man, of nation rather than of national leader personified as Mao.

In an attempt to be seen to perform in accordance with the expectations of national reform, the trial proceedings closely followed the narrative of procedural propriety as set out in the CPL that had been passed by the NPC only months before. The Baotou text notes that first, the main parties in the proceedings were introduced one by one in the judicial ritual, starting with the four unemployed defendants on trial on multiple theft charges. The presiding judge confirmed the identity of the defendants as Xing Chengming, a twenty-four-year-old unemployed male residing in Donghe district, Guo Runcun, a twenty-five-year-old unemployed male residing in Donghe district, Sun Yu, a twenty-year-old male residing in Donghe district, and forty-eight-year-old Hou Yulian, the unemployed mother of Guo Runcun. Second, the collegial panel was introduced, comprising Li Wenkao himself as chief judge (the vice-president of the Baotou Intermediate Court) and two people's assessors, Xue Yuwen and Du Xumei. The Baotou text notes that Judge Ma Weigang acted as court recorder, and the Municipal People's Procurator, Guo Gang, acted as prosecutor. The three people acting as public defenders for the defendants were Li Zhunde, a former staff member of the Municipal Legal Advisory Office, Chang Songcun, a lecturer in Marxism–Leninism at the Baotou Medical College, and Lu Yide, a high school teacher at the New Town High School in the Outer Suburbs district.

Procedures in the September 28 trial were followed to the letter of the new CPL. The four defendants were informed of their rights: to have a defense, to demand withdrawal of any officers of the court, to introduce new evidence, to question the witnesses, to make a final statement, and to appeal. At the trial all four defendants admitted guilt, each one explaining the circumstances of his or her crime. After two rounds of debate (*bianlun*), and following the defendants' final statements, the court adjourned for a short time to deliberate. Judgment was then announced in detail: two of the defendants had committed sixteen counts of theft over the period October 1977 to July 1978, stealing a total of 1,284 yuan in cash and 110,000 yuan worth of goods, including various brands of watches, 106 items of clothing, 2 radios, and 2 "135" cameras, more than 300 *jin* of pork and lamb meat, 5 bicycles, more than 160 cartons of cigarettes, ration tickets, cotton, a record player, camera film, and alcohol. Xing Chenming was convicted on charges of theft and armed robbery and was sentenced to eighteen years imprisonment. Guo Runcun was convicted on charges of theft and was sentenced to fifteen years imprisonment. The final crime, in which the two accused were caught in the act, was described as "particularly heinous," because the resident whom the accused assaulted with a tool caught the pair, thus constituting a crime of armed robbery. Xing's mother, Hou Yulian, was found to be fully aware of her son's criminal activity and had harbored the criminal, covered up the crimes, and even made use of some of the stolen goods. Despite this, both she and Sun Yu were dealt with lightly and did not attract a criminal record.[73] The Baotou text's description of the model trial concludes with the following comment.

> The courts have conscientiously implemented every aspect of the system of legal procedure. All cases, which, according to law, should be tried in open court, have been tried in open court. Judgments on cases that by law are not tried in open court are nevertheless announced publicly, and at every opportunity, the courts propagate the law in order to improve the social effectiveness of the law.[74]

This description indicates that the post-1978 trial is to convey a clear message: justice is no longer attained through the "uninstutionalized" and unmediated will of the masses as characterized in the "lost" years of court work from 1958 to 1976. Rather, *The Annals* portrays justice as increasingly institutionalized in the procedural and bureaucratic processes of trial work. Here we see how the moral authority of socialist legality—as the legitimizing force of punishment—continues to be presented as a reflection of the will of the masses. However, the conditions under which this new vision of moral authority is constructed in the 1980s require the vehicle of a judiciary, which fits closely within the larger institutional and political project of reform. We see that the conceptual goalposts of authority have been moved within the discursive boundaries of reformist ideologies and the basis of moral authority in unmediated revolutionary popular justice has been shifted back to reincorporate the institutionally-based claims legitimizing authority that were first promulgated in the period of institution-building in the 1950s.

Trials and Propaganda in 2001

One of the most significant changes to the presentation and mode of propagating law since the late 1990s has been the introduction of live and videotaped television coverage of important trials. Trial footage is used in three main television formats: standard news footage, documentaries, and live broadcasts of important trials. One of the first and most popular examples of a documentary series televised in 2000 and 2001 titled *Fawang: da'an jishi* (The Legal Net: A chronicle of major cases) provided far greater detail into police investigations and court procedures than similar "reality TV" Western television documentaries. The series, covering over fifty cases, includes police file footage of interrogation, public trials, sentencing, and public parading of soon-to-be executed criminals. More recently, reality TV series on law such as *Jinri shuofa* (Talking Law Today) and *Fazhi shenghuo* (Law and Life) have become as popular as they are in the West. Although more a form of entertainment than a propaganda program, series like these nevertheless afford a far greater coverage of police and judicial activities than would have been possible even a decade ago. Like the documentary series, live coverage of important trials, which began in 2001, is also an indication that the courts, the procuratorate and the public security bureau are increasingly confident of demonstrating their legal prowess to wide audiences. In 2001, due to nationwide public outrage and indignation toward a serial bank robber and murderer, Zhang Jun, politico-legal authorities for the first time allowed live TV and Internet coverage of the trial of the infamous Zhang and his gang who murdered twenty-eight people in over a dozen separate incidents.

Other efforts by the judiciary to develop public credibility and legitimacy include the decision in 2000 that judges change their official attire from military-style uniforms to Western-style judicial robes. The adoption of Western judicial robes, some judges argued, endows the judiciary with a sense of legitimacy that would not have otherwise been possible. For instance, one article written by an intermediate court judge appeared on the PRC judges' website in April 2000 praising the adoption of Western-style judicial gowns as the official attire for judges in China. The judge explained:

> In recent times, we have witnessed important changes in the dress code of judges. As from April 2000, the [military style] suit, epaulet and the judge's service cap have been abolished and in their place, judges now wear judges' gowns for the courtroom and western style suits for everyday business. The black robe symbolizes the solemness of the position, and the red stole and gold toggle represent the national colors of the PRC.[75]

The writer referred to the introduction of new robes as a way of bestowing judges with a more "civilized" (*wenming*) look, of giving them an air of "authority" (*quanwei*). This perception that a judge's authority and credibility relies on a cultured and civilized image, however, is heavily tested in the exercise of judicial authority during anti-crime campaigns. Over the last two decades, at the same time that professionalism has been promoted in the judicial ranks, the exercise of draconian degradation ceremonies by the judiciary have challenged the image of a sage-like judge. In Chapter Three, we see this "civilized" representation of the judiciary in dispute as we follow this socialist logic of propaganda and education into the realm of expressive punishment, the sentencing rally.

Conclusion

From the start of the reform era in 1979, court workers have had to negotiate a path of change to establish two new defining features for the courts. One is a new court culture and the other is legitimacy, based on an ideology of procedural propriety rather than on the ethos of revolutionary justice. In China, this development of court authority links the moral authority of courts to the sweeping national project of reform. Courts have sought to build a new organizational identity based on the promises of the national political and economic reform movement.

Like John Brigham's study of the American Supreme Court mentioned in the previous chapter, this chapter has problematized the idea that court work can be explained solely by conventional reference to its "surface" political functions. I have tried to counter the common assumption that, as institutions, courts and their practices exist and develop solely as the product of their formal political determinants. I have argued that we need a more nuanced understanding of the frameworks upon which institutional power is based. Institutions like the court may seem to exist on the basis of their "spontaneous claim"[76] to govern a particular aspect of social life, but as Peter Manning observed in his analysis of the social organization of policing, "these claims to prestige and legal rights are not normally easily claimed, easily won, or easily defended. The claims must be negotiated, won or lost, in a series of transactions between occupational groups and their significant audiences."[77] This is because institutions like the court are constructed on the basis of social, as well as political, expectations and understandings. In this chapter, I have explored the relationship between the court and its messages of judicial authority by examining how the internal "doings" of the court are intended to affect the external environment of these "doings" via propaganda programs and symbolic messages, particularly public trials.

I have considered how the Baotou Intermediate Court uses propaganda programs and the symbolic rituals of public trials as vital media for defining and depicting its authority to the general public. The Baotou court's authority to administer justice—and by extension this court's public identity as a legitimate administrator of justice—is conditioned by the "professional, political and public expectations that delineate the institution."[78] In examining the court's authority and institutional identity to administer justice in the reform era in Baotou we have considered the structural ties, procedural formats, organizational make-up, and politico-legal agendas operating within the historical circumstances of open reform. This historically specific analysis of the practices of the Baotou court exemplifies how the nation's courts, having superseded appeals to mass revolution, have appropriated the rhetoric, visions, and agendas of the wider social, political, and economic catchcries of open reform.

Notes

1. An earlier version of this chapter was previously published in an article form as the following: Susan Trevaskes, "Propaganda Work in Chinese Courts: public trials and sentencing rallies as sites of expressive punishment and public education in the People's Republic of China," *Punishment and Society* 6, no. 1 (2004), 5–21. Copyright (©Sage Publications, 2004). Reprinted by kind permission of Sage Publications.
2. Zhu Guozhi ed., *Shenpan guanli caozuo guifan* (Operational standards for trial management) (Jilin: Renmin fayuan chubanshe, 1995), 53–54. Note that in 2006, these official tasks were modified. See Chapter Eight for details.
3. Zhu, *Shenpan guanli caozuo guifan*, 216.
4. Zhu, *Shenpan guanli caozuo guifan*, 216.
5. Zhu, *Shenpan guanli caozuo guifan*, 216.
6. As Wuthrow et al. put it: "[T]he legitimacy of the modern state no longer rests on tradition or absolute values, but is rooted in conceptions of proper procedures—procedures deemed legitimate if they have been established according to norms of legality and constitutionality and if they conform to certain conceptions of citizenship and representation." R. J. Wuthnow, A. Bergesen and E. Kurzwell, *Cultural Analysis* (London: Routledge, 1984), 222, cited in *Representing Order: Crime, Law, and Justice in the News Media*, ed. Richard V. Ericson, Patricia M. Barnanek and Janet B. L. Chan (Buckingham: Open University Press, 1991), 9.
7. Ronald C. Keith, *China's Struggle for the Rule of Law* (London: St. Martin's Press, 1994), 9.
8. Zhao Ziyang, cited in Keith, *China's Struggle for the Rule of Law*, 22.
9. The term "glorious social engineering" was a term used by former politburo member Qiao Shi in 1986. See Qiao Shi, Speech made at the Second National Conference on Legal Education and Propaganda, 1986, in "Quanguo puji falu changshi shi lishi chuangju," (The National Legal Education Drive is Historically Significant Pioneering Work) *Renmin Ribao* (People's Daily), 12 December 1986, 1.

   This function of educating and imparting socialist values is linked to what Donald Munro describes as a "fosterage" role of government in affecting the socialist transformation of society. For a discussion of this fosterage role and related beliefs about the concept of the individual and his/her relationship to the social whole, see Donald Munro, *The Concept of Man in Contemporary China*, pp. 84–89 and Donald J. Munro, "Belief

Control: The Psychological and Ethical Foundations," in *Deviance and Social Control in Chinese Society*, ed. Amy Auberacher Wilson et al. (New York: Praeger, 1977), 22.

10. Phillip M. Chen, *Law and Justice: The Legal System in China 2000 B.C. to 1960 A.D.* (New York/London: Dunnellen Publishing Company, 1973), 115.

11. Wu Lei ed. *Zhongguo sifa zhidu* (China's Judicial System) (Beijing: Renmin daxue chubanshe, 1992), 234. *Fazhi xuanchuan* activities were first employed to propagate first the suppression of counter-revolutionaries in 1949, then the Land Reform Law in 1950, and the Constitution and the Marriage Law in 1954. *Fazhi xuanchuan* lost its appeal during the Anti-Rightist campaign of the late fifties and was given little credence during the Cultural Revolution when written law was deemed a bourgeois enterprise. Following the Third Plenum of the 11th Central Committee in 1978, it was brought back onto the agenda of courts, and from 1982 its status was promoted to an integral part of court work.

12. Spiritual civilization refers to a type of ethical and cultural process to develop in the citizenry an ideologically and culturally correct conduct on a national scale. The construction of ideologically-correct citizens for this spiritual civilization includes the inculcation of Marxist and Communist morality and values, and a positive attitude toward labor, patriotism, and internationalism. The construction of culture refers to the promotion of the education, science, literature, art, the print, radio and television media, health and sport, libraries, museums, and other cultural institutions. The role of socialist spiritual civilization in the big picture of reform is to help fulfill the requirements of socialist modernization, to promote citizens who are "idealistic, moral, cultured and disciplined," and to help to advance the "quality of the ideology and morality of the Chinese people." Lin Hua ed., *Zhongguo falu jichu* (The Foundations of Chinese Law) (Guangzhou: Zhongshan daxue chubanshe, 1992), 30. Also see Wu, *Zhongguo sifa zhidu*, 234, and Lin, *Zhongguo falu jichu*, 30.

13. Wu, *Zhongguo sifa zhidu*, 234–35. Legal consciousness in China refers to a set of general views and attitudes toward law and legal phenomena. See *Zhongguo dabaikequansh: faxue* (Encyclopaedia of China: Law) (Beijing/Shanghai: Zhongguo dabaikequanshu chubanshe, 1984), 104. Ronald Keith notes that in China, "Legal consciousness (*falu yishi*) formally includes both legal psychology (*falu xinli*) or just knowing the law, and legal consciousness (*falu sixiang*), legal thought, implying an understanding of the conceptual roots of law in society." Keith, *China's Struggle for the Rule of Law*, 16–17. In this respect, the idea of "legal consciousness," in the way it is articulated in the official literature, has some similarities to the concept of legal consciousness explored in recent socio-legal studies. Legal consciousness includes both conscious thought processes and unconscious acceptance in such a way that perceptions of the world "require no self awareness, that seem so much part of the natural order of things that the self never reflects on them, never needs to rationalize their truth nor consider the possibility that they may be false." David M. Engel, "How Does Law Matter in the Constitution of Legal Consciousness," in *How Does the Law Matter?*, ed. Bryant G. Garth, and Austin Sarat (Evanston, IL: Northwestern University Press), 1998: 116.

14. "Making Law a Household Word in China," *Beijing Review* 31, no. 28 (1985): 26.

15. Primary schools conducted "law classes" (*falu ke*), secondary schools adopted "general legal knowledge" classes as an integral part of the curriculum, and universities conducted more comprehensive classes on the legal system. See Wu, *Zhongguo sifa zhidu*, 236.

16. "Zhu Mingshan fuyuanzhang zai bufen gaoji fayuan fazhi xuanchuan gongzuo zuotanhuishang de jianghua," (SPC Vice-President Zhu Mingshan's Speech at the Semi-

nar for Higher Courts on Propaganda Work) in *Renmin fayuan nianjian 1988* (Yearbook of the People's Courts 1988), ed. Renmin fayuan nianjian bianji weiyuanhui (Beijing: Renmin fayuan chubanshe, 1992), 795.

17. "Zhu Mingshan de jianghua," 796.

18. Lin Zhun, "Zongjie yanjiu zai jiezaiyan nuli ba renmin fayuan yu shehui zhi'an zonghe zhili gongzuo tigao dao yige xin de shuiping," (Summarizing The Experiences of People's Courts and of Comprehensive Management of Public Order Work in Striving to Reach New Standards) in *The People's Courts Yearbook 1991* (*Renmin fayuan nianjian 1991*), ed. Renmin fayuan nianjian bianji weiyuanhui (Beijing: xinhua chubanshe, 1994), 547.

19. Lin, "Zongjie yanjiu," 547. For instance, in April 1983 in Shanghai, five hundred judicial workers participated in a law publicity week where more than thirty advisory booths were set up on streets. See "Shanghai publicizes the legal system." *Beijing Review*, 33 (1983): 22.

20. "Shanghai publicizes the legal system," 23. The article notes that a 1983 exhibition in Shanghai on opposing corruption and bribery inspired a number of lawbreakers to turn themselves in. Other educative and propaganda tasks performed by courts include visitation activities by courts where court staff visit jails to publicly announce sentence reductions and parole of individuals to an audience of prisoners in order to demonstrate the just nature of the law. Courts are encouraged to use this opportunity to promote the cause of justice by focusing heavily on the message that good behavior and a repentant heart is rewarded. See Lin, "Zongjie yanjiu," 547.

21. A detailed examination of the sentencing rally is given in Chapter Five.

22. David Garland, "Punishment and Culture: The Symbolic Dimensions of Criminal Justice," *Studies in Law, Politics and Society*, 11 (1991): 194–95.

23. David Garland, *Punishment and Modern Society: A Study in Social Theory* (Chicago/Oxford: University of Chicago Press and Oxford University Press, 1990), 67–70.

24. Song Zhansheng, ed., *Zhongguo gongan baike quanshu* (Encyclopedia of Public Security in China). (Jilin: Jilin renmin chubanshe, 1990), 339.

25. "Zhu Mingshan de jianghua," 796.

26. Xingshi susongfa jiaocheng bianxiezu ed., *Xingshi susongfa jiaocheng* (A Course in Criminal Procedure) Beijing: Qunzhong chubanshe, 1989), 60–61. These stated benefits of trials and sentencing procedures concur with analysis by Thomas Mathieson of the three key messages of punishment. He says that, first and foremost, punishment is a deterrence message that says that "crime does not pay." Second, punishment is a moral and educative message that highlights certain modes of behavior that should be avoided because they are morally improper. Third, punishment's message suggests habit formation; "that you should get into the habit of avoiding certain acts." Thomas Mathieson, "General Prevention as Communication," in *A Reader on Punishment*, ed. R. A. Duff and David Garland (Oxford: Oxford University Press, 1994), 221.

27. Lin, "Zongjie yanjiu," 546.

28. Lin, "Zongjie yanjiu," 546–47.

29. Lin, "Zongjie yanjiu," 547. (my emphasis)

30. As Richard Ericson argues, "How something is communicated precedes what is communicated. Each medium of communication has distinct formats, defined as procedures for the selection, transmission and reception of knowledge. Each medium differs in the way it transcends the limits of time and space to make knowledge available, and thereby creates a different social environment and context for thinking." Richard V. Eric-

son, "Why Law is Like News," in *Law as Communication*, ed. David Nelken (Aldershot: Dartmouth, 1996), 206.

31. The process of communicating messages, as Mathieson explains, involves the transfer of meanings from the sender to the receiver. Meanings, he notes, are not transferred directly but through signs or "carriers of meanings." These include language, visual representations and bodily expressions. Meaning is produced through the interaction of three main components of communication: the "external reality" of objects or events, the signs that carry meaning and the interpretation of signs by the receiver. In the context of the criminal trial, carriers of meaning can include spatial arrangements, the specific timing of events, and modes of address. See Mathieson, "General Prevention as Communication," 222–23. Also see Ericson, "Why Law is Like News," 217.

32. As Peter Winn notes, a legal ritual actually constitutes a legal event. The legal ritual provides the scaffolding necessary to articulate actions in a particular legal context. Rituals, Winn argues, are not merely a verbal expression of regulatory rules, they are the "formalized social actions" that give meaning and context to the operation of rules. Peter A. Winn, "Legal Ritual." *Law and Critique*, no. 2 (1991), 216–19. Richard Ericson has observed a similar relationship between the news and the law, claiming that, "the reality created through the use of a medium is a matter of how it presents knowledge in its established formats, rather than of what it presents. Content must always fit the format, and it is therefore always secondary to the format." Ericson, "Why Law is Like News," 206.

33. Pat Carlen uses a dramaturgical approach to consider the presentation of authority relations in magistrate's courts in England. Carlen argues that the specialized performances of judicial actors systematically results in the ritualistic control of court activities, where "[f]ormal delineations of behavioral, motivational and justificatory meanings are translated into a judicial language and logic which assigns legitimacy to one set of social relationships." Pat Carlen, *Magistrate's Justice* (London: Martin Robertson and Co., 1976), 12. She argued that not only relationships and roles, but also furniture and props are inscribed with consequential social meanings that are organized to achieve presentational control over events. Spatial arrangements, she says, "define the special territorial rights and duties of those designated as occupiers of a particular social space." The spacing and placing arrangements of people "is strategic to their ability to effectively participate in [these arrangements]." Pat Carlen, "The Staging of Magistrate's Justice," *British Journal of Criminology* 16, no. 1 (1976), 50, and Carlen, *Magistrate's Justice*, 49–50.

34. "Guanyu geji renmin fayuan shenpan ting jianshe wenti yu yijian" (Problems and Opinions Concerning the Construction of Courtrooms in People's Courts) in *Xingshi shenpan shouce* (*Handbook on Criminal Trials*), ed. Zuigao fayuan xingshi shenpan diyiting (Beijing: Renmin fayuan chubanshe, 1989), 449.

35. "Shenpan tiaojian de guanli" (Management of Trial Conditions) in *Fayuan guanli gailun* (Outline of Court Management), ed. Guo Jisheng (Beijing: Renmin fayuan chubanshe, 1992), 203–206. For a more detailed exegesis of the requirements of standard courtroom furniture and facilities, including a breakdown on the required dimensions for the judicial bench, prosecution bench, defense bench, and measurements pertaining to the required height and distance of the judicial bench in relation to the other benches, see the SPC regulation, "Zuigao renmin fayuan, zuigao renmin jianchayuan guanyu renmin fayuan shenpan fating shenpantai, gongsutai, bianhutai weizhi de guiding." (May 25, 1985) in *Renmin fayuan guanli gongzuo shouce* (Handbook of Court Management Work) ed. Zuigao renmin fayuan "renmin fayuan guanli gongzuo shouce" bianxiezu (Beijing: Renmin fayuan chubanshe, 1998), 1230–31.

36. Michael R. Dutton, *Policing and Punishment in China: From Patriarchy to the People* (Cambridge: Cambridge University Press, 1992), 263. Dutton adds, "From their

controlling position, they not only survey the criminal and the court but are also at the centre of any exchange between the prosecution and defense. This particular spatial arrangement signifies both the ascribed impartiality of investigation by the judges, and their centrality to 'all the facts.' The process does not turn on mass indignation of popular will but on the excavation of 'truth.'" (p. 263)

37. Dutton, *Policing and Punishment in China*, 263. Pat Carlen describes the actors and the expression of authority relations in the English magistrate's court in a similar way: "In contrast to their unceremonious and coercive presentation of defendants, magistrates, policemen, solicitors and other court personnel all project visual images of themselves, and verbally embellished images of each other which are designed to personify the absolute propriety of their situated (judicial) actions." Carlen, "The Staging of Magistrate's Justice," 53.

38. This is not unique to China. See Carlen, "The Staging of Magistrate's Justice," 53.

39. Mirjin Damaska, *The Faces of Justice and State Authority: A Comparative Approach to the Legal Process* (New Haven/London: Yale University Press, 1986).

40. Damaska, *The Faces of Justice and State Authority*, 82.

41. Damaska, *The Faces of Justice and State Authority*, 18–23.

42. Kanishka Jayasuriya, "Corporatism and Judicial Independence Within Statist Legal Institutions in East Asia," in *Law, Capitalism and Power in East Asia: The Rule of Law and Legal Institutions*, ed. Kanishka Jayasuriya (London: Routledge, 1999), 198.

43. Jayasuriya, "Corporatism and Judicial Independence," 199.

44. Jayasuriya, "Corporatism and Judicial Independence," 199.

45. Jayasuriya, "Corporatism and Judicial Independence," 198–99

46. Jayasuriya, "Corporatism and Judicial Independence," 195.

47. Damaska, *The Faces of Justice and State Authority*, 48–50.

48. Mark Findlay, "'Independence' and the Judiciary in the PRC," in *Law, Capitalism and Power in East Asia: The Rule of Law and Legal Institutions*, ed. Kanishka Jayasuriya (Routledge, London, 1999), 284.

49. Article 17 of the Organic Law of the People's Courts states that: "The Supreme People's Court shall be responsible and report to the National People's Congress and its Standing Committee . . . Local people's courts shall be responsible and report to local people's congresses at corresponding levels and their standing committees. The judicial work of the lower levels shall be subject to supervision by the people's court at higher levels."

50. Du Xichuan and Zhang Lingyuan, *Chinese Legal System: A General Survey* (Beijing: New World Press, 1990), 79.

51. Du and Zhang, *Chinese Legal System*, 79.

52. Article 35, Organic Law of the People's Courts of the People's Republic of China (1979).

53. Susan Finder, "The Supreme People's Court of the People's Republic of China," *Journal of Chinese Law* 7, no. 2 (Fall 1993), 155; Perry Keller, "Sources of Order in Chinese Law," *The American Journal of Comparative Law* XLII (1994), 754; and Chen, *Law and Justice*, 123.

54. "Two trials" refers to one case tried in the first instance with the opportunity for one appeal.

55. Susan Finder explains the concept of "supervision" as it applies to the SPC's role in court work in China: In Chinese politics and law the term "supervision" (*jiandu*) encompasses guiding, monitoring, criticizing, and making charges against, or exposures of a state organ or functionary and many come from the top down or bottom up. It con-

trasts with the term "lead" (*lingdao*), which implies that the "leading" organs or functionary is empowered to give orders to subordinate personnel or organs who must obey. "Leadership" means that the leader has the authority to appoint subordinates to, and remove them from office. Finder, "The Supreme People's Court," 163.

56. The SPC establishes and supervises procedures in the lower courts by issuing interpretations to lower courts in the form of nine different types of administration documents that clarify new or existing laws and regulations: "'official opinions' (*yijian*), 'explanations' (*jieda* or *jieshi*), 'official answers' (*pifu* or *dafu*), 'letters' (*fuhan*, also sometimes *han*), 'notices' (*tongzhi* or *tonggao*) and 'conference summaries' (*yiyao*)." Finder, "The Supreme People's Court," 166.

57. Damaska, *The Faces of Justice and State Authority*, 148.

58. Damaska, *The Faces of Justice and State Authority*, 147–80.

59. Damaska, *The Faces of Justice and State Authority*, 165.

60. Article 9, Organic Law of the People's Courts. A revision of the law in 1983 made people's assessors officially optional.

61. Du and Zhang, *Chinese Legal System: A General Survey*, 95.

62. Zhu, *Shenpan guanli caozuo guifan*, 8.

63. Zhu, *Shenpan guanli caozuo guifan*, 37–42.

64. Lian Shanggang ed., *Ban'an guifan* (Standards for Case Management) (Beijing: Renmin fayuan chubanshe, 1995), 10–11. The victim's testimony can be used as the basis of a case if the statement has gone through a process of verification. In the situation in which the victim's statement is the basis for determining a case, both parties are to be given adequate opportunity to question and cross-examine the victim. Before the victim's statement is read out, the presiding judge confirms the identity of the victim and explains their rights and obligations. The victim is permitted to allow a legal counsel to speak on his/her behalf. Once the presiding judge or other members of the collegial panel have finished questioning the victim, the procurator, defender, or defendant can question the victim. (p. 12)

65. Lian, *Ban'an guifan*, 12.

66. Lian, *Ban'an guifan*, 12. If, in the event that the parties or the defender makes a request to summon a new witness, new material evidence, or new expert witness statements to be produced in court, the collegial panel shall first inquire as to the identity of the witness or the location of the material evidence and their relation to the case. If it is deemed that the new evidence or witness will directly influence the outcome of the case, the collegial panel shall agree to the presentation of the new evidence and will call an adjournment. If the collegial bench does not agree to the presentation of new evidence, the presiding judge shall explain the bench's decision and will announce the continuation of the trial. Lian, *Ban'an guifan*, 13.

67. If the content of the final statement is repetitive, the residing judge can dissuade the defendant from repeating the same content. If the defendant's final statement contains any contemptuous statements relating to the court or prosecution, or if any statement violates the interests of any particular individual or society in general, the presiding judge will order the defendant to cease. If any statement made is not relevant to the case or if it involves the private affairs of an individual or state secrets, the defendant will be ordered to cease. Lian, *Ban'an guifan*, 14.

68. "Putting into Effect the System of Criminal Procedure," *The Annals*, 38.

69. Article 2, Criminal Procedure Law of the People's Republic of China (1979).

70. "Summary of Criminal Trial Work," *The Annals*, 26–27.

71. "Putting into Effect the System of Criminal Procedure," *The Annals*, 34.

72. "Putting into Effect the System of Criminal Procedure," *The Annals*, 34.

73. "Putting into Effect the System of Criminal Procedure," *The Annals*, 39.

74. "Putting into Effect the System of Criminal Procedure," *The Annals*, 40.

75. <http://www.Chinajudge.com>, accessed on 29 April 2001.

76. Peter Manning, *Police Work: The Social Organization of Policing* (Cambridge, MA: MIT Press, 1977), 30.

77. Manning, *Police Work*, 30. Manning's study on the social organization of police work makes the point that, while agencies of social control may have jurisdictional control over certain aspects of political and social life, their claim to power is predicated on their ability to maximize the appearance of their authority through the utilization of both presentational and operational strategies. Peter Manning, *Police Work*, 23–37.

78. Brigham, *The Cult of the Court*, 8.

Chapter Three

Expressive Punishment: The Court Sentencing Rally[1]

Introduction

> On 7 September 1983, mammoth public sentencing rallies were held in Baotou city. Separate rallies were conducted in Kundulun and Donghe districts with sentences being pronounced on eighty serious criminals. At the rallies, forty-two criminals guilty of the most heinous crimes were sentenced to death, evoking an intense reaction throughout the city. . . . More than one hundred thousand people attended the rallies. . . . The venues were so packed that some people had no alternative but to stand outside. Despite these circumstances, the rallies ran smoothly from start to finish. More than one hundred thousand people lined the streets in the pouring rain to voice their indignation at the criminals on their route to the execution grounds. Families brought along their young and their old, and they all paved the streets to "send off the gods of plague." The task of frightening potential criminals was accomplished and the masses breathed a sigh of relief. People were elated, clapping and cheering, and afterwards, numerous letters of praise were sent to the politico-legal organs.[2]

In China, two judicial actions, the courtroom trial (*shen*) and sentencing (*pan*), comprise the complete judicial event *shenpan*. In Chapter Two we explored the educative function of trials. In this chapter we examine the educative and deterrence function of the public sentencing rally. This chapter looks at the public sentencing rally as an integral part of the operational and symbolic function of criminal court work in post-Mao China, particularly in relation to anti-crime campaigns. The excerpt above from *The Annals* is an example of a rally during China's first "Strike Hard" (Yanda) campaign in 1983. The successes of this campaign, along with smaller "specialized struggle" campaigns (*zhuanxiang douzheng*) are promoted as a series of public spectacles that draw attention to the crime situation and to the government's hard-line response.

This chapter explores the role and development of the rally, first in relation to its educative and symbolic functions. This involves examining the medium, messages, and social actors in the rally. Second, it examines the rally in relation to the broader themes and rhetoric of Dengist institutional reform as they apply to courts in the post-1978 period. A tension developed in this period between the rhetoric of reform and the "civilizing" of rallies on the one hand, and the perceived imperative to continue with hard-line, draconian law and order practices on the other. This theme is taken into the third section with an examination of the present-day status of the rally as a symbol of hard-line law and order power and politics in the theatrics of Yanda 2001.

The Procedure and Functions of the Sentencing Rally

The sentencing rally in China is a shaming ritual acted out in public for educational and deterrence purposes. It is a judicial event in which the judgment and sentence of a convicted criminal is announced in a public forum. The audience, ranging from a few dozen to more than a hundred thousand, is usually organized to attend *en masse* by work units and local Party committees. The rally is not a site for adjudication and determination of guilt, as the judgment of a case has already been decided in court. It is, rather, a judicial format in which the emotive acts of public shaming and gestures of moral indignation can be acted out to the general public. In short, it provides an important organizational format through which the communicative acts of blaming and shaming are constituted and relayed to their social audience as a message from the state that "crime does not pay."

The sentencing rally is removed from the formal and unemotive trial proceedings of the courtroom and is usually held away from the courthouse in a venue that belongs to the public, not the court. It is conducted at sites such as market places, stadiums, community halls, at the crime site, or the criminal's workplace. It can be convened to pronounce sentences on a few individuals or a large group of convicted criminals, usually for serious crimes that attract some public attention or specific crimes that are the targets of anti-crime campaigns. The rally usually opens with a succession of offenders brought out on to a platform or stage, handcuffed and under the guard of a line of court police. Offenders sometimes wear placards around their necks and tied to their backs, which detail the criminal's name, the nature of the offence, and the sentence. The offenders usually stand at the front of the stage under guard, while Party and government dignitaries stand or are seated behind them at the center of the stage or in other prominent positions. Senior heads of the police, procuratorate, and courts stand or sit together with local government and Party dignitaries as a sign of unity. After a succession of speeches, a senior judge or court president is called upon to declare sentencing. Offenders are then placed in court vehicles, sometimes in open trucks, and led either to their deaths at the local execution grounds or to prison.

Apart from an excellent but all too brief analysis of the symbolic functions of court practices by Michael Dutton in his study of policing and punishment, the study of public sentencing in China has been largely unexplored.[3] In contrast, the symbolic nature of adjudication and sentencing is a subject that has gained widespread importance in the field of criminal justice and socio-legal studies outside China studies in the past few decades. Scholars of the sociology of law and punishment such as David Garland, Pat Carlen, Richard Ericson, and others have been interested in developing new ways of understanding the representational significance of judicial and penal practices, seeing these as mediums that regulate social values and meanings through signification.[4] David Garland's study of penal practices and institutions in relation to their instrumental and symbolic functions and effects, for example, is particularly relevant to a study of expressive punishment in Chinese social control practices. He says that in relation to judicial and penal practices, communities "look to such procedures not just as instrumental mechanisms which will process the single offender in question, but as symbolic reassertions of order and authority which help to deal with the feelings of helplessness, disorder and insecurity which crime introduces into their lives."[5]

The symbolic dimensions of criminal justice in studies such as Garland's have been viewed as part of the ideological and constitutive nature of law. This view of punishment coincides with a socio-legal approach to law that attributes more to law than its conventional conception as an external force that simply imposes physical constraints on human conduct. It sees law as a set of practices that regulates social relations and social values by providing a rhetorical and symbolic framework that organizes social, moral, and political understandings of order, punishment, crime, and even judicial authority. The following analysis of sentencing rallies in China fits into this conceptual schema in a number of ways. The sentencing rally provides a symbolic reassurance of the capacity of the state both to protect its citizens and to reflect the prevailing moral order, and it also serves to establish and develop judicial legitimacy and authority by providing a theatrical setting in which the legal ritual is conducted and authority roles are acted out. Judicial and political actors present current criminal justice policies and narratives as *the* legitimate social or moral norm and, in doing so, they seek to increase their own credibility in society by claiming to embody the morality of the public at the same time that they educate and deter.[6] The rally, like other penal and legal rituals in general, therefore, "teaches, clarifies, dramatizes and authoritatively enacts some of the basic moral-political categories and distinctions which help to form our symbolic universe."[7]

The symbolic potential of judicial practices to affect social meanings, attitudes, and understandings is not, of course, lost on politico-legal authorities in China, in a political system that has made an art form out of public degradation and shaming over the last fifty years. Since the 1950s, public sentencing rallies in the PRC have been an integral part of government socialization programs that explicitly aim to guide the manner in which people behave and think about crime and punishment. This symbolic role of judicial practices has come under the rubric of the "propaganda work" (*xuanchuan gongzuo*) of the criminal justice organs. As a shaming ritual, the rally is a product of official reasoning that assumes that human behavior and attitudes toward crime can be successfully manipulated by conscious acts of persuasion and ideological education, using representational formats that project both positive and negative models as a guide to attitudinal and behavioral change. Hence, courts are advised by politico-legal authorities to select model cases strategically in order to "give wide publicity and magnify their social effectiveness."[8] Courts are encouraged to select cases that both frighten would-be criminals and inspire the masses to action, cases that send a clear message about the state's response to crime.

Scholars exploring the concept of law as communication and law as representation have described the procedures of trials and sentencing declarations in Western settings as legal rituals that actually *constitute* a legal event.[9] Rituals, in this sense, provide the conceptual scaffolding necessary for the articulation of actions in a particular legal context. This is a process of representing various authority and non-authority roles through the performance of regulative procedures. One of the most detailed recent accounts of a rally, at the climax of the first month of the Yanda 2001 campaign in April in Tianjin, we find that the legal ritual is carefully constructed, through the performance of social actors in a sequence of stages from preparation to execution, and through depictions of authority relations between the state and the criminal, the state and the masses, and the criminal and the masses. The court police, with their military-style rigor and precision, represent the rally as an act of war against the criminal, providing a corporeal image of the coercive nature of the law. The local government and Party dignitaries, at center stage, represent the political authority of the act, and the criminal justice officials represent the authority of the law. The crowd represents the moral authority of the act as a reflection of the will of the masses. The criminals themselves, shamed and many of them led off to their deaths at the local execution grounds, represent a moral and political victory both for the state and its citizens.

In the first stage of the construction of the event, the authority of the judges and court police is established by their ceremonial attire, punctuality, efficiency, and in the horsepower of their motor vehicles:

> The sun had not yet risen when judges and judicial police at the Tianjin No. 1 Intermediate Court in Nanma Road and No. 2 Intermediate Courts in Weiti Street had gathered. . . . Judicial police were busy adjusting their epaulets and putting on their green armbands inscribed with the word "enforcement" [*zhixing*], as today they would indeed be performing a special task. At around 4.30 a.m. the gates of both courts opened and a motorcade of court vehicles emerged.

> . . . Judges from both courts, along with judicial police, congregated outside the Tianjin Higher People's Court and proceeded to the Tianjin No. 1 Lock-up. The sound of the motorcade broke through the morning silence, providing an appropriate prologue to the main event of the day.[10]

In the second stage, the authority relations between court workers and condemned criminals are established. Next, the fate of the condemned criminals is juxtaposed against the ordinariness of morning life on the streets.

> It was almost 6 a.m. when dozens of judicial police vans and sedans entered the gates of the lockup . . . the soon-to-be sentenced prisoners emerge . . . timidly and with heads bowed, they are forced into the waiting vans as their names are called. Their foot shackles clang on the floor of the van. Some have a resigned look of dread on their face, some in a trance-like state. . . . It's 7 a.m. and the motorcade of nearly one hundred vehicles leaves the lock-up, with police lights blazing but with sirens silent. The motorcade follows the main road to the location of today's rally, the People's Sport Stadium, just as people on the street emerge on their way to work. More than ten thousand workers in transit see the passing motorcade.[11]

Following this, the ritual destruction of the criminal begins, as elaborately robed judges read out the criminals' fates. The sound of the shackles of the offenders as they shuffle their way to the stage demonstrates an attempt to bend the criminals' will to the will of the masses who surround the criminals on all four sides, applauding the judgments.

> Soon after 8 a.m., the audience at today's rally arrive just as the vehicles reach the stadium. . . . At 9 a.m. precisely, the rally officially begins. On the raised podium located on the field at the center the stadium stand the judges who pronounce sentencing. Surrounding them on all sides are more than four thousand members of the masses who sit silently in anticipation. . . . The announcement of the start of the rally brings spontaneous applause from the crowd. The first batch of criminals to be sentenced are brought out onto the stage, their foot shackles clanging as they step onto the podium. Today's judges are wearing their judicial robes. One judge [at a time] faces the audience and begins reading out the written judgments, each judgment notice detailing the criminal act, the criminal charge and the sentence.[12]

Next, the relationship between the masses and the state (judiciary) is shown to be validated in the masses' spontaneous expressions of support. The educative purpose of the rally is deemed a success as the audience indicates that they have observed and understood the relationship between law and punishment. Moreover, the retributive goals of the law, satisfied in the announcements of the heavy sentences and the hard-line actions of Yanda, are thus endorsed by public opinion.

> At each announcement of a death sentence, the audience claps enthusiastically. One member of the audience, a Mr. Wang, remarked that "we are applauding to

show support for and confidence in the justice meted out by the judicial organs." A Mr. Li commented that "Yanda truly gladdens the hearts of the people" [*Yanda zhenshi dakuai renxin.*] . . . Another member of the audience, a Mrs. Fan also commented that "this is the first sentencing rally I have attended . . . the facts of the cases have been explained very clearly as have the laws applied to the cases and the sentencing rationale. All those punished have been given the appropriate sentence. This is what real justice is all about." Others noted that "Yanda has allowed the masses to vent their anger and we are all delighted at this."[13]

Finally, the victory is expressed through the post-rally celebratory noise of sirens as the motorcade heads to the execution grounds.

> The rally is over. The motorcade of more than one hundred vehicles turn on their sirens and a batch of sentenced criminals, whose execution orders have already been signed, are driven off straight to the execution grounds. On the road, waves of supportive cheers [for the judicial organs] come from the crowds on the streets as the condemned criminals are sent to their deaths.[14]

The descriptions above of the Yanda rally in Tianjin city in 2001 illustrate the process of representation as a means of constituting a legal event. This process represents concepts such as "law," "order," "justice," and "punishment" through performance of regulative procedures as "formalized social action that gives meaning and context to the operation of rules."[15]

Given the rhetorical value of this form of expressive punishment, it is no surprise that, following the declaration of war on crime at the start of the first Yanda campaign in August 1983, the number of rallies in Baotou increased sharply. In Baotou, 249 rallies, attended by 2,290,000 residents, were held from 1983 to 1986. Most of these rallies were for mass sentencing conducted on the largest scale from August to December 1983, as shown in Table 3.1. In just four months at the height of the campaign from late August to December, more than six hundred thousand people had witnessed the pronouncement of death sentences given to sixty-three criminals.

Sentencing rallies were conducted regularly throughout the three years of Yanda in Baotou. In 1984, sentencing rallies were still popular but not held as frequently as during the first five months of Yanda in 1983. On March 23, for instance, twelve thousand people attended a rally to watch fourteen offenders sentenced.[16] For the June 27, 1984, rallies, four hundred thousand people in the city either attended in person or heard them broadcast live on radio. From September 13 to 15, 1984, basic-level people's courts held separate rallies in various parts of the city with the sentencing of eighty-five criminals involved in fifty cases and a radio audience of four hundred thousand.[17] In 1985, the rallies were even less intense, with attendance exceeding forty thousand on only a few occasions. There was only one large-scale rally on August 6, and here only two offenders were sentenced before an audience of two hundred and sixty thousand. This rally attracted a large audience because one of the convicted offenders was a murderer who dismembered the victim's body, and the other criminal was convicted of raping a minor (and burying the victim alive).[18] In 1986, one sentencing rally was held roughly every month, with the largest on March 27, which attracted an audience of thirty thousand.[19]

Table 3.1. Sentencing Rallies in Baotou: September to December, 1983

Date	Location	No. of criminals sentenced	No. of criminals sentenced to death	Public attendance at rally (approx.)
September 7	Kundulun and Donghe	80	42	100,000
September 14	9 rallies in various basic courts across the city	393	–	110,000
October 21	Qingshan; Guyang	48	19	400,000
October 28	Intermediate Court	19	–	1,000
December 31	Intermediate Court	13	2	unknown

Source: "Chronicle of Events," *The Annals*: 132–33.[20]

Tianjin city courts had one of the fiercest sentencing agendas in the country in Yanda 1983–1986, as Table 3.2 attests.

During all Yanda campaigns since 1983, a common practice has been to parade criminals around the streets in trucks before leading them to prison or to the execution grounds. For example, on September 1, 1983, a "mass rally" (*qunzhong dahui*) was held in the Liaoning Provincial Sport Stadium in Shenyang city, in which sixty-six criminals were sentenced to death after which they were paraded around the city before being executed.[21] At the first Yanda sentencing rally in Tianjin, forty criminals who were sentenced to death were paraded in trucks on their way to the execution grounds. On the way to the grounds, the trucks took a detour around thirty-one of the largest roads in the city spanning six districts, where thousands of members of the public jeered at the criminals.[22] In some areas, criminals were even sentenced and shot at the site of their crime.[23] From August 1983 to January 1987, tens of thousands of rallies were conducted in China.

The discursive frameworks of action and the symbolic depictions of justice in the Baotou and Tianjin rallies described above can be considered to exemplify Harold Garfinkel's degradation ceremony, a description of expressive punishment that centers around the communicative actions and narratives of shaming rituals involving moral indignation and public denunciation which transform an individual's identity to one lower in social rank.[24] An early 1980s description of a sentencing rally demonstrates this process:

> In front of a very high podium for the pronouncement of judgment stands the criminal element, bound tightly . . . and held vigilantly by the guards of the court who exert all their strength to grasp and hold the criminals unwilling arms. Sometimes they press down on his head, sometimes they bear down on the small of his back. Once judgment is passed, they even grab the criminal and drag or pull him along. In other places, right up to this day, they go so far as to make the criminal wear a placard . . . and to kneel before the podium while awaiting judgment.[25]

Table 3.2. Sentencing Rallies Involving Pronouncement of the Death Sentence in Tianjin, 1983–1985

Date	Location	Sentencing Details
August 28, 1983	Tianjin Minyuan Sports Stadium	40 death sentences
September 24, 1983	Tianjin Minyuan Sports Stadium	82 death sentences
February 13–18, 1984	Tianjin Minyuan Sports Stadium	28 death sentences (nine separate rallies)
May 21, 1984	Tianjin Minyuan Sports Stadium	9 death sentences
September 15, 1984	Tianjin Minyuan Sports Stadium and at other basic courts	19 death sentences, and 163 sentenced to life imprisonment and other terms
January 28, 1985	Cultural Palace	11 death sentences
June 25, 1985	Tianjin Minyuan Sports Stadium	15 death sentences
December 15–31, 1985	Tianjin Minyuan Sports Stadium and at other basic courts	10 death sentences, and 14 sentenced to life imprisonment and other terms

Source: *Tianjin fayuan gongzuo dashiji* (*Tianjin Court Work Chronicle*) (Tianjin: neibu ziliao (internal restricted circulation document), 1986), 178–205.

Moral indignation expressed in sentencing declarations also effect the ritual destruction of the individual by constructing the status of the accused as being the antithesis of the values and moral order of the majority.[26] Great importance is placed on the role of the masses as the rally rouses them to struggle against the criminal. But like public trials, the ritual destruction of the individual in the rally is not presented as an unmediated relationship between the masses and the criminal. Rather, it is presented as part of the authority relations between the state and the people.[27] The hierarchical and procedural arrangements of order represented in sentencing ceremonies depict judicial, Party, and political actors as agents of the will of the masses in the form of state authority as exercised in law. The masses' support of the state's initiatives in punishing criminals is demonstrated in their enthusiasm for punishment at the rally, as described in a newspaper report in Sichuan province in 2001:

> This morning the Sichuan Provincial Sports Stadium became the focus of community attention with the province's first major public sentencing rally since the start of Yanda. Stadium attendance was at full capacity with a crowd of over ten thousand. Latecomers were unable to find seating and lined the streets outside the stadium in eager anticipation for the sentencing pronouncements. More than one hundred convicted criminals were led into the stadium for sentencing. As soon as Chengdu Intermediate Court vice-president Mao Shangui announced that today's sentencing included forty-five death penalty sentences, the crowd spontaneously broke out in thunderous applause.[28]

While sentencing rallies provide an avenue for a general expression of community condemnation and censure, and while in many cases the rally is an outlet for the expression of public anger and indignation, it is important to note that they are nevertheless *organized* rituals. This being the case, the sentencing rally exists not simply to provide a politically disinterested format for the raw expression of popular will. It provides, rather, a means through which authorities attempt to organize and order public sentiment and indignation into a content and format that complies with the objectives and agendas of existing crime control strategies. David Garland makes this point about public sentencing and penal practices in general: rather than seeing these practices as simply unmediated expression of public indignation, they should be envisaged as consciously planned mechanisms through which social values and emotions are structured and routinized into rituals depicting popular sentiment. In this way, judicial declarations can "set the tone for the public response at the very moment that they claim to express it"[29] by structuring the language of condemnation and retribution into already existing narratives of crime control rhetoric. In doing so, these declarations give popular sentiment "a degree of definition"[30] by linking the rhetoric of popular sentiment to the institutional rhetoric of law and order.

Messages about punishment addressed to the general public through rallies are formulated with a specific audience in mind. For criminals and would-be criminals in the audience, messages of general deterrence and public condemnation of crime are meant to frighten and to show that "criminal cunning cannot succeed in escaping the arm of the law."[31] In contrast, messages that attempt to frighten would-be criminals by conveying the severity of punishment will be read by the law-abiding citizen in a quite different way. To the law-abiding member of the general public, messages of condemnation are there to convey a more general and indirect message of reassurance that social order is safe in the hands of the judicial organs.[32]

Sentencing rallies also possess an educative function in relation to the propagation of criminal law.[33] Part of the process of public sentencing includes speeches given by politico-legal authorities on the importance of law and order. Public sentencing also entails the judge's pronouncement and explanation of the sentencing rationale for the crime. Therefore, those who attend mass sentencing rallies, like those who attend public trials, are given a lesson in the law: how to distinguish the types of behavior that constitute a crime, what rights are protected under the law, and the extent of harm that criminals inflict on society.[34] In exposing criminal activities to the masses, sentencing rallies, like public trials, serve to "educate the masses in improving their vigilance and conscious respect for the law."[35] Punishment-related messages in rallies include the general message that "crime does not pay," but they also incorporate specific warnings. Public sentencing provides a framework that enables the public to gauge the severity of punishment at a given period, for example at the time of the enactment of a new PRC law, or more importantly, during an anti-crime campaign when the severity of sanctions often varies greatly from those meted out in normal times.

Since the early 1980s, the public sentencing rally has also acted as an avenue through which the aims and outcomes of anti-crime campaigns are promoted. The first Yanda declaration of war on crime in August 1983 saw a marked increase in the severity of punishments given to major crimes targeted in Yanda, and it was these targets that were on display in rallies. In 1984, in one city alone, Wuhan in central China, the Wuhan Intermediate People's Court publicly sentenced 253 offenders, and over half a million residents attended the rallies. In one instance, an accused charged with murder was publicly tried and sentenced at his workplace, with those in attendance "receiving a practical lesson in the law."[36] In another case, a court in Wuhan publicly sentenced on site a number of thieves who were causing problems at the Han Zhengjie Markets. Six offenders charged and convicted of theft were publicly sentenced at a major intersection in the marketplace, to give a warning to criminals and reassurance to the public.[37]

1980s Judicial Authority and the Problem of "Civilizing" Rallies

The present-day format of sentencing rallies in China has its origins in the mass trials (*gongshen dahui*) of the revolutionary period and in the early 1950s. First convened in the revolutionary strongholds of Ruijin and Yan'an in the pre-1949 period and then during the Suppression of Counterrevolutionaries Campaign from 1950 to 1951, mass trials were public events conducted by local politico-legal committees of the Communist Party. Rows of criminals were lined up on center-stage, covering the masses' view of criminal justice officials who were in the background. Although the mass trial was very much a Party-organized activity, symbolically, the main actors in the event were the masses and their enemies.

Both in revolutionary times and in the 1950s, the masses were foregrounded as the center of presentational and symbolic judicial authority as they "prosecuted" in a line-up of political criminals on a stage format.[38] Unlike mass trials, the mass sentencing rally, which came into common use around the same time, has always been the official property of the courts. The rally emerged in the early- to mid-1950s as a common judicial practice during the mass movements, in particular the Three and Five-antis campaign, the Anti-Rightist campaign, and the Great Leap Forward. By the early 1960s, both adjudication and sentencing became less public and, during the Cultural Revolution, other degradation ceremonies such as accusation meetings (*kongsu dahui* and *douzhenghui*) took the place of the sentencing rally as the most common degradation ceremony.

When sentencing rallies first returned in the 1970s, Party and government dignitaries usually presided and gave the main speeches, and the courts played a less prominent role in proceedings. Sentencing rallies during this time were not controlled exclusively by the judiciary but were organized by the local Party politico-legal committees in cooperation with the public security bureau and the procuratorate. The symbolic presence of the judge during the rally was secondary to the principal role of government and Party dignitaries, and so the rhetoric of denunciation was largely the property of government and Party dignitaries. Judges merely confirmed the legal implications of judgment and denunciation already addressed in the speeches at the start of the ceremony, then would briefly announce the nature of the offence of each criminal on display and the sentence given for the crime.[39]

In the reform era of the 1980s, rallies became sites of two competing lines of politico-legal rhetoric: the discourse of the mass-line and that of legal reform and modernization. We therefore find a curious twist in the evolution of the mass sentencing rally in the 1980s: the rally gained unprecedented prevalence as a tool of crime prevention and education at the very time of an unprecedented push to establish and promote a socialist rule of law. So what developed in the 1980s within this new post-Mao persona of courts was a kind of tension in the way the authorities represented and promoted sentencing rallies: on the one hand, these were promoted as the unmediated reflection of mass indignation and the moral authority of the mass line. On the other, rallies were promoted as an efficiently organized, regulated, and legitimate stage in the legal process. We find, therefore, an interesting mix of practices developing in the 1980s and beyond that reflects this Janus-faced nature of law and order rhetoric and representation.

The spatial and symbolic arrangement of authority relations in the 1980s reflected this interplay between mass-line rhetoric and "rule of law" rhetoric. Judges now stood at the center of linguistic activity and chaired the meetings. Although rallies were still organized by local politico-legal Party committees, and although there was still a very strong police presence, the sovereignty of the judge was nevertheless clearly symbolized in the new spatial arrangements.[40]

Following this newfound authority given to the judiciary was a push to "civilize" judicial work in the 1980s, which came about as a response to the overuse of the death penalty by the lower courts that had gone into "overkill" with public sentencing and executions in the first months of Yanda 1983. Public overexposure to some of the more draconian methods of public humiliation of convicted criminals in August that year led to the issuing of a criminal justice circular explaining the do's and don'ts of education and deterrence work. The circular issued by a representative of the Ministry of Justice on September 27, 1983, to the criminal justice organs upheld an earlier policy directive from the Propaganda Department of the Central Party Committee. Both directives stated that Party committees within the criminal justice system were not to go overboard with the job of education and deterrence. The September circular made recommendations to accentuate the positive aspects of propaganda work (*cong zhengmian jinxing xuanchuan*) while at the same time using a variety of means to frighten criminals and potential offenders. Courts were therefore advised to "to flush out criminals and expose them" but to do this in a civilized manner.[41]

This focus of the "positive" side of law and order emphasizing strict adherence to the law was promoted as part of the "civilized trials" (*wenming shenpan*) promoted in the era of Dengist legal reforms. In contrast to the uncivilized practice of public execution, which was condemned by authorities in the early 1980s, courts were told that they were now to avoid explicit and open expressions of state violence. This included a ban on the traditional post-rally practice of publicly parading soon-to-be executed criminals along the streets en route to the execution grounds. Prohibited by authorities as early as 1984, the parading of criminals has been slow to disappear. A joint notice in 1986 issued by the Supreme People's Court, the Supreme People's Procuratorate, the Ministry of Public Security and the Ministry of Justice (collectively known as the *gongjianfa*), for example, laid out in clear terms the strict ban on the practice, reminding the *gongjianfa* that they had already been reminded once in 1984 that this was an illegal practice according to Article 155 of the Criminal Procedure Law. The circular noted that, although in many areas the *gongjianfa* had become "more civilized" in the practice of executions (*zai wenmingshang you henda de jinbu*), in a small number of areas uncivilized practices were still common. Parading criminals in trucks was prohibited not only because of the illegality of the practice but also because it "did not comply with the standards of socialist spiritual civilization" (*bu fuhe shehui zhuyi wenming de yaoqiu*).[42] In disengaging the public gaze from the violent spectacle of execution and prohibiting the parading of criminals following sentencing rallies, the new message going out to the community was that the coercive acts of the state are a necessary part of criminal court work, but that they were to be performed in a civilized manner by an authoritatively sound institution.

This push to civilize criminal court work is important to the issue of how judicial authority in post-1978 China has developed and how legal discourses and judicial events are an organized attempt to provide a system of meaning within which judicial authority is represented and constituted. The increased importance placed on the role of the judiciary in the sentencing rally has been part of an on-going process to define and depict the authority of the post-1978 court as residing in the legitimate capacity of judicial office. Post-1978 judicial authority, defined through the procedures and rituals of everyday judicial practices, has been promoted as a reflection of the new ethos of a new format of socialist rule of law, with the source of authority of courts being depicted as residing in the professional execution of judicial duties in accordance with the law. The underlying message here is that socialist law in the post-1978 period is represented as an organized and systematized rendition of the regulative rules of the socialist legal and political order. In other words, these messages are saying that, unlike the chaotic violence of Cultural Revolution punishment and state violence, in post-1978 China, state violence is controlled with the institutional strictures of court procedure. Social order is therefore to be sustained through institutional authority.

The civilizing of the rally reflects a more institutionally authoritative court, but this has not meant that popular justice and mass-line have lost their rhetorical appeal. Therefore, the authority of courts in rallies is depicted as having a dual source: it resides in the professional execution of judicial duties "in accordance with the law," but at the same time is promoted as a direct expression of the will of the masses.

Rallies and Yanda 2001

Criminal justice agencies in China today remain reliant on rallies to represent both the symbolic force of the state and the "will of the masses" in anti-crime drives. Hence, the tension between the push for "civilized" criminal court work and the concomitant promotion of hard-core degradation practices continues to be played out in the public arena of the rally. All of the degradation ceremony no-no's that were discouraged and outlawed in the 1980s have come back in force in 2001 in the latest Yanda campaign that began in early April.

On April 2–3, 2001, for the first time since 1978, the entire national leadership, including Jiang Zemin, Li Peng, Zhu Rongji, Li Ruihuan, and Hu Jintao, attended a National Conference on Public Order in Beijing in a gesture of unprecedented support from the Central Party Committee for an anti-crime campaign. Calling for a new two-year assault against crime to protect the economic reforms and long-term national security, president Jiang Zemin signaled in no uncertain terms the significance given to crime control as paramount to the very future of the CCP's political dominance in China.[43] According to subsequent calls-to-arms from the three arms of criminal justice, Yanda 2001 would focus on three broad areas of crime: crimes committed by organized crime gangs, serious violent crimes including bombings, murder, robbery, and kidnapping, and crimes of theft that pose a serious threat to the security of the masses.[44]

Aided and abetted by the media, the rally has again played a key role in Yanda as the No. 1 national symbol of brute law and order force with reports from the *People's Daily* and other local papers consistently couched in theatric tones. On April 11, within days of the national declaration of war against crime, the first batch of sentencing rallies were convened across the country. One early report from the provinces commented that "the curtain of Yanda was drawn" in Guangdong at the Yuexiushang Sports Stadium in Guangzhou on April 11, 2001. The Guangzhou Intermediate Court announced a number of death sentences that had already been approved by the Guangdong Higher People's Court. Those sentenced to death were led off to their execution immediately following the rally. Included amongst those to be shot were criminals convicted of willful murder, intentional assault, armed robbery, and drug trafficking. The report noted that despite the fact that Guangzhou was experiencing a cold snap in the weather, more than thirty thousand members of the public turned up to applaud enthusiastically after each death sentence was announced, adding that "the noise of their clapping resounding throughout the skies, so loud that it set off the police dogs present at the rally into a fit of howling."[45] The city mayor gave a speech at the rally declaring that, "the issue of social order is not only an enormous social problem but is also an important political problem. . . . We need to set off an upsurge of force 'striking hard' to such a degree that criminals will shudder in their boots when they hear the name 'Guangzhou.'"[46] Another local report of the same rally noted that the prisoners were made to stand in the center of the grounds on a platform wearing neon-yellow-colored vests so as the crowd could differentiate them from the judicial police standing beside them. After sentencing, criminals were placed in open trucks, one criminal per truck, each prisoner handcuffed to the rails of the trucks with the trucks forming a motorcade off to the execution grounds.[47] The one-criminal-per-truck idea was possibly to avoid the ban on parading large batches of criminals in a truck and possibly to enhance the magnitude of the event by creating a train effect. Meanwhile, a mass sentencing rally was convened in Shenzhen on the same day to pronounce sentence on forty-five convicted criminals at the Shenzhen Sports Stadium.[48] At the same time, courts across Shanghai held sentencing rallies to pronounce sentencing given to 136 convicted criminals involved in seventy-five separate cases including robbery, kidnapping, and other serious violent crimes.

Three main formats of sentencing rallies particular to Yanda 2001 have dominated news reports and politico-legal circulars: simultaneously-convened rallies (*jizhong gongpan dahui*); rallies convened for a specific audience or "special sentencing rallies" (*zhuanxiang gongpan dahui*); and "joint public arrest and sentencing rallies" (*gongkai deipu gongkai xuanpan dahui*). Simultaneously-convened rallies are part of the campaign strategy orchestrated by central authorities to act collectively and in a comprehensive manner and to magnify the effects of public sentencing.[49] The policy of simultaneously-convened rallies was especially popular in the first stage of Yanda 2001, from early April to late May. The Xinjiang Higher People's Court, for example, decided that they would direct their Yanda propaganda work at simultaneously convening three or four very large-scale rallies in Urumqi and three other cities.[50]

Other provinces also seem to have taken this as their battle plan for the first stage of Yanda. The same strategy was employed across Liaoning on May 20, where nine courts convened rallies to publicly sentence thirty-eight criminals. Similarly, on May 25 in Zhengzhou, basic and intermediate courts simultaneously convened rallies, and on the following day, intermediate and basic courts across Shenyang city followed suit, simultaneously sentencing criminals guilty of armed robbery, theft, and fraud. Likewise, intermediate courts across Yunnan province convened rallies on May 29, and on May 30, three intermediate courts in Guizhou convened sentencing rallies along with forty-nine intermediate and basic courts across Jiangxi province. On the same day, the Tianjin No. 1 and No. 2 intermediate courts simultaneously convened rallies to sentence more than one hundred criminals involved in fifty-two separate cases. The following day, May 31, the Xuzhou Intermediate Court and lower courts held six rallies to sentence criminals involved in seventy-seven separate cases.[51] More than a month after the first batch of rallies, on June 27, Shanghai courts at all levels simultaneously convened rallies in which ninety-eight criminals involved in seventy-nine separate cases were sentenced. On the same day, courts all over Harbin simultaneously convened sentencing rallies in which ninety-two criminals in total were sentenced.[52] Earlier on in the campaign on April 27, in a creative twist to the conventional simultaneous rallies, the Changsha Intermediate Court in Hunan province convened a rally that was simultaneously broadcast to various "branch rallies" (*fenhuichang*) in four local county courts, where forty thousand of the masses were gathered in various venues to sit and listen to the Changsha rally broadcast on the radio.[53]

A second and less common rally format in Yanda 2001 is the rally convened for a specific audience or purpose. "Special purpose Yanda sentencing rallies" (*Yanda zhuanxiang gongpan dahui*) vary in scale and style. One of the best examples of this format was a rally held on April 25 at the No. 68 High School by the Haizhu Basic People's Court specifically to educate high school students and to frighten would-be criminals in the audience. More than thirteen hundred students and teachers attended the rally in which three armed robbers were sentenced. The rally was said to have had a "positive effect" on the school environment. Those students who had been troublemakers suddenly experienced an attitudinal change (*dou laoshile*) and troublemakers hanging about outside the school all fled in fear.[54] The *Xian Daily* reported that, on May 29, the Baqiao Basic People's Court held a rally at the Qinghua Machinery Factory's sports field, and among those sentenced were criminals convicted of theft at the factory.[55] Similarly, on July 13, the Datian Basic Court convened a rally to sentence criminals for illegally selling explosives. The rally was convened not in the city in which the case was tried but in the small town where the crime took place.[56] A special purpose rally was convened on June 25 in Zibo city, Shandong, at the site of a local driving school to sentence criminals involved in thirteen negligent driving cases in which eleven people had died. This occurred despite the fact that negligent driving was not even a targeted offence in the Yanda campaign.[57]

Other special purpose rallies are convened to publicize certain crimes in a particular area, such as drug-related crimes in southwest China. Three days prior to the annual international anti-drugs day, on June 23 Chengdu police publicly burnt off thirty thousand grams of heroin, the same day that ten criminals convicted of drug trafficking were executed. A joint drugs-burn-off and sentencing rally was convened at the Pixian Sports Stadium on the morning of June 23 attended by three thousand members of the general public and military police.[58] Similarly, in Zhanjiang, Guangdong province, a rally was convened to mark the international anti-drugs day on June 23, when 102 criminals were sentenced and 158 suspects publicly arrested. During the rally, a batch of illegal firearms and a large quantity of drugs were destroyed.[59]

The rally in Zhanjiang described above incorporates the third and most popular format of sentencing rally in Yanda 2001: the joint public arrest and sentencing rally (*gongpu gongpan dahui*). The joint rally is a Yanda 2001 innovation, a hybrid of the public arrest show (*gongpu dahui*) popular in the 1990s and the conventional sentencing rally. In this rally format, the public security bureau (PSB) publicly arrests a batch of suspects, and the court sentences a separate batch of criminals, very often convicted of crimes that are similar to those for which the suspects have been charged. The work of the police and the court are combined in these joint rallies to demonstrate in no uncertain terms that those arrested will be punished severely. A typical procedure for this rally format begins with a line-up of suspects who have already been detained at an earlier date and who are taken out onto a stage or podium and publicly arrested by PSB officers, handcuffed, and (sometimes) paraded around the grounds of the rally site.

Other major centers began joint rallies a week or so later, many of which took the opportunity to arrest or "deal with" (*chuli*) suspects charged with misdemeanors and minor offences, lighter crimes which would normally not be put on show at a conventional rally. On the morning of April 18, for example, cities and districts across Guangdong convened simultaneous rallies to publicly "deal with" 5,485 suspects in total, arresting 2,769 suspects, remanding 1,294 in criminal detention, sending 935 to "reform through education" facilities, and issuing community service orders to 487 individuals or sending them to detox clinics.[60] Again, on the morning of April 18 in Zhanjiang city, a public arrest rally (*chuli dahui*) was held to arrest suspects, announce reform through education, and impose terms of imprisonment and detention to 471 individuals involved in murder, assault, armed robbery, theft, drug trafficking, rape, and smuggling cases.[61]

By June 2001, joint arrest and sentencing rallies had become so commonplace in the Yanda itinerary that in many places they were now called simply "Yanda rallies" (*Yanda dahui*). More simultaneously-convened Yanda arrest and sentencing rallies were occurring in Yanda hot-spots such as Guangdong, Wuhan, and Sichuan. In Guangzhou, for example, on June 9 in twelve districts across the city, the *gongjianfa* together convened simultaneous Yanda rallies with twenty-five thousand "public witnesses" (*jianzheng*) present. Eleven basic courts announced the death penalty on behalf of the Guangzhou Intermediate Court. In addition, the courts publicly sentenced 171 other convicted criminals whose cases had been tried in the first instance, and the procuratorate approved arrests of 285 suspects. In all, five hundred vicious criminals "received their just desserts."[62]

By the end of the first phase of the Yanda campaign at the end of May and early June, major cities were publicizing their "fruits of battle" (*zhanguo*) in an attempt to keep up the momentum for the second phase of the campaign from early June to late August. Heading the figures for the greatest number of sentencing rallies from April to May was Sichuan province with over 1,270 rallies convened and with a total public attendance of over 990,000. Over 1,250 criminals had been sentenced in Hebei with over one million of the masses attending rallies to witness 1,253 criminals sentenced. In Anhui, in four weeks alone, there were fifty-six separate rallies sentencing criminals involved in 545 cases with six hundred thousand in attendance. More than 880 criminals involved in 490 cases were sentenced in the first six weeks of the campaign to May 31. Xinjiang witnessed sixty-two separate rallies compared with sixty-eight rallies in Fujian.[63]

Conclusion

This chapter has looked at one way in which the criminal justice organs in the PRC project images of law, justice, deviance, punishment, and authority outwards to a community of spectators and participants. The educative and deterrent tasks of sentencing rallies have been examined as an attempt by criminal justice authorities to change this community of spectators into a community of "believers."

The general messages in the ritual of sentencing in China contain themes common to many symbolic legal-penal events in other modern legal systems. The theatrics of the act of sentencing, whether in a magistrate's court in England or in a local court in China, carry messages and images about the state, order, and institutional legitimacy as well as the consequences of punishment. Penal and sentencing practices therefore provide:

> moral guidance, patterns of discernment and languages of condemnation which have wider social effects in organizing conduct in all walks of life, as well as

> their role in feeding back more directly their support for the established institutions of punishment.[64]

In China, however, these messages and images are organized around the rhetoric and authority relationships of socialist law and order politics. This being the case, the messages of trials and sentencing, while speaking of general themes and claims about crime and punishment, are articulated within the political context of a particular vision of (socialist) national development, a context in which social stability is a precursor to successful economic reform. So, while the messages of trials and sentencing rallies are primarily about crime—about how the state responds to crime and how crime does not pay—they are also about institutional power and the power of the state to manage social instability. Sentencing rallies provide an arena in which the authority of criminal justice institutions can be defined and projected to the larger community through a process reflecting both post-1978 professionalism and a strict adherence to the law and Maoist mass-line-type popular justice. Mass-line politicking in the post-1978 era is invoked as a rhetorical reminder of the law's moral authority (as representative of the will and interests of the masses), but the *means* by which justice is attained is not represented in the unmediated will of the masses. It is portrayed, rather, as increasingly institutionalized in the procedural and bureaucratic processes of trial work. So, while the moral authority of socialist legality has continued to be represented as a reflection of the will of the masses as the legitimizing force of punishment, the conditions under which this new vision of judicial authority has been constructed in the 1980s are nevertheless more closely connected to the larger institutional and political project of reform. It is in this respect that, within the discursive boundaries of reformist ideologies, the representational "goalposts" of authority have been moved from a basis of unmediated revolutionary popular justice to reincorporate the institutionally based claims of legitimacy that were first promulgated in the period of institution building of the mid 1950s.

Despite the fact that crime has consistently and dramatically increased after every Yanda campaign since 1986, Yanda strategies will most probably continue to be used as the key political response to social change in China well into the first decade of the new century. The rhetorical heart of the campaign will continue to rely on mass-line justice and the main players in the degradation event will continue to be the three organs of criminal justice, along with the masses versus the enemies of the people and the enemies of socialism. The socialist faith in overt acts of public degradation as a way of changing a community of onlookers into a community of believers will continue to be publicly touted as a key rationale of campaigning. This is despite the fact that China has been, for over two decades now, in an environment in which the "invisible hand" of the economy is so evidently much more powerful in deciding on the fate of social order than any hard-line social control strategies. As this chapter has shown, public sentencing and executions have as much or more to do with a show of state strength, and even the very survival of the CCP, as they have to do with crime control. Even Jiang Zemin himself alluded to this in his Yanda call-to-arms speech in early April 2001 when he called for the new assault against crime, to protect not only the economic reforms and the long-term national security but most tellingly, the very future of the CCP's political dominance in China.[65]

Notes

1. An earlier version of this chapter was previously published in an article form as the following: Susan Trevaskes, "Public Sentencing Rallies in China: the symbolizing of punishment and justice in a socialist state," *Crime, Law and Social Change* 39 (2003), 359–82. Permission to reprint from Springer Science and Business Media is gratefully acknowledged.

2. "Summary of Criminal Trial Work," *The Annals*, 30–31.

3. See Michael R. Dutton, *Policing and Punishment in China: From Patriarchy to the People* (Cambridge: Cambridge University Press, 1992), 262.

4. Pat Carlen, "The Staging of Magistrate's Justice," *British Journal of Criminology* 16, no. 1 (1976), 48–55; Pat Carlen, *Magistrate's Justice* (Martin Robertson and Co., London, 1976); Richard V. Ericson, "Mass Media, Crime, Law and Justice," *The British Journal of Criminology* 31, no. 3 (1991), 219–49; Richard V. Ericson, "Why Law is Like News," in *Law as Communication* ed. David Nelken (Aldershot: Dartmouth, 1996), 195–230; Richard V. Ericson, Patricia M. Barnanek, and Janet B. L. Chan, *Representing Order: Crime, Law, and Justice in the News Media* (Milton Keys: Open University Press, 1991); David Garland, *Punishment and Modern Society: A Study in Social Theory* (Chicago: University of Chicago Press and Oxford University Press, 1990); David Garland, "Punishment and Culture: The Symbolic Dimensions of Criminal Justice," *Studies in Law, Politics and Society* 11 (1991), 191–222.

5. Garland, *Punishment and Modern Society*, 68.

6. Garland, "Punishment and Culture," 191–222.

7. Garland, "Punishment and Culture," 195.

8. "Sichuansheng fayuan yanli daji yanzhong xingshi fanzui gongzuo huiyi," (Sichuan Province Court Work Conference on Striking Hard at Serious Crime) in *Renmin fayuan nianjian 1990* (The Yearbook of the People's Courts 1990) (Beijing: renmin chubanshe, 1993), 630.

9. Peter A. Winn, "Legal Ritual," *Law and Critique* II no. 2 (1991): 214–18.

10. Ajuan Wu, "E you e'bao: gongpan dahui ceji," (Evil Reaps what Evil Sows: Sidelight on a Public Sentencing Rally) *Tianjin Ribao* (*Tianjin Daily*), April 23, 2001, 1.

11. Wu, "E you e'bao," 1.

12. Wu, "E you e'bao," 1.

13. Wu, "E you e'bao," 1.

14. Wu, "E you e'bao," 1.

15. Winn, "Legal Ritual," 214.

16. "Chronicle of Events," *The Annals*, 135.

17. "Chronicle of Events," *The Annals*, 136.

18. "Chronicle of Events," *The Annals*, 139.

19. "Chronicle of Events," *The Annals*, 141.

20. These were the rallies recorded in the Baotou document, but it is very likely that many more rallies occurred during this time that were not detailed in the "Chronicle of Events."

21. *Shenyang gonganju diaocha yanjiushi* (*Annals of Shenyang Public Security Bureau Investigation Research*) (Shenyang: neibu ziliao, 1988), 338.

22. *Tianjin fayuan gongzuo dashiji* (*Tianjin Court Work Chronicle*) (Tianjin: neibu ziliao, 1986), 178.

23. *Tianjin fayuan gongzuo dashiji*, 178–79.

24. Harold Garfinkel, "Conditions of Successful Degradation Ceremonies," *The American Journal of Sociology* 51, no. 5 (1956), 420–24.

25. Dutton, *Policing and Punishment in China*, 262.

26. Garfinkel, "Conditions of Successful Degradation Ceremonies," 420.

27. Dutton, *Policing and Punishment in China*, 267.

28. Zheng Degang, "Sichuan Kuangbiao xingdong diyiyi" (Operation Hurricane Begins in Sichuan) at <http://www.people.com.cn/GB/shehui/43/index.html>, April 21, 2001. Hereafter cited as RMW43.

29. Garland, *Punishment and Modern Society*, 58.

30. Garland, *Punishment and Modern Society*, 58.

31. Xingshi susongfa jiaocheng bianxiezu ed. *Xingshi Susongfa jiaocheng* (A Course in Criminal Procedural Law) (Beijing: Qunzhong chubanshe, 1991), 61.

32. Garland, "Punishment and Culture," 206–207.

33. *Xingshi Susongfa jiaocheng*, 60–61.

34. *Xingshi Susongfa jiaocheng*, 61.

35. *Xingshi Susongfa jiaocheng*, 61.

36. Dangdai zhongguo lishi weiyuanwei, ed., *Dangdai Zhongguo de shenpan gongzuo* (Trial Work in Contemporary China) (vol. 1) (Beijing: Dangdai zhongguo chubanshe, 1993), 172.

37. *Dangdai Zhongguo de shenpan gongzuo*, 172.

38. This information is gained from photographic evidence in the publication *Quanguo laodong gaizao zuifan gongzuo zhanlanhui huace* (Catalogue of the National Exhibition on Reform Through Labor Work) (Beijing: neibu ziliao faxing, 1959), 4–5.

39. Interviews conducted with public security bureau and court staff in Beijing by the author in 1996.

40. Interviews conducted with public security bureau and court staff in Beijing by the author in 1996.

41. "Sifabu guanche zhongxuanbu 'guanyu daji xingshi fanzui de xuanchuan wenti' de jidian tongzhi," (Ministry of Justice Notice on Some Points Regarding the Implementation Propaganda Department's "Problems Relating to Propagating the Attack on Crime") in *Xin Zhongguo sifa jieshi daquan* (Anthology of Judicial Interpretations in the New China), ed. Liang Guoqing (Beijing: Zhongguo jiancha chubanshe, 1994), 292–93.

42. "Zuigao remin fayuan zuigao renming jianchayuan gong'anbu sifabu guanyu zhixing sixing yanjin youjie shizhong de tongshi" (July 24, 1986) (Joint Notice from the Supreme People's Courts, the Supreme People's Procuratorate, the Public Security Bureau and the Ministry of Justice on the Strict Prohibiting of Parading Criminals Prior to Execution) in *Xin Zhongguo sifa jieshi daquan* (Anthology of Judicial Interpretations in the New China), ed. Liang Guoqing (Beijing: Zhongguo jiancha chubanshe, 1994), 452. A similar circular was issued two years later in 1988 reminding the courts, procuratorate, and public security bureau yet again that the practice was forbidden according to Article 155 of the Criminal Procedure Law. The 1988 notice noted that courts had already been informed on a number of occasions that this practice was forbidden. For example, in 1984, a joint notice was issued asking the judicial organs to "take precautions against the

[foreign] media spreading rumors regarding the practice of executing criminals." (see p. 455).

43. "Jiang Zemin Calls for Law, Order to Safeguard Social Stability, Reforms Process," *Xinhua News*, April 3, 2001, FBIS-CHI-2001-0403.

44. "Gongjian bushu yanda douzheng, zhongdian daji sanlei fanzui," (Court and Procuratorate Announce Yanda Policy to Focus on Three Broad Areas of Crime) *Fazhi bao* (Legal System News), April 10, 2001.

45. "Guangzhou juxing gongpu gongpan dahui," (Joint public arrest and sentencing rally held in Guangzhou), *Renmin ribao* (People's Daily) (hereafter *RMRB*), April 12, 2001, 1.

46. "Guangzhou juxing gongpu gongpan dahui," 1.

47. *Yangcheng wanbao* (Yancheng Evening News), April 14, 2001.

48. Chen Wen, "Shenzhen xuanpan sishiwuming fanzui fenzi," (Forty-five criminals sentenced in Shenzhen), *RMW43*, April 12, 2001.

49. Numerous reports on this type of rally have noted that these rallies have been convened in accordance with the central policy of Yanda.

50. News bulletin site at *Renmin fayuanbao* (People's Court News, hereafter *RMFYB* online search), April 13, 2001 at <http://www.rmfyb.com/search/index2.asp>, May 23, 2001.

51. *RMFYB* online search. See dates indicated in text.

52. <http://webpage.sina.com.cn>, June 27, 2001.

53. <http://211.90.109.78/mag6/20001111/colart18168.htm>, April 27, 2001.

54. *Yanchang wanbao*, <http://ycwb.com.cn/1998/11/17/xkb/zhxw/ka2b1715.html>, April 25, 2001.

55. *Xian Ribao* (Xian Daily), <http://webpage.sina.com.cn>, May 29, 2001.

56. *RMFYB* online search, July 13, 2001.

57. *RMFYB* online search, June 25, 2001.

58. Xinhua, "Chengdu Jingfang fendu san wan ke, shimin zuifan bei zhixing sixing," (Chengdu police burn off 30,000 grams of heroin, ten criminals are executed), People's Daily online (*RMW43*), June 24, 2001.

59. "Guangdong zhanjiang zhaokai xuanpan chuli dahui, bile yipi sichou shaole hei qiang dupin" (Rally convened in Zhanjiang: a batch of criminals are executed, guns and drugs destroyed), *RMW43*, June 24, 2001.

60. "Guangdong gedi gongkai chuli 5,000 yifan," (5,000 suspects publicly arrested across Guangdong province) *RMRB*, April 19, 2001, 1.

61. "Yanda zai xingdong" (Yanda in Action), <http://www.people.com.cn/GB/ shehui/44/index.html>, April 19, 2001. Hereafter cited as *RMW44*.

62. "Guangzhou wubai e'ren jinri de e'bao," (500 vicious criminals in Guangzhou today receive their just desserts) *RMW 43*, June 9, 2001.

63. *RMFYB* online search, April to June 2001.

64. Garland, *Punishment and Modern Society*, 68.

65. "Zhonggong zhongyang zongshuji, guojia zhuxi, zhongyang junwei zhuxi Jiang Zemin zai quanguo sheihui zhian gongzuo huiyishang zhongyao jianghua" (Party General Secretary, National President, Chairman of Party Central Military Commission, Jiang Zemin's Key Note Speech at the National Conference on Public Order Work), *Renmin Ribao* (The People's Daily), April 4, 2001, 1.

Chapter Four

The Rise of the Anti-Crime Campaign in Post-Mao Court Work

During the Cultural Revolution, Mr. Wang Guihe, a laborer and Party member from the Baotou Municipal Iron and Steel Works, was accused of acting as a counter-revolutionary. He was given a five-year jail term and thrown out of the Party for expressing dissatisfaction with the "formalism" (*xingshi zhuyi*) of Lin Biao and the Gang of Four. Subsequently, his wife left him, his father went blind, and his two children became destitute and homeless. In 1979, after the Baotou Intermediate Court redressed his case, Wang addressed the large public forum and, in an emotion-packed speech, he told the crowd repeatedly how thankful he was to the CCP Central Committee for redressing his case. Wang blamed Lin Biao and the Gang of Four for all anti-Party activities that had led to his arrest and urged the crowd to join with him in "looking ahead to the future and to contributing to the construction of the Four Modernizations."[1] From 1979 to 1981, the Intermediate Court in Baotou, like courts all around China, conducted public forums to propagate court successes in achieving what they described as "bringing justice out of the chaos of the Cultural Revolution." The courts used former victims of the Cultural Revolution as props to display their newfound procedural propriety. This description of the rehabilitation of Wang as one of many thousands of residents rehabilitated in China in the three years from 1979 to 1981, exemplifies the promotional and political cache in exculpating the victims of one political regime to promote the establishment of a new regime.[2] The decision in late 1978 to redress (*pingfan*) cases and rehabilitate victims was meant to signal to the public that people's courts had metamorphosed from a draconian mass-line organization to a reformed institution. This attempt to develop institutional authority for the courts in the immediate post-1978 period relied heavily on elevating the discourses of modernization and reform. Hence, while the people's courts played a key role in the nationwide rehabilitation campaign, developing their institutional authority was also a crucial means by which courts proceeded to reinvent themselves as reformist agents of justice and legitimate legal arbiters.

In the previous chapters we considered how the courts employed reformist rhetoric in an attempt to rebuild a new type of judicial authority based on procedural propriety. The promotion of a new persona of judicial authority emerged, represented as a process of moving from the shackles of leftism to the liberation of reformist politics, from darkness to light. The redress and rehabilitation campaign from 1979 to 1981 mentioned above was essentially concerned with the politics of reconstruction, a way of providing a clear line of demarcation from Maoist to Dengist practices. This process was significant for enabling the courts to redevelop their authority in the latter period as it provided courts with an important stage from which they could be *seen* publicly to be performing with a renewed sense of authority and legitimacy.

The motive for the drive was to construct a clear line of demarcation between Maoist and Dengist justice, between "campaign style popular justice" and "rule of law" justice. Yet, within a number of months after the start of the rehabilitation drive, China embarked on the first of dozens of anti-crime drives that have occurred over a period of nearly three decades since the reform era began. Since 1979, there has not been one year in China in which a national anti-crime drive or "specialized struggle" has not occurred. These campaigns have their rhetorical and operational foundation in the mass campaigns of the 1950s. This chapter, using Baotou as the exemplar court, traces the emergence of the early 1980s campaigns, exploring their historical antecedents and examining how the practice of campaign-style court work informs judicial practice today. We do this through a walk backwards in history from the twenty-first century to the 1950s.

The key focus of this chapter concerns the "praxis" of socialist law in action in three anti-crime campaigns that dominated the day-to-day work in the Baotou criminal court divisions from 1979 to the end of 1982. We examine how courts were employed to pursue the key goals of China's reform period by relying on the rhetoric, targets, and strategies of popular justice to "attack" the enemies of socialist modernization. In terms of the rhetoric and practice of socialist law, the rationale, targets, and strategies of the three campaigns have much in common with anti-crime campaigns in China today. Anti-crime campaigning in the post-Mao period and today involves four main strategies:

(1) to announce at a national conference that crime rates are unacceptably high and that only "striking hard" at crime will control crime rates;
(2) to announce a discrete set of targeted enemies for each offensive;
(3) to make the criminal justice process flexible in order to punish criminals "severely and swiftly";
(4) to create a "great momentum" for the campaign by "mobilizing the masses" and by acts of expressive punishment, in particular, mass sentencing rallies attended by thousands of "the masses."

This chapter examines in particular two of these features—features also present in 1950s criminal court work—which help to develop our understanding of the nature and practice of campaign work in China in the 1980s and today. These shared features concern the key strategies of the campaigns. First is the targeting of criminals as "the enemy." During campaigns, courts apply the criminal law using the socialist concept of "social harm" as the rationale for judicial decisionmaking and sentencing. Social harm is the harm caused to socialist social relations. On this basis, courts target predetermined "enemies" of socialist construction. Second is the adoption of "flexible" judicial practices. The courts employ "flexibility" in procedure and sentencing practice and a policy of "mutual coordination" between the three criminal justice agencies.

As a prelude to the main analysis, and to bring home the relevance of 1980s justice to court work today, the first part of this chapter briefly outlines campaign-style justice today and in the 1990s. The second part provides factual context by describing the unfolding of events of each of the three early 1980s campaigns nationally and locally in Baotou. The remainder of the chapter analyzes the conduct of these three campaigns in relation to the two distinct strategies mentioned above: the targeting of criminal categories as enemies of economic modernization; and the *modus operandi* of "flexibility." This analysis of the campaign strategies traces rhetoric and practices in the contemporary period to their roots in the 1950s. It is important to our understanding of courts today because the early 1980s set the foundation for campaign-style justice beyond the twentieth century into the twenty-first century.

Campaigning in the Twenty-first Century

In April 2001, China launched a nationwide Yanda ("Strike Hard") anti-crime campaign, officially termed the "Strike Hard and Rectification Struggle" (*Yanda zhengzhi douzheng*). As outlined in the introductory chapter, Yanda is a campaign that "attacks" (*daji*) outbreaks of crime or worrying crime trends. The three agencies of criminal justice, the Public Security Bureau (PSB), the procuratorate, and the courts, perform case work collaboratively for a specified period of time. From April 2 to 3, 2001, for the first time in post-1978 history, the entire national leadership, including Jiang Zemin, Li Peng, Zhu Rongji, Li Ruihuan, and Hu Jintao, attended a National Conference on Public Order in Beijing in a gesture of unprecedented support from the Central Party Committee for an anti-crime campaign. Calling for a new two-year assault against crime to protect the economic reforms and long-term national security, president Jiang Zemin signaled in no uncertain terms the significance given to crime control as paramount to the very future of the CCP's political dominance in China.[3] In line with subsequent calls-to-arms from the three arms of criminal justice, Yanda 2001–2003 focused on three broad areas of crime: crimes committed by organized crime gangs; serious violent crimes including bombings, murder, robbery, and kidnapping; and crimes of theft that posed a serious threat to the security of the masses.[4] Thousands of criminals were sentenced to death from 2001–2003, tens of thousands were imprisoned, and millions of people attended mass sentencing rallies.[5]

Campaigning in the 1990s

Yanda 1990

Yanda 2001 was not the first "strike hard" drive in the PRC. As noted previously, from 1983 to 1986 China embarked on a nationwide Strike Hard campaign. Initially intended as a campaign to eliminate serious crime in China, it was not foreseen at the time that it would become the subsequent model for three more nationwide campaigns and dozens of small-scale anti-crime drives. The tactics employed in the Yanda campaign from 1983 to 1986 were credited with being instrumental in the drop in the national crime rate from 8.9 per 10,000 in 1981 to between 5.0 and 5.2 per 10,000 from 1985 to 1987.[6] However, by 1988 a different picture was emerging. In 1987 there were 570,439 registered criminal cases in China. As the Table 4.1 indicates, by 1988 the figure had increased to 827,595, and in 1990 it was over 2.3 million.[7]

Table 4.1. National Registered Crimes, 1987–1991

	1987	1988	1989	1990	1991
Registered cases	570,439	827,594	1,191,901	2,365,709	1,582,659
Homicide	13,154	15,959	19,590	23,199	24,132
Assault	21,727	26,639	35,931	57,478	59,901
Arson	2,792	3,283	5,089	8,074	7,407
Bombing	1,236	1,407	3,141	3,146	3,051
Rape	37,225	34,120	40,999	50,331	49,829
Robbery	17,775	36,318	72,886	105,132	125,092
Theft	435,235	658,683	1,673,222	1,922,506	1,142,556

Source: Guo Xingguo ed., *Jianguo yilai gongan gongzuo dashi yaolan* (National Overview of Public Security Work since the Establishment of the People's Republic (Beijing: Qunzhong chubanshe (zhengfa jiguan neibu faxing), 2003), 680–889).

The Minister for Public Security, Wang Feng, made a number of points about the state of public order in a report to the NPC in 1989. He noted that criminal cases, especially serious crimes, were on the increase; social crimes such as gambling and prostitution continued to increase despite all efforts to counter the trend; public demonstrations, street fights, and crimes such as looting had increased rapidly and were adversely affecting social order; and arson and traffic accidents had increased substantially.[8] The smell of a Yanda drive was in the air.

On May 5, 1990, the Party Central Committee's politico-legal committee convened a nationwide teleconference in which the head of the committee, Qiao Shi, announced that once again crime was rampant and it was necessary to launch a Yanda campaign. The campaign was to run from May to the National Day holidays in October that year. Deputy secretary of the committee, Ren Jianxin, designated the following areas as the geographical focus of the campaign:

- large and medium sized cities
- ethnic minority areas where public disorder was rampant
- border areas
- highways and freeways where robbery was rife
- economically developing areas south of the Yangtze River where crime was a problem
- small coastal cities and large coastal townships[9]

In an address to courts in 1990, SPC President Ren Jianxin underscored the importance of the general public in anti-crime activities, describing the work of the court and the masses in crime campaigns as a cooperative effort in political struggle.

> Attacking crime and protecting social order is of direct concern to every individual in every household. In order to maintain social order, the politico-legal organs must coordinate a specific mass-line approach. . . . To ensure a victory for the Yanda campaign, all of society must participate and all work units must support it. When the masses rise up, there will be no place for criminals to shelter. When the judicial organs unite with the mass-line, it will produce great force in frightening criminals.[10]

The crime targets were murder, bombing, theft and robbery of firearms, crimes using firearms, robbery, major theft, highway robbery, damaging state-owned electrical and communications equipment and construction equipment, drug trafficking, trafficking in firearms, trafficking in women and children, major fraud, major smuggling, hooligan gang ringleaders, ringleaders of prostitution rackets, and counter-revolutionaries (from the Tiananmen incident). Ren Jianxin also announced that regions could select their own Yanda targets according to the crime problems in their area. Criminal justice agencies were told to maintain the policy of "severity and swiftness in accordance with the law" while at the same time maintaining the policy of acting "surely, accurately, and relentlessly" (*wen, zhun, hen*).

The campaign began immediately after the conference. In the first few months of the campaign in May and June 1990, united operations (*tongyi xingdong*) were implemented at the municipal or provincial level. Following this, united operations were adopted on a larger scale in four main geographical regions across the country including the "northern operation" (Heilongjiang, Jilin, Liaoning, and Inner Mongolia), the "Southern China Sea" operation (Guangdong, Fujian, Hainan), the "water net" operation in provinces in close proximity to the Yangtze River (Hubei, Hunan, Anhui, Jiangsu, Zhejiang), and the "Railways operation" on ten major rail lines. In this part of the campaign, itinerant criminals (*liucuan*) and fugitives (*taofan*) were targeted. Yanda concluded on September 30, 1990, with 966,002 suspects brought in for questioning, 796,171 cases cracked (including 155,725 major crimes), and 337,098 members of gangs apprehended. At a national teleconference in October that year, Qiao Shi congratulated criminal justice agencies on their Yanda success, but added that they needed to maintain the Yanda momentum. Ren Jianxin added that crime had not dropped substantially and major crime in particular was rampant. Hence, he announced that in the coming years the Yanda policy of severity and swiftness would not be relaxed. Immediately following the conference, two more specialized struggles were announced.[11]

National "specialized struggles" (*zhuanxiang douzheng*) were launched in the 1990s on a continuous basis. Yet, the crime rate continued to increase. As Table 4.2 shows, by 1995, the rate had increased to 1.69 million. It was time for another Yanda.

Table 4.2. National Registered Crimes, 1992–1996

	1992	1993	1994	1995	1996
Registered cases	1,582,659	1,616,879	1,660,734	1,691,256	1,600,716
Homicide	24,132	25,380	26,553	27,362	25,411
Assault	59,901	64,595	67,864	72,280	68,992
Arson	7,407	6,166	6,572	7,088	7,997
Bombing	3,051	2,904	2,926	3,059	2,893
Rape	49,829	47,033	44,118	41,833	42,820
Robbery	125,092	152,102	159,253	164,478	151,147
Theft	1,142,556	1,122,105	1,133,682	1,133,401	1,043,982

Source: Guo Xingguo ed., *Jianguo yilai gongan gongzuo dashi yaolan* (National Overview of Public Security Work Since the Establishment of the People's Republic (Beijing: Qunzhong chubanshe (zhengfa jiguan neibu faxing), 2003), 926–1105.

Yanda 1996 and Specialized Campaigns

On the morning of June 10, 1996, thirteen years and one month after the start of the first Yanda anti-crime campaign, a report on the city's third Yanda battle led the front-page news of the *Baotou ribao* (Baotou Daily). The article reported a mass sentencing rally at the Baotou Iron and Steel Works Sports Stadium where the Baotou Intermediate People's Court had publicly pronounced sentence on thirty-eight criminals involved in eleven different cases. Of the thirty-eight sentenced, nine criminals "who committed the most heinous crimes" were executed. Another article on the front page that day, titled "Yanda Wins Popular Support," described the use of the law in the latest Yanda campaign in Baotou as "proof of the mighty power of the people's democratic dictatorship." It stated that the latest Yanda campaign was based on the "objective needs of the current circumstances" and had been launched in response to the requirements that the broad masses placed on the government to strengthen the socialist legal system.[12]

As always, the 1996 Yanda campaign was launched on the tailcoat of a national law and order conference. CPC politico-legal committee deputy secretary, Ren Jianxin, announced that the state of law and order across the country was appalling and, particularly over the previous few years, the emergence of "Mafia-style" criminal syndicates and other heinous organized crime groups had contributed substantially to the increase in murder, robbery, and drug crimes. The decision to "Yanda" yet again was made by the politburo. All Party and government organizations across the nation were to unite in leadership to concentrate their strengths on mobilizing the masses and ensuring that enthusiasm for Yanda on the part of criminal justice workers would not wane.[13]

Initially, Yanda was set to run for three months from April to June 1996, with a focus on crimes that seriously damaged public order and serious crime and public order misdemeanors that were a threat to the public. The objective was to use the speediest means available to effect a turnaround in public order. The campaign gained a powerful kick-start with an urgent meeting of criminal justice workers called on April 22, in which China's president, Jiang Zemin, ordered all local Party secretaries to take personal command over Yanda in their area.[14] The campaign was extended to many parts of the country until August that year, as the results of the campaign from April to June were not substantial enough. Blame was placed on Party secretaries who had failed to effectively lead criminal justice agencies in the fight against major crime, crimes committed by fugitives, and organized crime. This Yanda campaign fizzled out in August with little fanfare and few Yanda success stories.[15]

"Specialized struggles" (*zhuanxiang douzheng*), are mini-Yanda campaigns implemented periodically in between Yanda campaigns to fight outbreaks of particular types of crime. As Table 4.3 shows, since 1987, there has not been one year in which China has not experienced either a Yanda campaign or a specialized offensive against one type of crime or another.

In all Yanda campaigns outlined above, the objectives of the drives are rationalized as a key means of crime prevention and social control using the policy of employing "severity and swiftness" (*congzhong congkuai*) to deal with criminal cases considered a serious threat to public or social order. "Severity" is applied as a sentencing rationale and essentially means meting out comparatively severe punishment within the scope of the law. "Swiftness" refers to the accelerating and simplifying of criminal procedure to deal with targeted criminals. Swiftness is rationalized in terms of its perceived deterrence value: the shorter the time that expires between the committing of a crime and the punishment thereby inflicted, the greater are said to be the social benefits of punishment in terms of its deterrence value, and the more conspicuous the relationship between crime and punishment in the minds of the public.[16] An examination of the 1983–1986 Yanda campaign, which is the subject of Chapters Five and Six, needs to be made with reference to the historical and theoretical foundations of crime control in the PRC and in relation to Yanda's immediate predecessors. The following is an outline of the main events of three campaigns that occurred between 1979 and 1983, followed by an examination of two of the campaign strategies: targeting the enemy and making criminal procedure "flexible."

Table 4.3. List of Nationally Implemented "Strike Hard" and "Specialized Campaigns"

Year	Specialized Campaigns
1987	Specialized drive against theft and smuggling of antiquities
	Specialized drive against prostitution
	Specialized drive against trafficking in women and children
1988	Specialized drive against gambling, bombings, and other violent crimes
	Specialized drive against robberies committed on major highways and freeways
1989	Specialized drive against itinerant criminals
	United operations against the "six harmfuls"
1990	The "Six Harmfuls" campaign
	Specialized drive against trafficking in women and children
	Specialized drive to catch fugitives
	The Yanda campaign
1991	Specialized drive against prostitution
	Rectification campaign focusing on hotels and clubs
	Specialized drive against theft

Table 4.3 (continued)

1991 (cont.)	Specialized drive against trafficking in women and children
1992	Specialized drive against crime on trains
1993	Specialized drive against robberies committed on major highways and freeways
	Specialized drive against trafficking in women and children
	Specialized drive against prostitution
	Specialized drive against illegal border crossing
1994	Specialized drive against manufacturing fake business receipts
	Specialized drive against damaging railway tracks, major transportation routes, and oil fields
	A National Urban and Rural Offensive to Strike Hard at Crimes and to Rectify the Public Order
1995	Specialized drive against trafficking in women and children
	Springtime Yanda Offensive
1996	The Yanda Campaign
	Wintertime Yanda Offensive
1997	National Anti-drugs campaign
	Yanda Offensive (in some provinces)
1998	Specialized drive against bombing, illegal possession, and selling of explosives
1999	Specialized drive against the Falungong and superstitious sects
	Specialized drive to apprehend fugitives
2000	Specialized drive against trafficking in women and children
	Specialized drive against counterfeit currency
	A "Typhoon Offensive" against counterfeit trademarks
	Specialized drive against prostitution
	Specialized drive against tax evasion
	Specialized drive against "Mafia-style" crime

Source: Guo Xingguo ed., *Jianguo yilai gongan gongzuo dashi yaolan* (National Overview of Public Security Work since the Establishment of the People's Republic (Beijing: Qunzhong chubanshe (zhengfa jiguan neibu faxing), 2003), 645–1299.

A Survey of Baotou Campaigning

Campaign No. 1 (1979–1980)

The story of the first post-1978 anti-crime campaign in Baotou begins in the national scene, in June 1979, with a conference involving eight national work units and social organizations.[17] The conference was convened to discuss the problem of juvenile delinquency and to report findings to the Central Committee of the CCP. Various politico-judicial units and organizations reported that, in many urban areas, minor juvenile offences such as petty theft, street fights, and hooliganism were developing into serious crimes such as armed robbery, rape, and murder. It was reported that some criminals were becoming habitual offenders and some youths were committing crimes in gangs.[18] Juveniles were reported to be adopting Western ways of thinking, including "so-called democracy, freedom, and human rights," and leaving behind their loyalty to and faith in the socialist system, including the dictatorship of the proletariat, the leadership of the CCP, and Marxism–Leninism–Mao Zedong Thought.[19] The conference report recommended that the Party take a "soft" option in preventing juvenile crime through education, and using punishment only in serious cases.[20]

However, by November 1979, the crime situation was said to have worsened so much that the soft option of deterring juvenile and youth crime was replaced with a "call to arms" from Peng Zhen (the head of the Politico-Legal Committee of the Central Committee of the CCP). In an address given that month at the "National Conference of Municipal Authorities on the Public Order," Peng called for a struggle to be waged against criminals who sabotage the public order and endanger the social order, in particular, criminals who commit murder, rape, armed robbery and arson, and those who set off explosives. The national policy directive on dealing with juvenile and youth offenders was to handle these cases through "education" (for the majority) or punishment (for the minority). The policy differentiated clearly between petty offences and serious offences to determine charges for crimes such as theft and hooliganism. Petty offences would be dealt with administratively through the public security organs (reform through education facilities) and serious offences would be prosecuted.[21]

The first anti-crime drive in Baotou in the post-1978 period was initiated in response to Peng Zhen's call to arms at the November 1979 national conference. "The Summary" notes that a struggle designed to "severely and swiftly" punish criminal elements was officially launched in late December 1979.[22] The sequence of events in Baotou followed a pattern similar to that advocated by Peng Zhen. First, the Baotou Municipal Party Committee organized a conference on "Strengthening the Public Order" in December 1979 to bring into effect the spirit of the "National Conference of Municipal Authorities on the Public Order." At the Baotou conference, the Leading Party Group from the Intermediate Court analyzed the state of public order in Baotou over the last six months of 1979 and relayed to court cadres and court police the spirit of the municipal conference. Conference organizers also disseminated to all court levels (banner, county, and district), a report by the Municipal Party Committee on "Strengthening the Public Order in Baotou."[23] On this basis, the conference participants agreed to mount an anti-crime campaign in line with national anti-crime campaign directives. The targets of the campaign were identified as criminals whose "object" (*keti*) of crime was social order and public order. Five main categories of crime were targeted: murder, arson, rape, armed robbery, and setting off explosives.[24]

"The Summary" in *The Annals* records how the three agencies of criminal justice then came together in a spirit of cooperation. Baotou Intermediate Court president Batucang was given overall responsibility for the tasks of the anti-crime drive in the city, and each president of the basic-level courts was made responsible for the attack on active criminals in their area. The Public Security Bureau, the procuratorate, and the courts were brought together to coordinate a series of successive "attacks" on the five main categories of crime that endangered the social and public order.[25] From December 13 to 31, thirteen public sentencing rallies were held in Baotou in both the intermediate and lower courts to sentence those arrested and convicted during these attacks. The courts pronounced judgment and sentencing on eight-two varying cases involving one hundred and twenty convicted criminals. Over half (59 percent) of the cases that were sentenced over the two-week period involved murder, rape, armed robbery, and other serious crimes.[26] By late December the propaganda machine was in full swing. For example, on December 29, the Intermediate Court broadcast a well-publicized mass sentencing rally live on radio across the city to more than three hundred thousand listeners. The rally was convened to announce the sentences of convicted murderers Zou Jiabao, Feng Jianying, and fourteen others. Zou and Feng were sentenced to death, and the others received punishments that included the death penalty with a reprieve, life sentence, and term sentences from four to fifteen years.[27]

Campaign No. 2 (1981)

Despite these recorded successes of the previous campaign, by mid-1981 the social and public order was again deemed to be under threat. Targets were again selected and a second campaign on public order and social order crimes was mounted. This time, the Criminal Law and Criminal Procedure Law were amended to accommodate an even tougher stance on crime. On June 10, 1981, the Standing Committee of the NPC adopted the "Decision of the Standing Committee of the National People's Congress Regarding Approval of Cases Involving the Death Sentence." The decision modified the stipulations of the Criminal Procedural Law on the jurisdictional requirements for approving the death sentence. Originally all cases involving the death sentence had to be given to the Supreme People's Court for approval. The June 10 decision allowed (initially, until the end of 1983) for the sentencing of capital cases involving murder, robbery, rape, arson, and setting off explosives to be sent for final approval to the provincial higher people's courts instead of the SPC.[28]

Once measures were in place to "legalize" an impending further crackdown through "swift and severe punishment," national media reports on the crime situation and policy reports on the government and Party's response to crime became more frequent. On August 17, the *People's Daily* published an editorial titled "Push forward the high tide of victory to strengthen public order."[29] The editorial affirmed that, "The state of public order—whether it declines or improves—will have a direct impact on the very success of the Four Modernizations. One of the central concerns of the masses is to be able to live in peace and security."[30] The editorial also claimed that, once the public order had been improved, it would still be imperative "not to let down our guard" and to continue the fight against crime.[31]

In Baotou, the courts employed "severity and swiftness" and combined "punishment with leniency" in the second anti-crime campaign which lasted approximately six months from mid-1981 to the end of the year. In this second drive to stamp out crimes against social order and public order, the Baotou courts used mass sentencing rallies as a vital tactic. The mass sentencing rally provided a crucial link between the masses and the court. It allowed the courts to propagate fear of non-compliance among the masses and effectively co-opted into submission some who might have otherwise committed crimes. The final part of the campaign was to broadcast its success. A report that SPC president Jiang Hua gave to the NPC at the end of the year outlined the success of criminal court work in cracking down on serious criminal offenders. His report noted that the people's courts firmly believed that "the authority of the law should be reflected not only in the making of laws but more importantly, in the effective implementation of these laws."[32]

Campaign No. 3 (1982)

Within a few years of the start of the economic reforms, a small number of Party and government officials "who had come under the corrosive influence of capitalist ideas"[33] were said to be threatening the spiritual civilization of the Chinese people and the very success of China's economic modernization.[34] This prompted criminal justice agencies nationwide in 1982 to implement the third campaign. Like the two previous anti-crime drives against offenders who endanger the social and public order, the third campaign targeted a specific caliber of criminal, those "who endanger the socialist economic order." Like the previous two campaigns, this campaign moved through a particular sequence that began with an official declaration from central authorities about the severity of the situation. Particular categories of criminals were targeted, and a "call to arms" against the offenders was made in the media both before and after the "legalization" of the campaign through legislative changes. Next came the concrete implementation of the campaign through trial and punishment. Under the policy of "punishing the minority and winning over the majority," courts clamped down on serious economic crime, focusing on important cases involving large sums of money, especially cases involving government employees. Of the crimes codified in the Criminal Law as crimes that endanger the socialist economy—smuggling, speculation, swindling, bribery, tax evasion, theft of state property, graft, and embezzlement—nationally, the economic crime that was the catalyst for the campaign was smuggling.[35] However, the most common economic crimes in Baotou at the time were bribery, profiteering, and corruption through theft of state property.

In the introduction to a description of the campaign against economic crime in Baotou, the "Summary of Criminal Trial Work" situates the problem of corruption in a context of tremendous national import—the very success or failure of national economic reforms. Here is a description of both the material and ideological damage to the nation as a result of smuggling, speculation, swindling, and bribery by government employees. These economic crimes are described in relation to the criminals' intent and in terms of the economic and social effects of the crimes. It is explained that offenders who committed economic crimes took advantage of the economic situation "to sabotage the socialist economic order, and to damage the reforms and the smooth progress of the open door policy."[36] These crimes "corroded the ideological standing of cadres and . . . poisoned the positive atmosphere within the Party and in society in general."[37] Here was the apologia that "if these criminals were not dealt a swift and severe blow, the economic enterprises growing out of the 'Four Modernizations' would have suffered and failed just when they were on the cusp of success."[38]

After the announcement of the NPC Decision, a call to arms was initiated across the nation, and the campaign against economic crime was launched in the newspapers on March 10. A *People's Daily* editorial stressed the imperative of cracking down on economic crime, claiming that the "corrosive influence of capitalist ideology" was a threat to the socialist cause and to the people's interests.[39] On March 13, the adjudication committee and the court administration office of the Baotou Intermediate Court met to study the *People's Daily* editorial and to formulate measures for the crackdown.[40] On March 15, the Supreme People's Court issued a circular urging all people's courts to study and implement the NPC decision and to give primary importance to handling economic crime.[41] As a result, the Leading Party Group of the Baotou Intermediate Court held three meetings to discuss the specifics of implementing the NPC Standing Committee decision. In a meeting on March 23, seven decisions and provisions were made about processing economic crimes in the No. 1 Criminal Division of the Baotou Intermediate Court, and accordingly, increasing numbers of judicial personnel in this area were co-opted to handle the heavier workload. Specific targets of the campaign were confirmed through fieldwork and investigation. A number of government officials and businesspeople were arrested, prosecuted, and publicly sentenced, and the campaign (which did not officially finish until 1986) was declared a success.

The Targets of 1980s Campaigns: The Enemies of Modernization

In his recent account of the history of policing in the PRC, Michael Dutton proffered the following statement about the "us" and "them" nature of Chinese politics and social control.

> If you want to understand the concept of the political, turn to the first line of the first page of the first volume of Mao Zedong's Selected Works. There, one finds an article originally written in 1926, that expresses in the form of a question to our (revolutionary) selves the quintessence of politics: "Who are our enemies, who are our friends? That is the question germane to the revolution." This is, of course, more than a question; it names a divide that assumes and leads toward a way of understanding. As the Chinese revolution demonstrates, it also leads to a way of living. Living turns into action and, in making revolution, one's actions are caught firmly in life's grip. The intensity of revolutionary action forces life into a simple binary choice of friend and enemy and imprints that choice upon the mind such that it becomes the only question worth asking.[42]

The rationales of punishment in the PRC have historically relied on utilitarian dialectics—"the people" versus "the people's enemies"; the "majority" versus the "minority"; "the general enemies" versus the "immediate enemies"—and policies such as "combining punishment and education" and "leniency and severity." As Ronald Keith explains,

> On the one level, Mao's strategy of "dividing and breaking up criminals" (*fanhua wajie fangzui fenzi*) seeks to educate and reform the majority of criminals, while, on another level, there is a targeting and isolation of a supposed minority of intransigent criminals, which requires the swift application of severe punishment.[43]

In the post-1949 period, the courts' means of determining criminality and sentencing was based on two of Mao's key political concepts for dealing with social contradictions; "democracy" as the means of dealing with the contradictions among the people, and "dictatorship" as the means of dealing with contradictions between the people and the enemy. Contradictions among "the people" could be dealt with in a non-antagonistic manner through the democratic means of "discussion, criticism, persuasion and education."[44] Whereas contradictions among the people were non-antagonistic and could be resolved by peaceful methods, antagonistic contradictions could not. The mode of "dictatorship" was applied to the "enemy" as a means of solving antagonistic contradictions in a coercive manner.[45] Those who belonged to the category of the enemy were "the social forces and groups which resist the socialist revolution and are hostile to or sabotage socialist construction." Enemies of the people were those "exploiters" who resisted the socialist revolution, including counter-revolutionaries and those who were hostile to socialist construction.

Criminal and non-criminal acts were to be differentiated by the court determining the nature of the crime (in terms of the degree of social harm caused by the act) and the circumstances of the criminal. According to Mao, the nature of the crimes committed by "exploiters who resist the socialist revolution" involved acts of subversion, theft of state property, political and state secrets and so on. Importantly, the classification of the offender as an enemy of the people was determined by the degree to which the particular act committed contravened the agendas of socialist construction and the public or social order. Those people whose intent it was to sabotage socialist construction including "thieves, swindlers, murderers, arsonists, criminal gangs, and other scoundrels who seriously disrupt public order,"[46] were, by the nature of the harm (or potential harm) they caused, enemies of the people. The method of "dictatorship" was considered the only appropriate means of resolving conflicts between the enemy and the people because the nature of the criminal act was considered a manifestation of class conflict and, as such, required a resolution through antagonistic class struggle.

Because the criminal statutes of the 1950s did not contain any details of the boundary between a criminal and non-criminal act, it was left to academic texts and Party and judicial policy documents to fill the gap in interpretation by providing guidance on differentiating criminal from non-criminal acts. According to one such source, *The Lectures on the General Principles of Criminal Law in the People's Republic of China*, written by four scholars at the Teaching and Research Office for Criminal Law of the Central Political-Legal Cadres' School, a crime is defined as a socially dangerous act. The degree of social dangerousness of an act is the main criterion for demarcating the boundary between criminal and unlawful acts. An act is considered a crime based on three main factors: the nature of the crime (as defined by the seriousness of the act), the amount of damage caused by the act, and the state of mind of the offender. Judicial interpretation of the "seriousness" of the act, which determines whether the act is a crime or a misdemeanor, altered from one political period to another. For instance, during periods when socialist construction was emphasized as a national priority, economic offences would be seen as more serious than would normally be the case. As such, behavior which normally may not be considered a crime in one period might be determined as a criminal offence in another period.[47]

Today in China, criminal liability in a criminal case is established on the basis of a claim by a representative of the state that the act for which the individual is prosecuted has caused a particular type of social harm. The type of social harm assigned to a particular behavior is defined in terms of how the act has harmed socialist social relations (*shehui zhuyi shehui guanxi*). Social harm is, therefore, the harm caused when the act under prosecution has violated one or more socialist social relations.[48] In the official literature on socialist law in the first thirty years of the PRC, the concept of social harm was closely connected to the cause of class struggle. However, in the 1980s, the idea of social harm is linked to the reformist objectives of economic modernization and social stability.[49] We see then that while criminal court work in the 1980s continued to serve political ends, these ends had been changed in line with the national reform program. We see the shift in context from mass movements to national economic construction and its pre-condition, social stability. Thus, in post-1978 Baotou, the political ends served by criminal court work were no longer ideologically linked to "liberating" the forces of production, but were correlated to the changing modes and relations of production required for economic restructuring.

Accordingly, notions of social harm in the reform period continued to underlie the principles, functions, and implementation of criminal law from 1978. However, under the reform program, the notion of the "social" was recast to incorporate the ever more complex social relations that economic modernization engendered. Post-1978 socialist criminal law theory dictates that the object of a criminal act to be the socialist social relations the act violates.[50] Social relations can be either material relations (*wuzhi guanxi*), which are part of the economic base, or ideological relations (*sixiang guanxi*), which are part of the superstructure. They include relations associated with the sovereignty and territorial integrity of the state, the people's democratic dictatorship, the socialist revolution, socialist construction, property owned by the whole people, and individual citizens' "rights of the person," including their democratic rights, rights to lawfully owned property, and so on. Chen Xinglian and Qiu Xinglong explain:

> A crime always has some social relationship to the object of its violation. Various kinds of social relations differ in their objective degree of danger. For example, counterrevolutionary crime has national security as its object of violation, aiming directly at the proletarian dictatorship and the socialist system, while the crime of violating personal rights only violated the personal rights of individual citizens, so the objective degree of danger of the latter can hardly be compared to that of the former.[51]

The concept of social harm informs the definitions of the main categories of criminal offences in the 1979 Criminal Law to the extent that, in this law, crimes are categorized in relation to the objects (*keti*) of crime (i.e., the social relations the crime has violated). This law has eight main categories of offences. The types of crimes are outlined in Part Two of the Criminal Law, where they are ordered according to the degree of social harm attributed to the crime.[52] The types of crimes tried in Baotou in the early 1990s are in Table 4.4.

Table 4.4. Offences in the Baotou Intermediate People's Court No. 1 Criminal Division, 1992–1993

Category of Crime	Offences
Crimes of counter-revolution	No counter-revolutionary offences committed in Baotou in 1992–1993.
Crimes of infringing upon the rights of the person and the democratic rights of citizens	Willful murder; negligent killing (manslaughter); rape; rape of minor (including consensual sexual relations with a juvenile under 14 yrs); serious assault (grievous bodily harm); assault (intentional bodily injury); abducting and trafficking in women and children; unlawful detention and deprivation of personal freedom; extorting confession by torture.
Crimes of endangering public security	Arson; sabotage of electric power or gas facilities; causing serious accidents (workplace accidents); causing serious accidents as a result of violation of transport rules and regulations; illegal manufacturing, trading, and transportation of armaments, ammunition, and explosives.
Crimes of property violation	Robbery (taking property by force); theft of public property; theft of private property; swindling public property; swindling private property; corruption; embezzlement.
Crimes of undermining the socialist economic order	Profiteering; tax evasion; counterfeiting registered trademarks.
Crimes of obstructing the administration of public order	Hooliganism; illegal gambling; obstructing a state functionary from carrying out duties; luring women into prostitution or sheltering women in prostitution.
Crimes of dereliction of duty	Accepting bribes (for state functionaries only); neglect of duty (causing loss of public property or state interests).
Crimes of disrupting marriage and family	Forcibly interfering with another's freedom of marriage; bigamy; abuse or maltreatment of a family member.

Source: Internal data provided by Baotou Court judges.

In all three campaigns in the early 1980s, the Baotou courts, like courts nationwide, participated in a "political struggle" (*douzheng*) to eliminate the enemies of socialist modernization. All three campaigns in Baotou during this time share a common rhetorical basis: all were represented as being essential to maintaining and upholding the people's democratic dictatorship and defending the modernization drive and national reforms. The three campaigns in Baotou, and nationwide, were launched against criminals "who seriously endanger the social order" and who "seriously endanger the socialist economic system." Each campaign had a list of targeted "criminal categories," and the majority of offenders prosecuted during the campaigns fitted the description of the campaign targets.[53]

Targets of Campaign No. 1 and No. 2

"The Summary" describes Baotou criminal court work in the 1980s within the narrative framework of two key criminal targets: those who sabotage the economic order and those who sabotage the social and/or public order. During the campaigns, the social order (*shehui zixu*) and the public order (*shehui zhi'an*) were articulated in the rhetoric of socialist criminal law theory as the main *objects* of criminal activity (*fanzui de keti*) in this period. Let us consider these two "orders." The "social order" is a general term that refers to a state of stability in society characterized by a highly ordered and stable social environment. A sound social order is manifest in orderly and stable economic production and social relations in the community. The "public order," according to Chinese criminologist Liu Hua, is regarded by most Chinese scholars in criminological circles as a phenomenon that encompasses both the material and the ideological/behavioral realm. The public order includes the physical space of public places as well as the "common standards of behavior observed by people in common life," the moral consciousness and social conduct of individuals.[54]

In the first anti-crime drive in Baotou in the post-1978 period, launched in December 1979, the targets of the campaign included hooligans, armed robbers, thieves, rapists, and murderers. In (socialist) legal terms, the object of their crime was the social order or the public order. The campaign was conducted in a spirit of cooperation between the three agencies of criminal justice who acted in close coordination in a series of successive attacks on offenders in the main categories of crime.

The second Baotou campaign in 1981 began with a "call to arms" from the Central Committee of the CCP at a Five City Public Security Conference in Beijing in May 1981. The spirit of the campaign principles was discussed at the conference and consequently disseminated to courts throughout China, including Baotou city. The basic purpose of the campaign was to attack serious criminal elements and to procure a sharp decline in crime rates by the judicial practice of applying "severe and swift" (*congzhong congkuai*) punishment to set categories of criminals as a means of deterrence and retribution.[55] The assessment of the degree of "severity" and "swiftness" that would be applied in trying and sentencing particular criminals depended on how court workers perceived the degree of social dangerousness caused by the criminal act.

In the post-1978 period, juvenile and youth offenders (aged between fourteen and eighteen years and eighteen and twenty-five years respectively) were designated as the most significant category of criminal. They replaced the politico-ideological criminal as the main target of crime control and became the new focus of fear and loathing. A number of reasons explain this shift to juveniles and youth. Borge Bakken, for example, notes that in demographic terms, juveniles and youth belonged to the baby-boom generation of the Cultural Revolution, and the sheer increase in the number of those inside the age bracket defining juvenile crime—from 137 million in 1966 to twice that figure in the mid-1980s—meant that there was a significantly greater number of juveniles than before and they were growing up in an environment of unprecedented mobility and social change.

Since crime is more prevalent in urban than in rural areas, the urbanization of this segment of the population was also a factor. Youth sent to the countryside during the Cultural Revolution returned to urban areas in search of work and a better life in the city. This urban migration by the young was accompanied by an increase in the proportion of crimes committed by juveniles and youths. The change in how criminal activity was construed by the authorities and represented to the people—from the pre-reform conception of crime as a manifestation of class struggle to the reformist conception of crime in terms of the social and economic order—increasingly linked juveniles and youth to community and government perceptions of social order and disorder. The nature of four of the main crimes of this period—rape, hooliganism, armed robbery, and larceny—is also significant in understanding the juvenile and youth target. All four of these types of crime had a much more direct impact on the lives of ordinary citizens than had crimes in the past, and the large bulk of offenders were juveniles and youths. For example, in 1981, 70 to 80 percent of those who were convicted of crimes of "seriously endangering the public order"—including gang rape, gang warfare, rape, and armed robbery—were juveniles and youths aged fourteen to twenty-five.[56]

Representing crime as endangering the social order (*weihai shehui zhixu*) and violating the public order (*pohuai shehui zhi'an*), and responding to crime through hard-line crackdowns can be regarded as a defense mechanism that authorities mobilized against what they saw to be an encroaching revolution. This was a social revolution that threatened the legitimacy of the new post-Maoist regime. As Borge Bakken argued, how the authorities perceived both the link between economic reform and social instability and its relationship to their hold on power is crucial in explaining the state's preoccupation with crimes against the social and public order.[57] Bakken explained the hard-line tactics of the 1980s crime policy in China as largely a "defense of moral and cultural values at a time of dramatic economic and social change." The state's hard-line response to crime focusing on juveniles and youths was a "central theme of the reform period" because this response related directly to the central question of "order" in society, "a question that should be seen as parallel to the question of economic growth."[58] For Bakken, "The legitimacy of the regime rests on both these issues—growth and order—and might explain why the Chinese are so preoccupied by crime. Even when the crime rates are some of the lowest in the world, crime seems to be on everyone's lips in China today."[59]

Targets of Campaign No. 3

The attack on the enemies of the socialist economy was launched at a national level through the policy of "punishing the minority and winning over the majority," targeting major crimes of bribery, profiteering, and corruption through theft of state property. Those guilty of crimes that "sabotage the socialist economic order," that damage "the reforms and the smooth progress of the open door policy," "corrode the ideological standing of cadres," and "poison the positive atmosphere within the Party and in society in general,"[60] were dealt with in "swift and severe blows."

In Baotou, specific targets of the campaign were confirmed through fieldwork and investigation. On March 21–22, 1982, vice-president of the Intermediate Court, Li Wenkao, took three other court workers to a number of offices around the city in order to investigate and prepare a written report on the economic crime situation. These offices included the Municipal Party Committee Office on Economic Crime, the Municipal Public Security Bureau, the Municipal Procuratorate, the Bureau of Industry and Commerce, and local lower banner, county and district procuratorates, and courts. The group analyzed 122 economic crime cases that had been uncovered. Eight of the cases related to smuggling and trafficking, thirty-four to profiteering and speculation, forty-nine to corruption and larceny, twenty-four were related to bribery, and seven were related to misappropriating public or collectively owned property. Of the 122 cases investigated, nine involved funds exceeding ten thousand yuan. Of the people found to be incriminated in these cases, sixty-eight were Party or government functionaries, including six at a senior level (county head or equivalent) and twelve at the level of section head.[61]

The analysis by Li Wenkao and his team confirmed that all of the cases had at least one of the following three characteristics:

(1) they involved schemes between government personnel and private citizens or between urban and rural government personnel;

(2) they involved Party and government functionaries and even senior-ranking government and judicial officials and others illegally holding lavish parties and giving gifts to curry favor; and
(3) they involved bribery.[62]

Using this knowledge, a conference, attended by all Baotou court presidents from both levels of the court, planned arrangements for the task of heavily punishing criminals who seriously sabotage the economy.[63]

Three days after this conference, the Baotou courts received the CCP Central Committee's Decision on "Cracking Down on Serious Crime" authored jointly with the State Council. The decision outlined the key strategies of the campaign: focusing on cases involving high-ranking officials; mobilizing the masses into action against corruption; and educating the Party and the masses through trials and sentencing rallies.[64] The decision urged court workers to follow through. Here the campaign targets, strategies—and gravity—were made clear for Baotou.

"The Summary" provides an example of one of the Baotou Intermediate Court's victories. This case involved the conviction of Xu Lianqun, who, from August 1981 to May 1984, alone and with others, committed seventy-four counts of theft and of stealing both public and privately-owned property valued at more than 26,000 yuan.[65] He was dealt with using the policy of "severe punishment in accordance with the law" and sentenced to death.[66]

The CCP Central Committee convened a forum on the economic crime campaign held from September 5 to 9 and declared the campaign a resounding success. The fruits of the struggle in this campaign included halting the offences of smuggling and corruption, successfully educating the masses and Party officials about the evils of economic crime, strengthening the Party's resolve "to be on guard against the corrosive influence of capitalist ideology," and advancing a positive social climate.[67] Here the struggle under way in this campaign is linked to the ideology of socialist spiritual civilization, with "corrosive Western influences" identified as part of the spiritual pollution of the West. To be sure, the targets of all three campaigns share this characteristic: their behavior, a result in part of caustic Western values that had permeated the social landscape, represents social and moral decay deemed a serious threat to the fabric of socialist society.

The History of "Flexibility" in PRC Criminal Court Work

Chinese socialist legal ideology had traditionally prescribed that changes in the concrete circumstances of social development be reflected in Party norms. Changes in law in response to changes in Party norms, and adjustments and changes in Party norms, are based on the "actuality" of the social conditions of socialist transformation, as interpreted by Party norms through Party policy. As law is to serve the interests of state-building and social development, it must be flexible in nature. The content and application of law is, in theory, to be continually amended and renegotiated on the basis of Party assessments of historical developments. The current circumstances and law should not be so fixed as to hinder the Party in directing state and social development. This was the basic rationale underlying the approach of flexibility and mutual coordination in court policy in anti-crime campaigns in Baotou in the 1950s and the 1980s. Crime control strategies in the 1950s and in the 1980s were based on a particular idea that, to best serve the people, law must be applied flexibly, in both procedure and sentencing practice. In applying the law, the three organs of criminal justice (*gongjianfa*) were to coordinate their efforts to achieve the most effective outcomes.

In the Anti-Rightist campaign of 1957, many Baotou court workers were labeled "rightist" and, as a result, the ranks of the judiciary were severely depleted of many younger, educated staff. The campaign was said to have disrupted the general flow of procedural regularity, and many court workers began to be afflicted with what researchers at the Contemporary Chinese History unit call the "disease of leftist paranoia" (*kongyoubing*).[68] With the recent memory of political culling of "rightist" judicial staff, those workers still in the courts enthusiastically adopted the ethos of the Great Leap Forward, espousing a "great leap forward in judicial work" with the policy of the "four nothings" (*siwu*). The policy of the "four nothings" decreed that, within one to three years, there would be "no counter-revolutionary offences, no property-related violations, no armed robberies; and no rapes occurring in Chinese society."[69] These policies resulted in a major increase in arrests.

A quota system based on the Great Leap Forward economic production quota system was put into effect in courts. Courts were required to dispose of cases in record time and, in some areas, judges were required to dispose of one hundred cases per month.[70] To meet quotas and to follow the communal work ethos of the Great Leap Forward, the public security bureau, procuratorate, and courts developed a system of joint handling of cases (*lianhe ban'an*).[71]

The practice of "joint handling of cases" included the practice of "one head representing three heads" (*yizhang dai sanzhang*). Particular jurisdictions were divided into zones in which one member of each of the public security bureau, procuratorate, or court would be responsible for a "case handling team" comprised of cadres from each of the three agencies. The head of the team would represent the authority of all three agencies from the stage of initial investigation to the execution of sentences. In practice, the individual members of each team would take a particular area, street, or prefecture and be responsible for investigating, trying, and sentencing offenders in that area.[72] The defendant was often simply handed over to the masses to be denounced and humiliated. The defendant could not state his/her case, and so-called evidence was presented by the crowds in open-air courts. Evidence could not be corroborated. In some remote areas, local communes or working teams took on the role of judicial officers and tried and sentenced people illegally. A number of cases of divorce were tried as criminal cases, with women being labeled as "capitalist roaders." In other areas, women who were already divorced were sent to "court" to be tried and sentenced.[73]

By the end of 1957, the democratic features of open trial and due process that were so widely touted in the mid-1950s as expressions of socialist justice were renounced as expressions of *bourgeois* overindulgence. The sins of "commandism," "subjectivism," and "bureaucratism" exposed during the Anti-Rightist campaign prompted a realigning of the rhetoric of mass-line away from the formalistic strictures of the courtroom to "on-the-spot" adjudication in factories, farms, and work units. In January 1958, two months after the Anti-Rightist campaign was initiated, regulations concerning the "simplified management of legal procedures" (*guanyu jianhua guanzhi falu shouxu de guiding*) were promulgated to the courts in Baotou. One instance of flexibility as a euphemism for simplified procedures through inter-agency coordination occurred in Baotou in March 1958. In an attempt to handle cases as efficiently and quickly as possible, the functions of Baotou court judges and presidents were altered. On one occasion, the division heads and judges of the Intermediate Court chaired the basic-level courts as provisional judges. The court president acted as court clerk and in one day, ninety-one criminal and civil cases were handled.[74]

Both rhetorically and operationally, simplifying judicial procedure closely followed the promotion of socialist catch cries of the mass movements of the late 1950s. For example, the reorganization of judicial procedures in Baotou in the late 1950s complemented a new emphasis on the Great Leap Forward ethos of mass production values of efficiency, productivity, speed, and cooperation. The police, procuratorate, and court in Kundulun district in downtown Baotou formally amalgamated into one office in November 1958. Under the united front of the *gongjianfa*, pre-trial and trial procedures were organized into "one package." A "judicial committee" was formed comprising "three chiefs" who were the heads of the police, procuratorate, and court, and the court president presided over the examination and approval of cases.[75]

The main politico-legal slogans of the time included catch cries such as "Go out in unison to arrest criminals and separate the various functions [of the three organs] only upon return"; "One cadre can represent all three organs"; "In the one hand grasp adjudication work, in the other hand grasp mediation"; and "Convene trials in batches in continuous waves." These catch cries accompanied slogans such as, "When there's politico-legal work to do, do it, but when there's none, go out and do physical labor for the cause of production."[76] At one point at the height of the Great Leap Forward, a group of judicial cadres in Baotou was sent to the countryside "to participate in and to protect production." Instead of trying cases, judicial officers were organized to "work hard in the production of non-staple foods."[77]

"Flexibility" and Simplifying Justice in the 1980s Campaigns

In all of the anti-crime campaigns in the 1980s, the Baotou courts' hard-line response to perceived increases in particular crimes such as murder, arson, rape, theft, and armed robbery was informed by changes in official circles in the "interpretation" of the social dangerousness of certain crimes in certain periods. For instance, when the unstable state of the social and public order was deemed to threaten the very success of national reforms, adjudication and sentencing practices were "simplified" and "quickened" to ensure the success of the campaign. Sanctions on "social order" and "public order" crimes were increased at times when these crimes were deemed a threat to the social order. Similarly, when corruption and profiteering were deemed a threat to the very success of the economy, sanctions increased substantially.

During the campaigns from 1981 to 1986, flexibility was manifest in two main policies. One was the policy of "severity and swiftness," *congzhong congkuai* (*congzhong* being the use of the harshest or most "severe" sentencing, *congkuai* being the use of "swiftened" judicial procedure). The second was the joint handling of cases between the courts, police, and procuratorate, under the rubric of "mutual coordination."

In 1981, a new policy of "comprehensive management of public order" (*shehui zhi'an zonghe zhili*) was promulgated as a key ideological and organizational tool for crime control in the new era. It was developed as an all-encompassing policy emphasizing education and punishment of criminals through mutual coordination and cooperation between political, social, legal, economic, cultural, and educational bodies in managing crime. The ideological and organizational rationale of "comprehensive management of public order" in criminal court work has its roots in judicial work practices during the mass campaigns of the 1950s. "Mutual coordination" of judicial activities was manifest in simplified trials and inter-agency coordination, through the flexible joint handling of cases with the police and procuratorate, in the Anti-Rightist campaign and the Great Leap Forward. This reliance on flexibility as a hallmark of criminal court work has its roots in the revolutionary era but was developed as a key component of criminal court work in the 1950s.[78]

In 1981 a new version of the "flexible" approach to criminal justice was promoted in the wake of an official reassessment of the causes and concept of crime. The interpretation of crime as essentially a political and class-based phenomenon was replaced with an interpretation that emphasized crime as a social phenomenon. The increase in crime in the post-1989 era was seen to be influenced increasingly by a myriad of social factors that were economic, political, and cultural. The multifaceted nature of crime required a multifaceted response from a variety of social institutions.[79]

"Comprehensive management of public order," a scientific term appropriated from the technical field of water conservancy, was a policy advocating the comprehensive management of crime through the proper management of the economy, politics, law, government administration, and ideology.[80] The rationale behind the policy was that, because criminal behavior was a complex social phenomenon (*fuza de shehui xianxiang*), and because its causes were equally complex politically, economically, ideologically, and culturally, this social illness or "syndrome" (*zonghezheng*) must be "cured" in a comprehensive manner, with the participation of all sectors of society.[81] The essence of comprehensive management of public order was, therefore, that under the leadership of the CCP, the politico-legal organs and other relevant work units and social organizations would "employ their influence using political, ideological, economic, educational, governmental, and cultural means, as well as legal means, to attack crime, reform criminals, save delinquents, and to educate the people."[82] The strategy was touted as a way to combine essential elements—the tactics of "attack" and "prevent," and the policies of "combining punishment with education," and "combining the cure of symptom and cause." This more unified approach would prevent crime from the grass-roots levels and help to restore the social order. Public security, administrative, and educational organizations would handle the "education" aspect, and the three organs of criminal justice would handle the "punishment" aspect.

Although the comprehensive management of public order policy was implemented officially in 1981, its roots were in historical practices of post-revolutionary China. The 1980s concept of comprehensive management owed much to 1950s policies to combine the work of the politico-legal organs with the "mass line" and to "combine punishment and education." The basic means for implementing "comprehensive management of public order" were similar to those set out in politico-legal folklore following Mao's treatise on "dictatorship," "democracy," "education," "punishment," and "reform" of the criminal.[83] The rationale of comprehensive management of public order was to improve the quantity and range of social and political organizations responsible for preventing crime. Work units from the grass roots up were to be held responsible for their own "patch," and had to establish their own system to protect and secure their own area. The policy's rationale and rhetoric even extended into the discourses of economic production; work units were to establish a system of rewards and penalties based on the ethos of comprehensive management of public order. The central idea here was to strengthen the grass-roots organization and work of the *gongjianfa*, local governments, citizens' committees, and village committees. It was "to allow the masses to make their own 'social contract' (*xianggui minyue*) at grass roots level, to allow the masses to develop a conscious respect for the law and public morals, and to strengthen the authority of local courts and (civil) mediation committees, in order that they resolve minor disputes before they become major disputes."[84]

Flexibility in the Policy of "Severity and Swiftness"

The first "project" under the rubric of comprehensive management of public order in the 1980s was to attack crime by "severely and swiftly punishing serious offenders in accordance with the law" in the 1981 campaign. The main rationale for using the heavy-handedness of severe and swift punishment instead of "education" and "prevention" was that "in times of social disorder and increased crime, only the punitive methods of 'swiftly and severely' punishing offenders can facilitate the proper implementation of all the other [non-punitive] aspects of comprehensive management."[85] Only by "severely and swiftly punishing in accordance with the law" could offenders fully appreciate and respect the sanctity of the law (*falu de zunyan*).[86] The two main categories of offenders targeted were criminals in the anti-crime campaigns and recidivists and escaped prisoners.[87]

The principle was to provide a "colorful warning to delinquents or potential offenders, encouraging them to get back on the right track." Policy measures would strongly encourage would-be criminals to do the right thing, which would transform undesirable social trends, enable the smooth development of socialist spiritual civilization and allow the political, governmental, and educational fields to do their part in comprehensively managing public order.[88] It was hoped that the principle would gain wide public support and thus effect a change in public attitudes towards crime "from a situation where the good people in society fear the bad ones to a situation where the masses actively participate in the political struggles against crime and in the comprehensive management."[89]

The concept of employing "severity" as a sentencing policy refers to the judge's application of the maximum penalty within the scope of the law when meting out punishment to the campaign targets, who formed the minority of serious criminal offenders. This concept is based on the premise that the degree of social harm caused by a criminal act is an important factor in the sentencing process.[90] Application of the concept is flexible to the extent that it relies on the discretion of the court to decide an "objective" assessment of the degree of social harm caused by the act. Interpretation of the degree of harmful social consequences of an act depends not only on the degree of the danger attributed to the crime but also on the subjective assessment of the criminal's character and behavior.[91] For both, the objective degree of danger is measured by considering the social relations that the criminal act has violated, the actual damage attributed to the crime or the potential damage of the crime, and the circumstances of the crime, such as its method, time, and location.[92] The subjective factors in determining punishment, the mental elements of a crime, include considerations such as intent and negligence, motive, and the general behavior of the criminal, including considerations of prior convictions.[93]

As in the 1950s, the 1980s policy of punishing certain criminals "severely" was aligned with the principle of "combining punishment with leniency" and the Maoist distinction between "general enemies" and "immediate enemies." As in the pre-1978 period, the "majority" of criminals were petty offenders, non-principal offenders, and so on, and the "minority" (the immediate enemies) were those who committed crimes that cause serious social harm and serious injury to individuals.[94]

Peng Zhen emphasized in his speech at the Five City forum in May 1980 that using the most severe penalty applicable (*congzhong*) in sentencing did not mean that a sentence was increased *outside* the scope of the range of sentences set down in the Criminal Law. Peng rationalized that there was a need for *congzhong* primarily because the Criminal Law was not precise enough to deal with the myriad of circumstances in every criminal offence, hence the need for wide-ranging judicial discretion from one period to another. Peng also pointed out that it was important to understand that because the "situation" in each period of social development is different, the state of public order in each period would necessarily be different, hence, the politico-legal organs would constantly need to adapt to the needs of each situation. The wide range of penalties already existing under the law and the discretionary freedom to apply the harshest possible penalty under the law, he argued, would allow for harsh sentencing policy in bad periods of social instability and less severe sentencing policy in good periods.[95]

The policy term "swiftness" (*congkuai*) refers to the speed that can be applied in handling serious criminal cases within the scope of time set out in the Criminal Procedural Law. The policy of swiftness was used in anti-crime campaigns in the 1980s to ensure efficiency in attacking certain categories of crime in a timely manner. The object or target of this policy changes from campaign to campaign, and the CCP Central Committee sets the targets in each campaign.[96] The policy of swiftness is based on a response to the circumstances of public order and the resultant "struggle" that would need to be waged against offenders in particular periods of instability. It is said to exist "to protect the interests and needs of the masses and to safeguard the requirements of the Four Modernizations."[97] Criminologist Shao Daosheng gives the official line on why this policy is still an important agent of deterrence, education, and retribution.

> At a certain stage of social development, it is necessary to adopt severe and rapid punishments for criminals guilty of serious crimes, and give this top priority in order to demonstrate the whole society's judgment and condemnation of criminal activities harmful both to the state and to the people's interests. This is necessary for social stability and the development of the country's legal system as well as its modernization program. Such measures can deter those on the

> verge of crime, thereby reducing the likelihood of their actually committing crimes. They can to a certain extent appease the victims of crime and strengthen their confidence in society; raise social consciousness in the fight against crime; and purify the social environment.[98]

"Severity and swiftness" remains a hallmark of anti-crime campaigns in China today. In Chapters Five and Six, we pursue "severity and swiftness" in its most dramatic manifestation, the 1983–1986 Strike Hard campaign, and aspects of flexibility in China's largest ever anti-crime campaign, "Strike Hard" (Yanda), which lasted for three years from 1983 to 1986.

Conclusion

This chapter has shown that the Third Plenum call to "systematize democracy" and to develop a socialist rule of law did not preclude courts from using past techniques and rationales of social control to regulate relations between "the people" and the enemies of the people. Courts in the post-1978 period continue to regulate social relations (*tiaozheng shehui guanxi*) in campaigns through targeting particular categories of criminals as enemies of socialism. As in the 1950s, the process of deciding the criminality of an act in the 1980s did not rely on immutable principles of criminal behavior set down in law. Rather it relied on a malleable idea about the *degree* to which an act is deemed "socially harmful," an idea that was not fixed in law but was constantly reinterpreted to fit the perceived changes in the "actual circumstances" of society in different periods according to policy dictates. As in the 1950s, the implication in the post-1978 period was of broad discrepancies in the punishment of social crimes at different times in the three years until 1983. For example, in times of relative social stability, crimes such as theft or fraud could be interpreted as only moderately harmful to society, whereas during times when the "actual circumstances" of society dictated a harsher response to crime, offences such as habitual theft were pronounced grievously harmful and were treated as capital offences, and serious cases of fraud were punishable by life imprisonment.

In this chapter we have explored some of the implications of the idea that criminal court work has historically been perceived as originating and operating from a broader and ever-changing social context rather than from formalistic, inflexible, and immutable rules and regulations. The openness of criminal law to interpretations of the broader social context has meant that, both historically and in the reform period, criminal law has necessarily had to serve different purposes. These were pursued through different strategies of regulation depending on understanding of the objects or targets of regulation at each stage in socialist development. We have seen how in times when mass-line and popular indignation is prioritized above the concerns of procedural propriety, sentencing policy is reconfigured to serve the interests of the anti-crime campaign then under way. We follow this theme into the following two chapters on the largest anti-crime campaign in post-1978 China.

Notes

1. "Summary of Criminal Trial Work," *The Annals*, 26.
2. 1.13 million cases from the Cultural Revolution were reexamined. For an examination of this campaign, see Sue Trevaskes, "People's Justice and Injustice: Courts and the Redressing of Cultural Revolution Cases," *China Information* 16 no. 2 (2002): 1–26.
3. "Jiang Zemin Calls for Law, Order to Safeguard Social Stability, Reforms Process," *Xinhua News*, April 3, 2001, FBIS-CHI-2001-0403.
4. "Gongjian bushu yanda douzheng, zhongdian daji sanlei fanzui," (Court and procuratorate announce Yanda policy to focus on three broad areas of crime), *Fazhi bao* (Legal System News), April 10, 2001.
5. A detailed examination of Yanda 2001–2003 is given in the following chapter and in Chapter Seven.
6. Han Yanlong, ed., *Zhonghua renmin gongheguo fazhi tongshi* (A Comprehensive History of the Legal System in the People's Republic of China) (Beijing: Zhonghua zhongyang dangxiao chubanshe, 1998), 870–71. Note that, compared to these figures, the nominal crime rate in Baotou was relatively high. The Baotou documents put the crime rate at 24 per ten thousand before Yanda and 9.7 per ten thousand after the second offensive in 1985. "Summary of Criminal Trial Work," *The Annals*, 29.
7. Guo Xingguo ed., *Jianguo yilai gongan gongzuo dashi yaolan* (An Outline of the Chronicles of Public Security Work Since Liberation) (Beijing: Qunzhong chubanshe, neibu faxing, 2003), 717.
8. Zhou Zhenxiang and Shao Jingchun, eds. *Xin Zhongguo fazhi jianshe 40 nian yaolan* (Outline of Forty years of the Construction of the Legal System in the New China) (Beijing: Qunzhong chubanshe, 1990), 809–10.
9. Guo, *Jianguo yilai gongan gongzuo dashi yaolan*, 797.
10. "Yanli daji yanzhong weihai shehui zhian de fanzui huodong, weihu zhengzhi jingji he shehui de jinyibu wending," (Strike Hard at Criminal Activity Which Gravely Endangers Public Order, Protect the Country's Political, Economic, and Social Stability) (Speech by Ren Jianxin, President of the Supreme Court, made at a national court conference on the Strike Hard Campaign on June 11, 1990), *Renmin fayuan nianjian* 1990 (Yearbook of the People's Courts 1990) (Renmin fayuan nianjian bianji weiyuanhui eds., 1993, p. 451).
11. Guo, *Jianguo yilai gongan gongzuo dashi yaolan*, 798.
12. *Baotou ribao* (Baotou Daily), June 12, 1996, 1.
13. Guo, *Jianguo yilai gongan gongzuo dashi yaolan*, 1052.
14. Guo, *Jianguo yilai gongan gongzuo dashi yaolan*, 1069.
15. Guo, *Jianguo yilai gongan gongzuo dashi yaolan*, 1078.
16. Susan Trevaskes, "Severe and Swift Justice in China," *British Journal of Criminology* 47 no. 1 (2007): 23–41.

17. These included the Propaganda Ministry of the Central Committee of the CCP, the Ministry of Education, the Ministry of Culture, the Ministry of Public Security, the State Bureau of Labor, the All-China Federation of Trade Unions, the Central Committee Youth League, and the All-China Federation of Women.

18. "Guanyu tiqing quandang zhongshi jiejue qingshaonian weifa fanzui wenti de baogao" ("Report on Reminding the Entire Party of the Resolution of the Youth Crime Problem"), in *Shehui zhi'an zonghe zhili zhengce fagui (huibian)* (Laws and Policies relating to the Comprehensive Management of Public Order), eds. Zhonggong fujiansheng zhengfa weiyuanhui and Zhonggong fujiansheng zhengce yanjiusuo (Beijing: Qunzhong chubanshe, 1992), 178.

19. "Guanyu tiqing quandang," 178. These problems were also blamed on the pernicious influence of Lin Biao and the Gang of Four and the culture of violence that emerged from the Cultural Revolution.

20. "Guanyu tiqing quandang," 180–81.

21. "Peng Zhen tongzhi zai quanguo chengshi zhi'an huiyishang de jianghua" (Peng Zhen's speech to the National Conference on Municipal Public Security) (November 22, 1979) in *Shehui zhian zonghe zhili zhengce fagui* (Laws and Policies relating to the Comprehensive Management of Public Order) eds. Zhonggong fujiansheng zhengfa weiyuanhui and Zhonggong fujiansheng zhengce yanjiusuo. Beijing: Qunzhong chubanshe, 1992, 40.

22. "Summary of Criminal Trial Work," *The Annals*, 28.

23. "Summary of Criminal Trial Work," *The Annals*, 28.

24. "Summary of Criminal Trial Work," *The Annals*, 28.

25. "Summary of Criminal Trial Work," *The Annals*, 28.

26. "Chronicle of Events," *The Annals*, 121.

27. "Chronicle of Events," *The Annals*, 121. The campaign continued into the new year. A forum for municipal court presidents and criminal division heads in Baotou was convened from April 15 to 19, 1980. *The Annals* records how, at the meeting, the spirit of the Inner Mongolia Autonomous Region Seminar on "Improving Public Order" was relayed, and court president Batucang gave a report on "Attacking active criminals with severity and swiftness according to the law, while keeping a firm grasp on examination and redressals of misjudged cases relating to the unjust case of Liu Shaoqi in order to achieve stability and unity, as well as safeguarding the construction of the 'Four Modernizations.'" On May 19–20, the Baotou Intermediate Court and the Kundulun District Court held two separate sentencing rallies that were broadcast live on radio. Judgment and sentencing were pronounced on sixty-one criminal cases, with 95.3 percent of criminals being juvenile and youth offenders. Another mass sentencing rally was convened on July 16. Here four criminals were sentenced: two to death, one to death with a reprieve, and the other was given a life sentence. Attendance at the rally exceeded thirty thousand. As part of the final stage of the campaign offensive that year, the campaign was appraised and its success summarized. "The Summary" records that, as a result of the campaign, there was an improvement in the social order in Baotou. Quoting Public Security Bureau statistics, the "Summary" notes that the number of registered criminal cases fell in January 1980 by 27.1 percent on figures for the previous month, and the February figure was 9.4 percent lower than the January rate. "Summary of Criminal Trial Work," *The Annals*, 28.

28. "Decision of the Standing Committee of the National People's Congress Regarding Approval of Cases Involving the Death Sentence" (Adopted at the 19th Meeting of the Standing Committee of the Fifth National People's Congress on June 10, 1981, translation in *The Laws of the People's Republic of China (1979–1982)* (Beijing: Foreign Language Press, 1987), 250.

29. Zhou and Shao, *Xin Zhongguo fazhi jianshe 40 nian yaolan*, 510.

30. Zhou and Shao, *Xin Zhongguo fazhi jianshe 40 nian yaolan*, 510.

31. Zhou and Shao, *Xin Zhongguo fazhi jianshe 40 nian yaolan*, 510.

32. Jiang Hua, "Work Report of the Supreme People's Court," *Law Annual Report of China 1982/3* (Hong Kong: Kingsway International Publications Ltd, 1982), 365.

33. Zhou and Shao, *Xin Zhongguo fazhi jianshe 40 nian yaolan*, 532.

34. "Decision of the CCP Central Committee and the State Council on Cracking Down on Serious Crime in the Economic Sphere." (April 13, 1982) Translation in *Issues and Studies* 20, no. 2 (February 1984): 102.

35. Keith Forster explained that, nationally, the crime that was the catalyst for the 1982 crackdown was smuggling. He claimed that the number of recorded smuggling–related crimes jumped from 13,400 cases (involving 7.3 million yuan) in 1979 to 45,000 cases (involving 100 million yuan) from January 1980 to June 1981. Keith Forster, "The 1982 Campaign Against Economic Crime," *The Australian Journal of Chinese Affairs* 14 (1985): 7.

36. "Summary of Criminal Trial Work," *The Annals*, 31.

37. "Summary of Criminal Trial Work," *The Annals*, 31.

38. "Summary of Criminal Trial Work," *The Annals*, 31. On January 11, 1982, CCP Central Committee issued an "Urgent Notice" that implored the whole Party to take decisive action against economic crime by organizing Party committees at every level to develop plans for tracking down and prosecuting high-ranking officials who took advantage of their office by misappropriating state funds and property. To launch the campaign, the CCP Central Committee dispatched Party representations to Guangzhou and Fujian provinces, where it appeared most of the smuggling activities were conducted. On March 8, 1982, the Standing Committee of the National People's Congress passed its "Decision Regarding the Severe Punishment of Criminals who Seriously Sabotage the Economy." The decision stressed the need to "deal firm blows" to economic crime and to severely punish offenders and state functionaries involved in crimes such as smuggling, arbitrage, speculation for profits, theft of public property and funds, sale of cultural relics, and extortion or acceptance of bribes. The decision amended a number of articles in the Criminal Law to intensify the severity of punishment for these and other serious crimes. The punishment for serious offenders convicted of smuggling, arbitrage and speculation, theft, sale of narcotics, and sale of precious cultural relics, was amended to a fixed term imprisonment of ten years or more, a life sentence, or the death penalty. State functionaries convicted of accepting bribes and embezzlement whose crimes were particularly serious would be sentenced to life imprisonment or death. The decision allowed for a one-month period of amnesty in which people who confessed their crimes and repented would be dealt with more leniently in accordance with the original provisions in the code. See "Decision of the Standing Committee of the National People's Congress Regarding the Severe Punishment of Criminals who Seriously Sabotage the Economy" (Adopted at the 22nd Session of the Standing Committee of the Fifth National People's Congress on March 8, 1982), *The Laws of the People's Republic of China (1979–1982)*, 345.

39. Zhou and Shao, *Xin Zhongguo fazhi jianshe 40 nian yaolan*, 532.

40. "Chronicle of Events," *The Annals*, 127.

41. *People's Republic of China Yearbook 1983*, 474.

42. Michael Dutton, Policing Chinese Politics: A History (Durham, NC: Duke University Press, 2005), 3.

43. Ronald C Keith, *China's Struggle for the Rule of Law* (London: St. Martin's Press, 1994), 154–55.

44. Mao Tse-tung, "On the Correct Handling of Contradictions Among the People," *Selected Works of Mao Tse-tung Volume 5* (Peking: Foreign Languages Press, 1973), 389.

45. Mao Tse-tung, "On the People's Democratic Dictatorship," *Selected Works of Mao Tse-tung Volume 4* (Peking: Foreign Languages Press, 1973), 417–19.

46. Mao, "On the Correct Handling of Contradictions Among the People," 387.

47. "The Teaching and Research Office for Criminal Law of the Central Political-Legal Cadres' School," translated in Jerome Cohen, *The Criminal Process in the People's Republic of China 1949–63: An Introduction*) (Cambridge, MA: Harvard University Press, 1968), 328.

48. Peng Ke, ed., *Xingfaxue zixue kaoshi dagang* (An Outline of Criminology for Self-Study) (Beijing: Beijing daxue chubanshe, 1992), 15.

49. "The Teaching and Research Office for Criminal Law of the Central Political-Legal Cadres' School" translated in Jerome Cohen, *The Criminal Process in the People's Republic of China 1949–63: An Introduction*) (Cambridge, MA: Harvard University Press, 1968), 328.

50. According to criminal law theory, both "objective" and "subjective" elements determine criminal liability and the seriousness attributed to an act in a given period of social development. These elements are roughly akin to *mens reas* and *actus rea* in common law theory. Objective factors are the physical elements of the crime. They include the object of the act (*keti*), the method used (*shouduan*), and the social consequences of the act (*houguo*). The subjective factors are the mental elements of the crime and include the form that the act takes (*xingshi)*, the motive of the act (*dongji*), and the intent of the act (*mudi*). Peng, *Xingfaxue zixue kaoshi dagang*, 15.

51. Chen Xianglong and Qiu Xinlong, "The Relationship between Crime and Punishment," *Social Sciences in China*, Third Issue (September 1988), 183.

52. Albert H. Y. Chen, *An Introduction to the Legal System of the People's Republic of China* (Hong Kong: Butterworths, 1992), 188. Social harm caused by counter-revolutionary crime is harm inflicted on the people's democratic dictatorship, which is treated as the most grievous crime. Crimes of Endangering Public Security are those in which an offender intentionally or negligently harms the lives, health, or personal property of an unspecified number of people. The main object of such crimes is public security. Crimes that undermine the socialist economic order are illegal activities related to the administration of the economy, in which the object of the crime committed is the socialist economic order. To constitute a crime of undermining socialist economic order, the act must have seriously undermined the smooth development of the economy or undermined the social order. In crimes of property violation, the object of the crime is the ownership rights of public and privately-owned property. This category of crime refers to acts of appropriating public or private property, committed with the intention of gaining illegal possession of that property. Crimes of obstructing the administration of public order are those crimes that infringe on the system of public order. The object of crime in these offences is the public order, not personal rights. See Peng, *Xingfaxue zixue kaoshi dagang*, 70–102.

53. For instance, of the 513 cases that went to trial during the first campaign in late 1979–1980, 70 percent belonged in one of the "five main categories" of criminals targeted in the campaign: those who committed murder, arson, rape, armed robbery, and setting off explosives.

54. Liu Hua, "Hooliganism," *Chinese Sociology and Anthropology* 27, no. 3 (Spring 1995): 57.

55. Qian Hui and Bi Jianlin eds., *Zhongguo renmin gongheguo fazhi dashiji* (Chronicle of Events of the Legal System of the People's Republic of China) (Jilin: Jilin Renmin chubanshe, 1992), 105–106.

56. Borge Bakken, "Editor's Introduction," *Chinese Sociology and Anthropology* 27, no. 3 (Spring 1995): 8. Also see Shao Daosheng, *Preliminary Study of China's Juvenile Delinquency* (Beijing: Foreign Language Press, 1992), 12.

57. Bakken, "Editor's Introduction," 3. Bakken argued that the hard-line response to juvenile and youth crime was a "central theme of the reform period as it is related in a direct way to the central question of 'order' in society, a question that should be seen as parallel to the question of economic growth." (p. 3)

58. Bakken, "Editor's Introduction," 3.

59. Bakken, "Editor's Introduction," 4.

60. "Summary of Criminal Trial Work," *The Annals*, 31.

61. "Summary of Criminal Trial Work," *The Annals*, 31–32.

62. "Summary of Criminal Trial Work," *The Annals*, 31.

63. "Summary of Criminal Trial Work," *The Annals*, 32.

64. "Decision of the CCP Central Committee and the State Council on Cracking Down on Serious Crime in the Economic Sphere" (April 13, 1982). Translation in *Issues and Studies* 20, no. 2 (February 1984): 103–108. The decision followed Deng Xiaoping's April 10 speech given to the politburo, in which he called for an increasingly intensive crackdown and urged political-judicial programs to address the economic crime situation using the principle of "swiftness and severity." With the idea of "with one hand, grasp the open door reforms and with the other, attack economic crime," the call was sent out to Party committees at all levels and the relevant political-legal organs to organize the crackdown. Han, *Zhonghua renmin gongheguo fazhi tongshi*, 709.

65. "Summary of Criminal Trial Work," *The Annals*, 32.

66. "Summary of Criminal Trial Work," *The Annals*, 32. The additional supplementary punishment of "deprivation of political rights" (see Articles 50–54, Criminal Law) given in capital cases was basically a symbolic gesture, especially given that the soon-to-be executed criminal, in being deprived of political rights, was simply giving up the right to vote and be elected.

67. Han, *Zhonghua renmin gongheguo fazhi tongshi*, 711.

68. Dangdai Zhongguo lishi weiyuanhui, eds. *Dangdai Zhongguo de shenpan gongzuo* (Trial Work in Contemporary China) (Beijing: Dangdai zhongguo chubanshe, 1993), 87.

69. *Dangdai Zhongguo de shenpan gongzuo*, 89.

70. *Dangdai Zhongguo de shenpan gongzuo*, 89.

71. *Dangdai Zhongguo de shenpan gongzuo*, 87.

72. *Dangdai Zhongguo de shenpan gongzuo*, 89.

73. *Dangdai Zhongguo de shenpan gongzuo*, 90.

74. "Chronicle of Events," *The Annals*, 98.

75. "Chronicle of Events," *The Annals*, 99.

76. "Summary of Criminal Trial Work," *The Annals*, 19.

77. "Chronicle of Events," *The Annals*, 102.

78. Patricia Griffin observed the use of flexibility in the revolutionary era: "The Communists viewed flexibility as a positive attribute necessary to respond to a changing revolutionary situation, and purposely built it into their legal system through imprecise legal codes, frequently changing laws and flexible interpretation of laws." Patricia Griffin, *The Chinese Communist Treatment of Counterrevolutionaries: 1924–1949* (New York: Princeton University Press, 1976), 6.

79. Han, *Zhonghua renmin gongheguo fazhi tongshi*, 871–72.

80. *Dangdai Zhongguo de shenpan gongzuo*, 165.

81. *Dangdai Zhongguo de shenpan gongzuo*, 166.

82. *Dangdai Zhongguo de shenpan gongzuo*, 166. Harold M. Tanner, *Strike Hard!: Anti-Crime Campaigns and Chinese Criminal Justice 1979–1985* (New York: East Asia Program, Cornell University), 1999.

83. Han, *Zhonghua renmin gongheguo fazhi tongshi*, 773–74. The "spirit" of comprehensive management of public order was said to be present in the immediate post-revolutionary period with the Suppression of Counter-revolutionaries. Prostitutes, gamblers, drug addicts, and others were reformed and used in a variety of ways to propagate and educate the masses. *Dangdai Zhongguo de shenpan gongzuo*, 167.

84. *Dangdai Zhongguo de shenpan gongzuo*, 166.

85. Keith, *China's Struggle for the Rule of Law*, 169.

86. Keith, *China's Struggle for the Rule of Law*, 169.

87. "Severely and swiftly punishing in accordance with the law" was also promoted as a way of discouraging inmates from escaping custody, through the policy of mandatory heavy sentencing for escapees and recidivists. Keith, *China's Struggle for the Rule of Law*, 169.

88. Keith, *China's Struggle for the Rule of Law*, 169.

89. Keith, *China's Struggle for the Rule of Law*, 169.

90. Article 57 states, "When sentencing a criminal, a punishment shall be imposed based on the facts, nature, and circumstances of the crime, the degree of harm done to society and the relevant provisions of this Law." Article 57, Criminal Law of the People's Republic of China (1979).

91. Chen and Qiu, "The Relationship between Crime and Punishment," 182.

92. Chen and Qiu explain the significance of the actual damage of a crime. They say, "For criminal acts of the same nature, the difference in their objective danger is mainly expressed in the difference in actual damage. The more serious the results, the greater the objective danger of the crime and vice versa." They give the example that the objective danger of a double murder is always greater than that of the murder of one of the people. They explain that the potential damage of a crime refers to crimes such as preparations to commit a crime and attempted crime that did not result in actual damage, in which case the objective danger can only be measured as the possible danger that would have occurred if the act had been completed. Chen and Qiu, "The Relationship between Crime and Punishment," 183.

93. Chen and Qiu, "The Relationship between Crime and Punishment," 183.

94. Du and Zhang, *China's Legal System*, 104, and Song, *Zhongguo gong'an baike quanshu*, 119.

95. "Peng Zhen tongzhi zai wu da chengshi zhian zuotanhuishang de jianghua yaodian" (jielu) (May 21–22, 1981) (Speech given in the conference to the five centrally administered cities) in *Shehui zh'an zonghe zhili zhengce fagui huibian* (Laws and Policies Relating to the Comprehensive Management of Public Order), eds. Zhonggong fujiansheng zhengfa weiyuanhui and Zhonggong fujiansheng zhengce yanjiusuo (Beijing: Qunzhong chubanshe, 1992), 42.

96. Han, *Zhonghua renmin gongheguo fazhi tongshi*, 869.

97. Song, *Zhongguo gong'an baike*, 362.

98. Shao, *Preliminary Study of China's Juvenile Delinquency*, 160.

Chapter Five

Striking Hard: The Politics of Law and Order

> Societies appear to be subject, every now and then, to periods of moral panic. A condition, episode, person or group of persons emerges to become defined as a threat to societal values and interests; its nature is presented in a stylized and stereotypical fashion by the mass media. . . . Sometimes the object of the panic is quite novel and at other times it is something which has been in existence long enough, but suddenly appears in the limelight. Sometimes the panic passes over and is forgotten, except in folklore and collective memory; at other times it has more serious and long-lasting repercussions and might produce such changes as those in legal and social policy or even in the way society conceives itself.[1]

The Yanda "Strike Hard" anti-crime campaign from 1983 to 1986 was the largest and most significant anti-crime campaign in China since the 1950s. In the three years of the campaign in Baotou, the courts dealt with 2,210 cases involving 3,825 people. Criminal sanctions were imposed on 97 percent of those put on trial (3,635 people) and, of these, 144 were given the death penalty. *The Annals* reports, "As a result of the attacks on serious crime and as a consequence of efforts to educate the citizens about legal matters, the general public's understanding of the concept of law had deepened and their enthusiasm for the fight against crime had been aroused."[2] Nationally, 1.7 million people were convicted and sentenced in courts, with over seven hundred and eight thousand handed down sentences ranging from five years in prison to the death penalty.[3]

As noted in the introductory chapter, Yanda has also been described as the "bloodiest chapter in post-Mao Chinese politics."[4] Some reports put the national figure of people sentenced to death over the three years at thirty thousand (including those sentenced to death with a two-year reprieve).[5] In Yunnan province alone, 780 people were executed as criminals in the first ten months of the campaign.[6] Far from meeting the initial aims of the campaign—creating the conditions necessary for social stability and economic prosperity—the results of the campaign created what Borge Bakken describes as a "brutalizing effect" in society. Here was a post-Cultural Revolution society where criminals were far more willing to use violence and revenge than ever before.[7] This is largely due to the way in which Party and politico-legal authorities tried to cope with what they saw as a threat to the reform movement and a threat to their very legitimacy. As Bakken describes:

> When the Yanda campaign was launched in September 1983, the crime rate was in fact the lowest since 1979, but . . . the crime rate "did not fall fast enough." The traditional belief in China is that parading evil—or, rather, bringing evil to justice for all to see—will lead to a decrease in crime. . . . The campaign had as a main target the newly emerging gang crimes, and the gangs' leaders (*touzi*). The aim was also to prevent further recruitment of juvenile criminals—though it was unclear whether removing the most actively delinquent "veterans" from gangs would indeed decrease significantly the recruitment of younger juveniles. . . . The networks survived, the gangs multiplied, and there was a fall in the age of the youths involved. . . . In 1986, a record-high figure of 93.3 percent of all gang members were 25 and under, almost half of them under the age of 18. All over the country, gang crime grew and thrived in the wake of the "Severe Blows" campaign. In the late 1980s gang crime accounted for 60–70 percent of all criminal offences in China.[8]

In this chapter we explore the management of the 1983–1986 Yanda campaign as a political strategy that involved Party leaders at every level, from policymaking to local implementation. A policy narrative of "severity and swiftness" (*congzhong congkuai*) was instrumental in the bloodbath that ensued over the three years, particularly in the first part of the campaign. We recall from Chapter Four that "severity" is applied as an assessment of a sentencing action and essentially means meting out severe punishment within the scope of the law. "Swiftness" refers to speeding up the process, particularly by simplifying criminal procedure for dealing with targeted criminals.

Yanda was conceived and implemented from "Party Central" for political purposes. The Baotou court records attest to the political nature of the campaign. "The Summary" describes the implementation of Yanda in August 1983 as a "political line," a term borrowed from Anti-Rightist and other campaigns from the 1950s. "The Summary" records Yanda as a victorious campaign to halt the war against the social and public order and to procure a turnaround in order by dealing with criminals "in one fell swoop." As this summary explains, with a dose of (apparently) self-serving rhetoric:

> Following the promulgation of the CCP's August 1983 "Decision to Strike a Severe Blow at Criminal Activities" and under the united leadership of the Municipal Party Committee and superior courts, each court across the city acted in cooperation with the other politico-legal authorities to resolutely implement the political line of "acting severely and swiftly in accordance with the law to capture all criminals in one fell swoop." They victoriously launched three large-scale offenses in a staunch attack on serious criminal elements lasting three years. The Yanda campaign reversed the irregularities in social conditions of the

> pre-Yanda campaign period that caused "evil people to strut around unhindered while the good folk have to endure feeling threatened and bullied and where activists feel disheartened and resentful and lower-level cadres lose morale." This reversal of conditions helped to consolidate and develop a stable and united political front. At the same time, a vast number of cadres were able to receive training and the political and professional quality of personnel showed marked improvement.[9]

Politicization of court work during this campaign went far beyond the presence of Party officials as the leaders of all local "Yanda command posts" (*Yanda zhihuibu*) in all Chinese counties and cities. It extended to politicizing common criminals as the enemies of socialist modernization: a charge paramount to treason that required the severest response on the part of the state. To be sure, criminal justice workers were called upon to "make the enemy surrender or annihilate them" (*weijian*). At the level of rhetorical strength, Yanda is imbued with not just political but military linguistic paraphernalia. Yanda policies are referred to as "deployment plans" (*zhanlue bushu*). The campaign itself, referred to in government and Party literature as "a political struggle" (*douzheng*), is divided into major "offensives" (*zhanyi*) and "battles" (*zhan*). Propaganda at the launch of each campaign often refers to the campaign as "a great decisive battle" (*weida de juezhan*). The concentrated powers of the PSB, courts, and procuratorate are referred to as the state's "concentrated military strength" (*jizhong bingli*), and the PSB's position in Yanda is called "the front line of battle" (*zhandou de zui qianxian*). Yanda's successes are referred to as "meritorious military achievements" (*zhangong*) and its outcomes as "fruits of battle" (*zhanguo*).[10] Of equal political pertinence is the act of public shaming that occurred in tens of thousands of separate sentencing rallies conducted in the three-year campaign.[11] Degradation ceremonies, as discussed in Chapter Three, are a deeply political experience in which the community itself becomes embroiled in the act of punishment. Rallies take on an even greater political potency during anti-crime campaigns where the criminal is politicized as public enemy number one.

Also discussed in Chapter Four, is the approach to anti-crime campaigning in the post-Mao period and today. This involves four main strategies:

(1) announcing at a national law and order conference that crime rates are unacceptably high and that only "striking hard" at crime will control crime rates;
(2) announcing a discrete set of targeted enemies for each offensive and making them the enemies of modernization;
(3) making the criminal justice process flexible in a number of ways in order to punish criminals "severely and swiftly";
(4) creating a "great momentum" for the campaign by "mobilizing the masses" and by acts of expressive punishment, in particular, mass sentencing rallies attended by thousands of "the masses."

Let us turn to consider each of the four strategies in relation to the implementation of the 1983–1986 campaign at the national, provincial, and municipal levels.

Strategy 1: Announcing Crime as a Major National Problem

Yanda began at the top echelons of power with Deng Xiaoping summoning the newly appointed Minister of Public Security, Liu Fuzhi, to a seaside resort at Beidaihe on July 17, 1983, to order Liu to launch a new offensive against serious crime. Deng complained that the current crime epidemic had much to do with the unwillingness of the public security forces to attack crime, the inability of the procuratorate to prosecute in a timely manner, and the courts' lenient treatment of criminals. Peng Zhen, head of the Central Party Committee's Central Politico-Legal Affairs Committee, who was also present at the meeting, complained that his repeated calls to attack crime "severely and swiftly" had gone unheeded by the three arms of criminal justice. He declared that any lack of enthusiasm and vigor in dealing with crime severely and swiftly would be interpreted by Party authorities as paramount to encouraging crime.[12] From July 29 to August 3, a National Public Order Work Conference was convened in Beijing with over four hundred officials in attendance, including provincial heads of Party committees, politico-legal affairs committees, provincial heads of courts, procuratorate and police, and heads of State Council and the military. They were called to plan the launching of province-wide "united operations" (*tongyi xingdong*), which involved a massive show of police force in the form of stings and raids on crime spots.[13]

The conference reached consensus on two issues. First, although crime figures indicated the public order had improved substantially in the past few years, it had not been restored to the level in the post-liberation period of the 1950s. Moreover, crime figures indicated that serious crime was on the increase. Second, to reverse the effects of taking a "soft option" against crime in recent years, the conference participants agreed to implement the policy of "severely and swiftly punishing offenders who endanger the public order." The rationale given for a heavy-handed approach to crime control in the Yanda campaign was that the problems of public order had been underestimated, producing an over-reliance on the function of education and persuasion and leaving the function of "dictatorship" under-utilized. This created a situation where the politico-legal organs had failed to adequately "deal severe blows" to serious crime. The period immediately before Yanda was described as a time in crime control when "accuracy" (*zhunque*) in following procedural guidelines was emphasized over and above "punishment," to the point where punishment was becoming ineffective (*chengda buli*) in deterring crime. In this situation, "those who should have been arrested were not being arrested" (*gai zhua bu zhua*), and "those who should have been punished were not being punished" (*gai pan bu pan*). To cure the problem of overemphasizing procedural "accuracy," even more "severity and swiftness" would be needed to intensify crime control.[14]

In reality, Yanda was put forward as a political response resuscitated from the bygone years of mass movements, not because those administering justice had slowed down the process of crime control or because judges overemphasized "accuracy" in criminal procedure, but rather because a series of events cumulatively provided public security leaders with what they articulated as a valid rationale to launch a bloody attack on hooligan gangs and other serious offenders, legitimized under the banner of "strike hard." These events included reportage in the media of an unusually high number of high-profile crime incidents and rising juvenile crime rates. The May hijacking of a plane to South Korea, a glut of savage crimes against women and children, including gang rapes, and other hooligan-related crimes inspired the August conference. Juveniles and hooligans were met with a combination of fear and loathing—fear of the power of gang control and loathing of a potential army of unemployed, uneducated, and disillusioned youth—that drove Party and politico-legal authorities to look to the past for a remedy of current social problems.

On August 21, a notice cowritten by the politburo's Propaganda Department and the politburo's Central Politico-Legal Affairs Committee announced an "Outline on Striking Hard at Crime to Bring about a Complete Turnaround in Public Order." It required all government and criminal justice agencies involved in this effort to publicize the contents of the notice in the press throughout the country, calling the masses and the Party to arms. Yanda's first offensive was now officially launched.[15] Four days later, on August 25, 1983, the Central Party Committee issued their "Decision Regarding Striking Hard Blows Against Criminal Activities" (Party Document No. 31, 1983), outlining the seven main categories of crime.[16] The decision was, in essence, "to organize over the next three years, a first, second, and third offensive in accordance with the policy of severely and swiftly punishing criminal offenders in one fell swoop."[17] The dates of the campaign offensives and battles were as follows:

Offensive 1 Battle 1	August 25, 1983–December 1983
Offensive 1 Battle 2	December 1983–March 1984
Offensive 1 Battle 3	April 1984–July 30, 1984
Offensive 2 Battle 1	September 1984
Offensive 2 Battle 2	January–February 15, 1985
Offensive 2 Battle 3	March 30, 1985–July 30, 1985
Offensive 1 Battle 1	January 1986–January 1987[18]

The Document 31 decision politicized the seven main targets of attack, blaming the current blow-out of crime on everything from the Cultural Revolution to "foreign bourgeois tendencies." Harold Tanner outlines the Document's rationale for Yanda:

> Explaining the need for a new and stronger crackdown on criminal activity, Document 31 pointed to the failure of the criminal justice system and of comprehensive management to bring about the desired "fundamental turn for the better" in public security. The Party leadership understood this as a failure of strength, the major reason being that the guiding principle of "severe and rapid punishment" had not truly been carried out and thus "blows against criminal elements have lacked force." Furthermore, the Party Center argued that the crime problem (which is ascribed to the lingering influence of Lin Biao and the Gang of Four and to the influx of foreign ideas since opening to the outside world in 1979) posed a threat to the moral tenor of Chinese society and thus to the ability of China to achieve modernizing economic growth.[19]

With the publicity machine now in full swing, the next move was to announce the targets of the campaign as the enemies of socialist modernization.

Strategy 2: Making Criminals the Enemy of Modernization

In the three offensives of Yanda from 1983 to 1986, the campaign targeted the following seven main types of offenders:

- members of hooligan gangs;
- recidivists;
- murderers, arsonists, bombers, drug traffickers, rapists, armed robbers, and criminals involved in serious theft;
- offenders who abduct and traffic in women and children, those who force, lure, or shelter women in prostitution, and those involved in the production and sale of pornography;
- offenders who organize reactionary secret societies;
- escapees from reform through labor camps, and wanted criminals; and
- offenders guilty of writing reactionary slogans, leaflets, anonymous letters, or correspondence with spies and offenders who continued to support Lin Biao and the Gang of Four.[20]

The first offensive of Yanda from August 1983 to mid-1984 propagated as public enemy number one the youth members of hooligan gangs (*liumang tuanhuo*). As the Central Party Yanda Decision explained:

> These hooligan gang elements are new dregs of society produced under the new historical conditions, elements of the underground society. By killing and impermissible behavior, by raping women, hijacking airplanes and boats, setting fires and explosions and other such cruel means, they cruelly injure and kill the innocent masses. They hate socialism and pose an extremely great threat to public security. We must recognize the nature of hooligan gangs. . . . Hooligan gang elements must be taken in one fell swoop, hooligan leaders must be resolutely killed off.[21]

Table 5.1. Yanda Targets of the First Two Offensives in Wuhan City

Offen-sive	Battle no.	Time	Targets	No. of suspects detained
1	1	4.8.83–3.12.83	Ringleaders of gangs, murderers, arsonists, armed robbers, traffickers in women and children, itinerant criminals	2,475
1	2	7.1.84–28.2.84	Ringleaders of hooligan gangs, murderers, armed robbers, rapists	2,131
1	3	11.6.84–20.7.84	Perpetrators of major theft crimes, members of criminal gangs, itinerant criminals	4,898
2	1	1.8.84–31.10.84	Itinerant criminals, fugitives, active criminals, bombers	3,058
2	2	1.11.84–31.3.85	Perpetrators of major theft crimes, itinerant criminals, perpetrators of serious economic crime	2,193
2	3	1.4.85–31.7.85	Fugitives, itinerant criminals	3,832
2	4	1.9.85–30.9.85	Itinerant criminals, perpetrators of serious economic crime and manufacturers of fake medicines and drugs	2,318
2	5	24.11.85–25.1.86	Smugglers, itinerant criminals	1,619

Source: *Wuhanshi gonganzhi* (Neibu chugao: unpublished restricted materials, 1988).

Rationalization for this particular enemy was that the harm caused by a hooligan would manifest in serious social disorder and moral decay.[22] Hooligan gangs were seen as offenders who had banded together to commit offences and, although they were not particularly well-organized and united, the social harm they caused to society in general, rather than to individuals in particular, was considered serious in nature and scope. In other words, the object of hooligan attack was not identified as an individual as such (and the attack not as an infringement upon the rights of the person) but as the public order itself.[23] Victims were not targeted specifically, and these crimes were not premeditated, so the object infringed upon was construed as the sense of "order" itself. The definition of "order" in this crime therefore extends beyond the conventional meaning of "public order"; it refers to both practical and moral order in the public sphere. Liu Hua explains it as "shared principles of life by people living in the community."[24] Campaign rhetoric upheld the notion that hooligan crimes endangered both public order and social morality. Crimes of hooliganism included criminal sexual behavior such as "luring and seducing women into having sexual intercourse" and "making lewd gestures and movements, and obscene talk," as well as the more obvious public order crimes of gang fights, and "instigation of trouble" in public places.[25] Assault resulting from a crime of hooliganism was not considered common assault, since common assault referred to assault in which the victim was a specified target, as the result of a specific dispute. In short, the unique characteristic of hooligan crime is that its manifest behaviors are relatively unpredictable, and it is this unpredictability that is considered a threat to the public and moral order.[26]

In many ways, then, the campaign set up the hooligan as the perfect enemy for the post-1978 period. He (mainly he) is socially dislocated, has allegiance only to his hooligan group, and is the antithesis of what is prescribed for social harmony and social security. The hooligan is, as Bakken describes, the manifestation of fear of social disorder: "Some observers have referred to the Chinese cultural preference for moderation, balance and harmony as a 'cult of self-restraint' . . . In Chinese analysis, 'loss of self-control' is often dominated by the fear of *liu* (drifting, moving) and *luan* (chaos), as in *dongluan* (disorder). . . . On one side is the disorder of *dongluan*, as represented by the new migrant population and their *liudong* (mobility). On the other side is the fear of modern Western ideas and their influence on youth, as represented by the fear of the *liumang*—the Chinese hooligan."[27] Although hooligan gang members were touted as the main target of the campaign, the Yanda hit list comprised a variety of targets. Generally, most provinces and cities had their own list of targets, as Table 5.1 indicates.

Strategy 3: Changing Criminal Procedure and Sentencing Practice

By early September, the nation's legislature was actively participating in the battle, producing three "decisions" that amended the nation's Criminal Law and the Criminal Procedure Law, thus smoothing the legal way for the courts' "swift and severe" punishment of criminals.[28] On September 2, the NPC "Decision of the Standing Committee of the National People's Congress Regarding the Severe Punishment of Criminals Who Seriously Endanger Public Security" was passed. It stated that, "[I]n order to maintain public security, and ensure the safety of the lives and property of the people and safeguard the smooth progress of socialist construction, it is imperative to subject criminals who seriously endanger public security to severe punishment."[29] The decision meant that punishment beyond the existing maximum punishment in the Criminal Law could be applied to a number of serious offenders. This included extending the death penalty to the seven main categories of criminals targeted in the campaign. The focus of the

NPC's second decision passed on September 2 shifted from punishment to prompt adjudication. This decision on "Procedure for Prompt Adjudication of Cases Involving Criminals Who Seriously Endanger Public Security" required courts to overstep certain provisions in the Criminal Procedure Law regarding time limits for delivering a bill of prosecution, summons, and an appeal. The NPC's third decision, on "Revision of the Organic Law of the People's Courts" lowered the level of the court of authorization for approval of the death penalty from the Supreme People's Court to the provincial level, the higher people's courts. This decision complemented an earlier joint notice on August 16, from the SPC, the Supreme People's Procuratorate, and the Ministry of Public Security, which gave basic-level courts the authority to conduct trials of capital cases involving criminals who gravely endangered public order.

The rationale for the three decisions was that decentralizing decisionmaking powers would help the politico-legal organs to coordinate efforts in the Yanda campaign. Changes to the laws of criminal procedure meant that, because the jurisdiction for sentencing and punishing cases of life imprisonment and capital punishment cases in the first instance would be handed down to basic courts for the period of the Yanda campaign, the intermediate court would be the court of final instance.[30] This was the first time in PRC history that the basic people's courts were required to hand down the death penalty.[31] Murray Scot Tanner explains the obvious implications of handing these powers to lower level courts.

> The circular increased exponentially the likelihood that defendants in death penalty and life imprisonment cases would not only have their *first* trial, but also their *appeal*, heard by a court which contained no judges or procurators with serious legal education, and that the decision would be ratified at the provincial rather than the central level.[32]

Flexibility of criminal justice practices during Yanda was particularly manifest in three main types of activities: Party control over local criminal justice work; joint handling of cases by the police, procuratorate, and courts; and speedy trials.

Party Control over Local Criminal Justice Work

As is the current practice, the Party then exercised leadership over courts through two types of committees: the Politico-Legal Affairs Committee (*zhengfa weiyuanhui*) that is part of the Communist Party bureaucracy, and local Party committees within courts and local government offices. The CCP Central Politico-Legal Affairs Committee supervises the courts and formulates legal policy. The Politico-Legal Affairs Committee is a subsidiary organ in the Party committee at each level of the hierarchy of administration. The Politico-Legal Affairs Committee at each level of government comprises the heads of the public security bureau, the procuratorate, the court, the Ministry of Justice, Ministry of State Security, and Ministry of Civil Affairs. Part of the Committee's work in coordinating politico-legal work is to try to solve through discussion particularly difficult or sensitive court cases.[33] The courts' own Party organization, the *dangzu*, operates at each administrative level under the central Party leadership in accordance with the principle of "dual leadership" over the courts. Dual leadership is defined as the "leadership of the local Communist Party Committee and government in matters of organization and personnel, leadership of the hierarchical central organs and hierarchical superiors in substantive matters."[34] In matters of organization (personnel), the Politico-Legal Affairs Committee acts in concert with another wing of the Party bureaucracy, the Organizational Department (*zuzhibu*), to select suitable candidates for leadership positions in courts before they are nominated formally by the people's congress at the corresponding level.[35]

Party control over the criminal process was greatly accentuated during Yanda, particularly in the first three months of the campaign. For example, in Xuzhou city, Jiangsu, on September 3, the municipal Party secretary called a meeting for all municipal heads of the police, procuratorate, and courts, along with local Party heads. A "Yanda Command Center" (*Yanda zhihuibu*) was established, with the municipal Party secretary, Li Cong, at the helm. The Command Center comprised the deputy municipal Party secretary, the city mayor, the city's politico-legal affairs committee secretary, the local military staff commander, the deputy military staff commander, and the head of the public security.[36] This was common practice in many areas.

A month earlier, even before the official start of the campaign, in Xining, Qinghai province, the Municipal Party Secretary, An Guimin, called a meeting of all senior heads of government and senior public security officers to transmit the politburo's directive on the launch of Yanda. Provincial Party Secretary Ma Wanli, the Deputy Governor, and the Mayor of Xining all attended the meeting. On August 14, a "Yanda Leaders Group" was established, comprising not the local criminal justice functionaries, but the municipal Party secretary, county Party secretaries, and district Party secretaries. The following day, the group announced the first "joint operation," to run from August 15 to 28. All police, procuratorate, and court staff were involved, along with representatives from the army and military police. There were 2,942 personnel involved in the sting and, over the two-week period, 1,528 people were detained for questioning including 539 suspects involved in organized gangs. The provincial Party secretary took personal command of the operation, and under his command were Yang Shufang, a consultant to the provincial government, and Mo Qian, the provincial politico-legal affairs committee secretary, as well as the provincial head of public security, the municipal Party secretary, the mayor, and two deputy Party secretaries. This group of political leaders was described as leading the campaign from the "frontline."[37] One source detailed in Murray Scot Tanner's study points to the danger of handing over the coordination of the Yanda campaign to local Party officials:

> One senior legal scholar explained that before the campaign, local Party Politico-Legal Committees were headed by the Party Deputy Secretary in charge of politico-legal work, who was usually the local chief of the Public Security or the People's Court Chief Justice. These people typically had a modicum of legal knowledge or at least bureaucratic respect for the formal and informal prerogatives of the local procurators and courts. But the campaign documents not only insisted that localities establish "Stern Blows Offices" (*Yanda bangongshi*) to oversee all politico-legal units, they also stipulated that the First Secretary of the region personally take charge of both the campaign and the work of these offices. These First Secretaries were rarely career politico-legal officials, but rather Party generalists or military holdovers from the Cultural Revolution who stressed campaign "results" over process, and often interfered with judges and procurators who might otherwise have tried to check on and control the work of the local police.[38]

Joint Handling of Cases by the Police, Procuratorate, and Courts

In China, the organizational and procedural connections between the police, the procuratorate, and the courts, known collectively as the *gongjianfa*, reflect the arrangements of a political structure in which supervision and mutual coordination are defining characteristics of inter-organizational relationships. The unified structure of the organs of criminal justice in the PRC, characterized by close cooperation between the police, procuratorate, and courts, provides for specialized stages of criminal procedure in which the trial is simply one episode in a course of proceedings. The proceedings are characterized by mutual coordination and cooperation between the three main judicial branches. The principle of applying unified judicial power under the unified leadership of the state enables separation of functions and responsibilities between the three main organs of justice based around the concepts of "mutual coordination" and "mutual restraint." During Yanda, cooperation between the three criminal justice agencies was greatly accentuated. Cooperation between the police, procuratorate, and courts during the campaign included the following configurations:

- joint handling of cases (*lianhe ban'an*);
- "the three heads of criminal justice" (*sanzhang*) making case-related decisions;
- the practice of courts "intervening in a case ahead of the standard time" (*tiqian jieru*). This practice also included the practice of members of the court judicial committee sitting in on court trials in person and not waiting until the case file was handed to them.

By mid-August, judges in Baotou began implementing "severity and swiftness" with vigor through the policy of "mutual coordination," involving "simplified trial procedure" and the "joint handling of cases" (*lianhe ban'an*) by the public security bureau, procuratorate, and courts. The Yanda campaign in Baotou was officially organized under the joint leadership of the local Party Committee and the Baotou Municipal Party Committee and Baotou Municipal Government. Under this leadership, the police, procuratorate, courts, and the Bureau of Justice joined forces to form "three-person case-handling groups." The "Summary of Criminal Trial Work" describes the efficiency and speed with which these case-handling groups meted out justice. For example,

> On August 16, authorities across the city moved in a united operation to arrest the first batch of criminals. The court immediately sprang into action forming 78 "case-handling groups" with the public security bureau and the procuratorate, involving 315 personnel. Within only a fortnight or so, 371 cases (involving 756 accused individuals) had been received. In no way affecting the quality of judicial work, a simplified trial process was adopted and after a fortnight or so of intensive investigation and verification of facts, 138 cases involving 230 individuals were sent to trial in the month of September.[39]

To further accentuate the united front of the *gongjianfa*, at a forum in Baotou for court police and cadres on October 14, it was decided that all court judges who participated in the joint handling of the Yanda attack would wear a police uniform, an important symbolic gesture of the unity of the three agencies of criminal justice and the para-militaristic character of the operation.[40]

In the first months of Yanda, the main method of dealing with Yanda offences in Miyang county, Henan province, was for one representative from each of the three arms of criminal justice to form a three-person case-handling group (*sanyuan lianhe ban'an*). All three members (one each from the police, prosecution, and court) took part in the preliminary findings and investigation of evidence. Having finished their investigation, they handed it on to their superiors, a group of four leaders (the heads of the police, prosecution, court, and bureau of justice), who met to decide the outcomes of cases. These four heads would decide on the conviction and sentence and then send the case back to the original three-person team to carry out the formality of investigation, prosecution, and sentencing on the heads' advice.[41]

In Hebei province, at the start of Yanda, the Hebei Higher Court decided to second eighty-two of their judges to form twelve collegiate benches to help adjudicate trials in the intermediate courts. They urged the lower courts to consult with the Higher Court on cases that were difficult or important, and only when this consultation did not result in a resolution were the lower courts permitted to consult the jointly-operated Yanda Head Office run by the Party. The Higher Court recorded that seconding their own judges to help adjudicate at the intermediate court level and moving intermediate court judges to help adjudicate at the basic court level were positive moves. The strategy was to solve problems on the spot and to help local judges to clearly differentiate between Yanda and non-Yanda crimes.[42]

Despite the Tianjin Higher Court's role as judicial authority for the approval of death sentences handed down by lower courts, on September 19–20, the Tianjin Higher Court nevertheless invited a number of representatives from the legislature's Chinese People's Political Consultative Conference (CPPCC) to take part in the deliberation of verdicts and sentences of a number of capital cases on file in the lower courts. After reviewing the cases, the CPPCC said that it would support the courts in handing down the death sentence in all eighty-two cases. On September 20–21, the Higher Court printed and distributed one hundred thousand open letters to work units, enterprises, schools, factories, and farm communities to ask the masses to discuss their views on the pending sentences of the eighty-two capital cases. Across the city, 11,500 "discussion meetings" about the cases were held involving over 2.5 million residents. With the exception of a few dissenting opinions from some individuals, almost all participants agreed with the courts' recommendation to execute the criminals. Unsurprisingly, the eighty-two were publicly sentenced to death on September 24, at a rally with twenty-five thousand in attendance.[43]

By October, Yanda excesses were beginning to make an impact on policy-making in Tianjin. The Higher Court designed new procedures for judicial decisionmaking in capital cases to tighten controls over the process. It decided that the collegiate bench of judges that would normally decide cases would now be required to take its recommendations to the head of the criminal court tribunal, the deputy court president, and the court president. The recommendations would then be taken to the court judicial committee and after that, to the municipal politico-legal affairs committee for review. The provincial politico-legal affairs committee would then need to convene a meeting with the public security bureau, the procuratorate, and Tianjin Higher Court president and head of the Bureau of Justice, who would together make a final decision. The problem with this process, however, was that capital cases would normally be tried at first instance by the Tianjin Intermediate Court. If a convicted criminal wanted to appeal a death penalty sentence, he/she would need to appeal to the Tianjin Higher Court. By virtue of the new procedures, however, the provincial-level Higher Court was essentially making the decision in the first instance, denying a convicted criminal any chance of an appeal. Moreover, it ensured that the final decision on a case would be made by the provincial politico-legal affairs committee along with the *gongjianfa*, not by the court in which the case should have been adjudicated and decided.[44] The following year, on April 6, the Higher Court president, Wang Yongchen, reported to the Tianjin People's Congress on Yanda progress, boasting that, "We have killed a large number of heinous criminals" and that, compared to the preceding year, a much greater proportion of criminals receiving a term of imprisonment were given heavy sentences.[45]

Speedy Trials

The majority of trials in the campaign were conducted during the first year, in 1983. Table 5.2 shows figures from one city (Nanjing) and one province (Liaoning) in Table 5.3 indicate something of the velocity and ferocity of adjudication and sentencing during the campaign. For instance, in Nanjing city in 1980, eleven death and life imprisonment sentences were handed down compared to 189 in 1983 and 258 in 1984.

Table 5.2. Criminal Trial Outcomes for Nanjing, 1980–1986

Year	Total no. of cases	Total no. of defendants	Death sentence or life	10–20 years imprisonment	5–9 years imprisonment	Under 5 years imprisonment
1980	1,283	1,637	11	7	230	994
1981	2,013	2,825	38	19	586	1,451
1982	1,839	2,522	23	13	348	1,302
1983	4,239	7,061	189	1,126	2,026	2,441
1984	3,689	6,325	258	628	1,477	2,421
1985	1,656	2,308	50	114	438	963
1986	2,050	2,836	33	114	490	1,193

Source: *Nanjing shenpanzhi* (Beijing: Fangzhi chubanshe, 1997), 168.

Table 5.3. Trials with Death Sentence or Life Imprisonment Outcomes for Liaoning Province, 1979–1985

Year	Total no. of defendants sentenced	Death sentence or life imprisonment
1977	7,919	248
1978	8,975	257
1979	9,568	284
1980	13,827	345
1981	15,782	404
1982	17,644	447
1983	41,487	2,145
1984	26,108	776
1985	12,082	495

Source: *Liaoning shengzhi jianchazhi* (Shenyang: Liaoning kexue jishu chubanshe), 369.

The "swiftness" of the Baotou courts' response to the Yanda call is evident in the number of cases these courts handled in the first six weeks of Yanda. On September 22, an overview of the campaign's implementation thus far was presented at a forum convened for all municipal court presidents. It was noted that, since beginning the joint handling of cases, 444 cases (involving 863 defendants) had been received and 89.2 percent of these were completed.[46]

Luoding county court, in rural Guangdong province, capitalized on its newfound authority to deliver death sentences and could boast of being one of the most enthusiastic practitioners of the death sentence in the first Yanda offensive, with eleven executions at the county level. It could also lay claim to one of the fastest executions recorded in Yanda. According to the *Annals of Public Security Work in Luoding*, on September 1, 1983, Chen Guangsen assaulted and raped a woman. The case was cracked on the same day with his immediate arrest. The pre-trial investigation, arrest approval, prosecution, trial, and approval of the death penalty by the intermediate court was completed within a period of seven days from September 1 to 8. He was executed the following day, September 9, eight days after the crime was reported.[47]

Hebei province staked its claim to Yanda fame by the practice of entering into the case management process "before the standard time" to ensure a speedy trial. The idea was for the court to work in close coordination with the prosecution and the police at the pre-trial stage to determine if more evidence was needed, allowing for further investigation before the case was brought before the court. In this way, cases could be moved through the court system expediently. Court time was also saved by sifting through cases to identify minor crimes that could be exempted from punishment, to make way for the speedy adjudication of Yanda cases. In the first offensive, from August 1983 to July 1984, the Hebei courts tried 20,300 cases, resulting in 34,700 convictions. This was roughly the same number of cases adjudicated by the Hebei courts in the entire three-year period from 1980 to 1983.[48]

Yunnan province's response to the rise in crime could also be seen as swift and relentless. In the first full month of Yanda, 4,102 criminal cases were tried in the courts. The writers of the Yunnan court history note that during Yanda, cases were tried following the policy of "severity and swiftness," within the limits stipulated by law. Yunnan court records reveal an example in the case of Qian Chuncai, who bombed a bus in Dali city on September 15, killing three people and injuring twenty-four. The Dali Procuratorate signed the bill of prosecution against the accused on September 23 and the Dali Intermediate Court tried the case the following day. That evening, he was sentenced to death and his death-penalty approval papers were sent to the Higher Court on September 25. On September 27, the Higher Court approved the death penalty and he was executed on September 30. The approval process took less than seventy-two hours. As noted at the start of this chapter, in the first offensive from August 1983 to July 1984,

780 criminals were sentenced to death in Yunnan, and over five thousand serious criminal offenders were found guilty of their crimes.[49]

Strategy 4: Creating a Momentum

The strategy of delivering "flexible justice" outlined above was implemented hand in hand with the simultaneous push to "mobilize the masses" to maximize the deterrence and educative effect of the campaign. In essence, this involved arranging for work units all over the country to organize staff to attend sentencing rallies. In Yunnan province alone, over nine million members of the public attended public sentencing rallies.[50]

After taking cases through the courts, the next prescribed move was to propagate the "success" of the campaign through mass sentencing rallies. Table 5.4 is a record from just one city of the hundreds in which rallies were conducted in Yanda.

Table 5.4. Public Sentencing Rallies in Baoji, Shanxi Province during Yanda, 1983–1986

Date	Rally details	Total no. of criminals sentenced	Sentences handed down
11.9.83	Simultaneously convened rallies at the Baoji Municipal Sports Stadium and in 8 county areas	44	34 given life imprisonment or the death penalty
23.9.83	Football field: rally convened by the Weibin District Basic people's court	17	Most serious crime given 15 years imprisonment
15.11.83	Baoji municipal theatre	14 (all members of hooligan gangs)	5 sentenced to death
28.12.83	Baoji Municipal Sports Stadium	4	2 sentenced to death for human trafficking and rape
3.1.84	Public forum convened to discuss the cases of 62 criminals who were about to be sentenced to death or given a heavy prison sentence		
5.1.84–	6 rallies convened by the	62	55 given death penalty,

Table 5.4 (continued)

13.1.84	Baoji Intermediate and 5 county courts		death penalty with reprieve, or life imprisonment; 17 given terms shorter than life imprisonment
12.5.84	4 rallies convened by the Baoji Intermediate and 3 county courts	7	7 given death penalty
25.8.84	7 rallies convened by the Baoji Intermediate and 6 county courts	95	27 given death penalty, death penalty with reprieve or life imprisonment
5.2.85	4 rallies convened by the Baoji Intermediate and 3 county courts	10	6 given death penalty, 2 given death penalty with reprieve and 1 given life imprisonment
7.5.86	Baoji Municipal Sports Stadium (after the rally, the prisoners were sent back to their original counties to the site of their crime and were publicly executed at the site)	9	5 given the death penalty
8.8.86	4 rallies convened by the Baoji Intermediate Court at the theatre and 2 county courts	37 (all theft cases)	1 death sentence and 1 life imprisonment
8.10.86	Weibin theatre in Baoji.	3	2 death sentences and 1 death with a reprieve

Source: Cheng Jianxing ed., *Baoji fayuanzhi* (Neibu ziliao: unpublished restricted materials, 2001), 44–51.

Back in Baotou, over two million people had attended rallies by the end of 1986. In all, the two tiers of the local courts conducted 249 public sentencing rallies throughout the three years of the campaign. More than 2,290,000 people attended the rallies and more than 580,000 public notices and leaflets about the trials were distributed in Baotou.[51] Of the criminals publicly sentenced during this period, 144 were given the death penalty. The first months of the campaign saw the most intense period of rallies. Indeed, one of the first and most detailed accounts of a rally during an anti-crime campaign in China is from the Baotou court history. The description exemplifies the significance attached to the rally as a shaming ritual that symbolically reflects the relationships between the state, the court system, the convicted criminal, and the masses. The history records that on

September 7, 1983, at the height of the first Strike Hard campaign, mammoth public sentencing rallies were held in two separate sites in Baotou city to pronounce sentencing on eighty serious offenders, forty-two of whom were sentenced to death:[52]

> To ensure the success of the sentencing rallies, court cadres and police from the intermediate court worked without let-up around the clock. In the early hours of the morning at 4 a.m., court and military police gathered together, braving an immense downpour of rain. They arrived at the site of the rallies at precisely 5 a.m.[53]

Attending the rallies were the municipal Party secretary, the mayor, and other Party and government dignitaries, along with the intermediate court president and the vice-president. The court distributed nine thousand copies of the judgment notices and twenty thousand leaflets publicizing the event, and more than one hundred thousand people attended the rallies. The court history recorded that members of the masses attended the momentous rallies in droves despite the heavy rains, and that "the venues were so packed that some people had no alternative but to stand outside."[54] The court's recording of the event relates how:

> [d]espite these circumstances, the rallies ran smoothly from start to finish. More than one hundred thousand people lined the streets in the pouring rain to voice their indignation against the criminals on their route to the execution grounds.[55]

In the three years of Yanda, the Qingxu county court in Shanxi province tried 433 cases (involving 391 people). The court executed seven criminals and gave a death sentence with a reprieve to one criminal. Their first Yanda sentencing rally was September 30, 1983, at the Dongbu stadium in the county capital, where five people were sentenced to death in front of an audience of ten thousand. Another two criminals were publicly sentenced to death on January 23, 1984. Reminiscent of the Cultural Revolution, the event was called a "mass rally" (*qunzhong dahui*).[56] Table 5.5 lists some details of rallies that were carried out in one county alone. There were over two thousand counties in China at the time.

Arguably the fastest and most furious response to the call to "Yanda" was in Tianjin. In the city's first public sentencing rally, convened at the Minyuan Sports Stadium on August 26 by the Tianjin Intermediate Court, forty people were sentenced to death in front of a crowd of twenty-five thousand. As noted in Chapter Three, after the rally, the soon-to-be executed criminals were placed in "propaganda trucks" (*xuanchuan che*) to be sent to the execution grounds. On the way, the criminals were paraded around thirty-one of the main roads of the city, spanning six main districts. Crowds gathered along the streets to applaud the sentencing action.[57]

Table 5.5. Sentencing Rallies in Qingxu County, Shanxi Province

Date	Location	Sentencing details
30.9.83	Dongbu Stadium, County capital	5 criminals sentenced to death
23.1.84	Dongbu Stadium, County capital	2 criminals sentenced to death; 12 given prison sentences
2.8.84	Wucun town	Criminals from the township convicted of robbery and rape
15.1.85	Mengfeng town	Criminals from the township convicted of robbery and harboring criminals
25.9.85	County capital town square	Criminals convicted of murder, rape, assault, arson, and theft
13.9.85	Annual county fair venue (on annual show day)	People convicted of illegal gambling
31.1.86	Dongbu county stadium	Mass rally for 15 criminals guilty of various common and economic crimes
25.6.86	Gaohua town	Mass rally chaired by county Party secretary and county government head, to sentence 8 convicted thieves
17.7.86	County capital cinema	Mass rally chaired by county Party secretary and county government head, to sentence 5 convicted thieves and 1 rapist
30.8.86		Mass rally to fight robbery and theft crimes, chaired by county Party secretary and county government head, to sentence 5 convicted criminals and 1 murderer
15.12.86	County cinema	A rally celebrating "Three Battles and Three Offensives of Yanda" chaired by county Party secretary and county government head, with the entire workforce of police, prosecution, and court staff present

Source: *Qingxu fayuan baogao* (Neibu ziliao: unpublished restricted materials, 1998), 79–81.

On another occasion, in Jianyang county, Sichuan province, the criminal justice organs organized over seventy open trucks to carry convicted criminals involved in 266 separate cases (including thirty-three people found guilty of Yanda-related crimes) around eighty people's communes and townships, with over two hundred thousand people lining the streets to watch. This was carried out as a Yanda promotional activity. The following year, on January 25, 1984, a public execution was conducted in Liulin Village. An offender, Wang Qinghong, found guilty of human trafficking and rape, was executed at the site where he committed the crimes of which he was found guilty. Wang had two prior convictions. He had bought eighteen people from Jianyang to sell on to people in Shandong province.[58] Public executions are illegal in China.

The National Scene 1984–1986

By early November 1983, the minister of Public Security had become increasingly alarmed at the rate and ferocity of Yanda's implementation at the grassroots of Chinese society, and particularly at the basic courts' application of the death penalty. The politburo's Politico-Legal Affairs Committee convened a public order work conference from November 7 to 14, with over five hundred national and provincial criminal justice dignitaries in attendance. Yet, even upon hearing their concerns, Committee Secretary Peng Zhen stated that he believed that "this campaign is still a healthy one." He endorsed glibly that if mistakes had been made, the people involved should simply correct them and be careful not to conceal problems. He re-emphasized that the Party committees at all levels must continue to take charge of Yanda leadership overall, and he reinterpreted Deng Xiaoping's slogan of "catching criminals in one fell swoop" (*yi wang dajin*) to mean "catching criminals in continuous swoops, one battle after another," thus signaling that he expected the Yanda leadership to begin making preparations for the second battle of the first offensive.[59]

Immediately after this meeting, Peng Zhen convened another week-long meeting for provincial criminal justice heads in which the experience of Yanda's first three months was summarized and discussed. It was concluded that the following battle must be focused much more narrowly than the first. Among the problems identified in the first battle was the failure of many courts to discriminate between

(1) real hooligan crime / fighting or tussling between family groups or between members of different work units;
(2) rape / "illicit relations" between males and females; and
(3) Yanda crimes (the seven categories) / non-Yanda crimes in sentencing practice.

Local leaders were urged to ensure that criminal justice agencies throughout the country continued the campaign with the appropriate degree of "severity and swiftness" expected of them by the Party Central Committee. They were to continue to pursue Yanda using the method of "intensive united operations" (*jizhong tongyi xingdong*) on crime to create a deterrence effect, while at the same time ensuring that all work for Yanda be carried out strictly in line with the law. They were reminded that they were under the united leadership of the Communist Party (not the leadership of the police, prosecution, and courts) and that all those detained from the first battle must be dealt with before the second battle could begin.[60] It was decided that the second battle, to begin around the time of the Spring Festival, would mainly target itinerant criminals.

In mid-February 1984, Peng Zhen again summoned the Minister of Public Security, Liu Fuzhi, to a meeting to discuss problems in implementing Yanda. Peng announced (probably to Liu's great surprise) that he had insisted from the beginning of Yanda, that the process of attacking and punishing crime was to be conducted "surely, accurately and relentlessly" (*wen zhun hen*), with "accuracy" (*zhun*) as the central focus. He made this statement even though it was he who complained, at the outset of the Yanda campaign in 1983, that the seriously damaging crime situation was partly the fault of courts that were slow to adjudicate trials because they zealously pursued "accuracy" at the expense of "swiftness." Peng summoned the heads of PSB in Jiangsu and Anhui provinces to insist that the policy of "severity and swiftness" was not working effectively because criminal justice agencies had failed to grasp the importance of "accuracy." He took the opportunity to insist again that Yanda be implemented under the leadership of the Communist Party at all levels.[61]

By March 17, 1984, the politburo had given approval to the plan of the Central Party Committee's Politico-Legal Affairs Committee for the second main offensive in 1985 along with the third battle of the first offensive in 1984. For both plans, the policy catchcry would now be "surely, accurately and relentlessly" with an emphasis on accuracy as the priority. A summary of the experiences and problems of the second battle of the first offensive was discussed at a Ministry of Public Security forum on May 3. A number of issues were put forward. First, it was concluded that, at the local level in the second battle, decisions about who to prosecute and who not to prosecute had been made with much more accuracy because the public security bureau, procuratorate, and courts were encouraged to discuss the specifics of cases before formal arrests were made. Second, the problem with overcrowding in police lock-ups was due in part to having to keep many convicted criminals there because the local prisons were full. Third, in two hot spots—government departments and industries, and places located on the outskirts of city areas—crime was still rife and needed to be contained.[62]

In July 1984, Peng Zhen again stressed the need for "accuracy" as the hallmark of Yanda implementation at the grassroots level. As he rationalized then, accuracy was not stressed as much in the first battle in 1983 because that battle had concentrated mainly on the more obvious "surface level" crimes and not so much on more complex (hard to solve) crimes that required more accurate targeting. He admitted that it was now widely acknowledged in public security circles that the first battle was sloppy and shambolic. He then sought to explain away problems by observing how local crime fighters, like the public in general, had become increasingly frustrated at the general lack of response to the crime situation prior to Yanda, and had let out their frustration and unleashed their fury on criminals in an overly exuberant manner. He added that their mistakes had been quickly correctly.[63]

The Ministry of Public Security held a conference for PSB heads from July 16 to 26, where it was relayed that, in the first year of Yanda from August 1983 to July 1984, over one million people had been detained for questioning. The crime rate had fallen but China had not yet experienced a complete turnaround in the state of law and order. Over one hundred thousand itinerant criminals were yet to be caught and all efforts were to go into solving long-pending cases.[64] From September 10 to 14, 1984, a three-day national sting aimed at rounding up itinerant criminals was launched, with 62,374 suspects detained. This three-day sting constituted the central focus of the first battle of the second offensive, which went from August 31 to September 30.[65]

In the second battle of the second main offensive, which began in January and ended in February 1985, all provinces with the exception of Henan and Tibet took part in "joint operations" and police stings. This second battle targeted crime in government departments and in areas on the outskirts of cities. The emphasis was on ensuring good quality investigation and prosecution of cases.[66] For the third battle of the second offensive, nineteen provinces again convened "joint operations" and police stings, and the remaining provinces convened "specialized campaigns" aimed at cracking cases. From August 5 to 11, 1985, the Ministry of Public Security convened a national meeting to summarize the experience of the second offensive. Yanda had then been running for twenty-two months and crime rates in general were falling, but major thefts and other serious crimes were on the rise. It was confirmed that a third offensive would be necessary in 1986 to curb this trend. Four principles were outlined for running the third offensive.

First, the principle of acting "surely, accurately and relentlessly" was to be given equal status with the policy of "severity and swiftness" and, in cases where it was unclear whether an individual should be detained for questioning, police were urged to err on the side of not detaining. Second, Party committees were to continue to head Yanda, and the system of joint processing of cases by the three criminal justice agencies was to be maintained. Third, regions were cautioned not to ignore the practice of launching joint operations against particular targets *en masse* throughout whole areas and regions. However, if some categories of crime were particularly prominent in that region, the region would be permitted to launch singular operations to combat the problem. Fourth, misjudged cases from the first and second offensives were to be redressed, but regions were warned that this did not mean that courts could go about undoing all the work of Yanda over the previous twenty-two months of the campaign. The focus of the third offensive was to be on public order offenses and major and violent crime. From August 1985 to the beginning of the third offensive, the focus was to be on gambling and prostitution.[67]

Three new national security heads were appointed by the politburo in September 1985 to take up new positions in the Ministry of Public Security and National Security. Qiao Shi was made a member of the politburo and secretary of the Central Party Committee Politico-Legal Affairs Committee. Ruan Chongwu was made Minister of Public Security and Jia Chunwang the Minister of National Security. All three were brought in from work areas outside public security. Peng Zhen reminded the newcomers that, "The main part of this job is implementing Party policy. You are therefore not strangers to this type of work. Of course, the criminal justice operations require specialist knowledge but you can learn that easily enough."[68]

The highlight of Deng Xiaoping's January 17, 1986, speech, "Talk at the Meeting of the Standing Committee of the Political Bureau of the Central Committee," was his call to continue to use the death penalty in China as the country's key means of crime deterrence. Questioning why the state, using the policy of severity and swiftness, should not execute not only murderers but also repeat offenders, criminals who traffic in women and children, and leaders of superstitious sects, he declared that, "Generally speaking, the problem now is that we are too soft on criminals. As a matter of fact, execution is one of the indispensable means of education."[69]

A decision to launch a third Yanda offensive was announced at a national conference on politico-legal work from February 21 to March 4, 1986. Provinces and regions were permitted to set their own targeted areas of crime for the third offensive but were required to maintain the system of intensive and simultaneous police operations and stings. Qiao Shi warned that the politico-legal organs were, in essence, the assistants and "staff officers" of the Party and government in the Yanda campaign. In terms of the operation of Yanda, "they must do as required of them with enthusiasm and vigor. They must uphold and support the dictatorship of the Communist Party and continue to serve the people."[70] The third offensive ran from March 1986 to January 1987.

Conclusion: 1950s and 1980s Criminal Justice Work—Spot the Difference

The announcement of a new era of socialist law at the historic Third Plenum of the 11th Central Committee in December 1978 prompted a speedy drive to reconstruct the new public image of courts as credible administrators of justice. As part of the hand-over of power from Maoist to Dengist institutions, the promotion of a new legal culture involved a process to develop a new credibility and authority to administer justice with regularity, procedural propriety, and bureaucratic rationality. Yet, as we have seen in this chapter, the political exercise of state and Party power—in the form of "severity and swiftness," speedy trials, flexible criminal justice practices, and "shock and awe" activities—placed the courts' burgeoning development of an authoritative and increasingly independent persona in serious jeopardy.

Crime control strategies, both in the 1950s were based on a particular idea that to best serve the people, law had to be applied in a flexible manner, both procedurally and in sentencing practice. In applying the law, the organs of criminal justice had to coordinate their efforts to achieve the most effective outcomes. Socialist legal ideology prescribed that changes in the concrete circumstances of social development be reflected in Party norms. Law changed in response to changes in Party norms and adjustments and changes in Party norms were said to be informed by the changing circumstances of social development, that is, based on the "actuality" of the social conditions of socialist transformation, as interpreted by Party norms through Party policy. As law served the interests of the state-building and social development, it had to be flexible in nature. The content and application of law was continually amended and renegotiated on the basis of Party assessments of historical developments and the current circumstances and law should not be so fixed as to hinder the Party in directing state and social development. Despite the heralding in of a new era of "rule of law" in the post-Mao period, this remained the basic rationale underlying the approach of flexibility and mutual coordination in court policy in anti-crime campaigns.

One of the dominant features of the anti-crime campaigns in the post-1978 period was the policy of using "flexibility" in the way in which procedure and sentencing were practiced in cases involving the *targets* of the campaigns. The policy of flexibility in applying the criminal law in judicial procedure was promoted as a legitimate means of adapting to changes in the political and economic conditions of social development and in reacting to the changing threats to the social order. In all the anti-crime campaigns from 1979 to 1986, the courts' hardline response to particular crimes such as murder, arson, rape, theft, and armed robbery was informed by changes in the official interpretation of the social dangerousness of certain crimes in certain periods. For instance, at times when the unstable state of the social and public order were deemed to threaten the very success of the national reforms, adjudication and sentencing practices were "simplified" and "quickened" to ensure the success of the campaign. Sanctions for "social order" and "public order" crimes increased at times during periods when these crimes were deemed a threat to the social order.

During the campaigns from 1983 to 1986, flexibility was manifest in two main policies; "severity and swiftness" and the joint handling of cases between the courts, police, and procuratorate, under the rubric of "mutual coordination." As in the 1950s, the rhetorical tools used to explain criminal court activities and crime control agendas in China in the post-1978 period were the programmatic agendas of "defending," "upholding," "protecting," "safeguarding," and "educating." The Yanda campaign borrowed much of its rhetoric and policy from the 1950s campaigns. For example, during the Yanda campaign, the interpretation of what is "socially harmful to the modernization drive" determined which objects of regulation were targeted.

The criminal justice system required a high degree of flexibility, not just in operations but also in understanding of the law and its purpose. To this end, a number of tactics were applied to achieve the goals of the campaign. In 1983, in response to the increased crime rate engendered by the changing social and political climate of reform, the criminal code was amended to accommodate these changing "objective" circumstances. The principle of "mutual coordination" between the three arms of criminal justice, which first applied in Baotou in the late 1950s, was resurrected during the Yanda campaign in the form of "case-handling groups" and in the rationale of "comprehensive management of public order." In the Yanda campaign, as in the mass movements of the 1950s, the programmatic goals of criminal court work were accentuated in the socialist rhetoric of the "people" and the "enemy." This policy of politicizing criminality ensured the continued use in the post-1978 period of some 1950s tactics and principles of campaigning.

In all the Yanda campaigns since 1983, but particularly in the first, the state of the public order—a common reference point and rationale for Yanda—has been linked to the glories of the past and the imperative of future modernization. This was public order in practice, based on a certain political and ideological morality. Rhetorically, the 1983–1986 campaign relied on an evocation of a simpler and safer past with reference to the social order of the glory days of the 1950s and early 1960s when "people didn't have to lock their doors at night."[71] But it also relied on the idea of the imperative of social stability as a precondition of economic reform. This is a perennial concern for Chinese authorities.

As with the rationales of the earlier campaigns from 1979 to 1982, the Party and politico-legal organs credited the Yanda campaign as capable of thwarting a serious threat to the very success of the modernization drive in China. In this sense, we can interpret Yanda to be as much about what the politico-legal authorities saw as the need to foster an authoritative and aggressive image as protectors of the social realm, as it was a response to the crime rate. This is especially so when we recognize that, although high by China's pre-reform period standards, the annual crime rate had actually declined since 1981.[72] Yanda can therefore be understood as a pre-emptive strike in response to a perception that increased crime during a time of rapid economic growth would produce a major threat to the social order. It was also an attempt to foster a public perception that the effects of both economic reform and social change were "controllable" by central management and that society would no longer need to "appear impotent in the face of crime."[73]

Compulsion to talk up the success of the campaign waned after the initial shock and awe campaign of 1983 but, at end of the campaign in early 1987, what the CCP cast as the fruits of success were again detailed in the press. For example, in April 1987, Chinese Legal System News (*Zhongguo fazhibao*) published an editorial citing the achievements of Yanda since 1983. The editorial stated that Yanda "had received enthusiastic support and praise from the general community. The three year struggle had also successfully dealt a heavy blow to a number of serious criminal offenders who were a grave risk to the public order and who had sabotaged the Four Modernizations and economic construction."[74] The campaign had also successfully dealt heavy blows to criminal offenders who committed economic crimes that sabotaged the open reforms. As a result of the campaign, large financial losses due to criminal activity had been retrieved. The campaign had advanced "the implementation of the policy of comprehensive management of public order," "the construction of socialist spiritual civilization," and "the construction of the socialist democratic legal system." It had improved both the "general social climate" and "the understanding of concepts of legality within both government circles and in amongst the masses."[75] But for all the vainglorious claims about Yanda's success, the court system was surely not among the beneficiaries of the campaign. As we will see in the following chapter, the conduct of Yanda dealt a costly blow to the Chinese court system.

Notes

1. Stanley Cohen, *Folk Devils and Moral Panics: The Creation of the Mods and Rockers* (New York: St. Martin's Press, 1980), 9.
2. "Summary of Criminal Trial Work," *The Annals*, 30.
3. Han Yanlong, ed., *Zhonghua renmin gongheguo fazhi tongshi* (A comprehensive history of the legal system in the People's Republic of China) (Beijing: Zhonghua zhongyang dangxiao chubanshe, 1998), 870–71; Tanner notes that other sources put the figure at over two million. See Murray Scot Tanner, "Campaign-style Policing in China and its Critics," in *Crime, Punishment, and Policing in China*, ed. Borge Bakken (Lanham, MD: Rowman & Littlefield, 2005), 175.
4. Murray Scot Tanner, "State Coercion and the Balance of Awe: The 1983–1986 'Stern Blows' Anti-Crime Campaign," *The China Journal* 44 (2000): 93.
5. Tanner, "Campaign-style Policing in China and its Critics," 175.
6. Qiu Chuangjiao, ed., *Yunnan shenpanzhi* (Kunming: Yunnan renmin chubanshe, 1996), 353.
7. Borge Bakken, *The Exemplary Society: Human Improvement, Social Control and the Dangers of Modernity in China* (New York: Oxford University Press, 2000), 394. For example, the increasing propensity for criminals to use violence and murder in property-related crimes, to leave no witnesses, is one of the effects of the hard-line campaign against property offenses in Yanda campaigns.
8. Bakken, *The Exemplary Society*, 392.
9. "Summary of Criminal Trial Work," *The Annals*, 28–29.
10. Hou Honglin, *Xingshi zhengce de jiazhi fenxi* (An Analysis of Criminal Justice Policy Values) Ph.D. dissertation (Zhongguo zhengfa daxue yanjiushengyuan, Zhongguo zhengfa daxue, 2004), 177–78.

11. In two provinces alone from 1983–1987, there were over five thousand rallies (2,336 in Liaoning and 2,780 in Guizhou). These figures are recorded in Zhao Ying, ed., *Guizhou shenpanzhi* (Annals of Trial Work in Guizhou) (Guiyang: Guizhou renmin chubanshe, 1999), 339, and Zhao Rixin, ed., *Liaoning shenpanzhi* (Neibu chugao, Draft document for internal circulation), 365.

12. Guo Xingguo, ed., *Jianguo yilai gongan gongzuo dashi yaolan* (An Outline of the Chronicles of Public Security Work Since Liberation) (Beijing: Qunzhong chubanshe, neibu faxing, 2003), 534. Note that this book is an internally circulated reference resource. All former heads of public security since the 1980s including Liu Fuzhi provided materials and verified the contents.

13. Guo, *Jianguo yilai gongan gongzuo dashi yaolan*, 534.

14 Guo, *Jianguo yilai gongan gongzuo dashi yaolan*, 534.

15. Guo, *Jianguo yilai gongan gongzuo dashi yaolan*, 536.

16. Guo, *Jianguo yilai gongan gongzuo dashi yaolan*, 536.

17. Han Yanlong, ed., *Zhonghua renmin gongheguo fazhi tongshi* (A comprehensive history of the legal system in the People's Republic of China) (Beijing: Zhonghua zhongyang dangxiao chubanshe, 1998), 713.

18. Guo, *Jianguo yilai gongan gongzuo dashi yaolan*, 543–618. Note that the exact dates of the implementation of offensives varied from region to region and there were even variations within provinces.

19. Harold M. Tanner, *Strike Hard: Anti-Crime Campaigns and Chinese Criminal Justice, 1979–1985* (Ithaca, NY: East Asia Programs Cornell University, 1999), 89.

20. "Summary of Criminal Trial Work," *The Annals*, 29.

21. "Zhongguo zhongyang guanyu yanli daji xingshi fanzui huodong de jueding—jielu (B)," p.133, cited in Tanner, *Strike Hard*, 91.

22. In the wider realm, "*liumang*" (hooliganism), as Geremie Barme notes, is described as both "a social phenomenon and a cultural refraction." The term has been used for at least a century in China to describe a type of underworld culture, and in the immediate post-1978 period developed into a cultural phenomenon known as "*liumang wenhua*." Geremie R. Barme, *In the Red: On Contemporary Chinese Culture* (New York: Columbia University Press, 1999), 63–64.

23. Han, *Zhonghua renmin gongheguo fazhi tongshi*, 712.

24. Liu Hua, "Hooliganism," *Chinese Sociology and Anthropology* 27, no. 3 (1995): 57.

25. Liu Hua, "Hooliganism," *Chinese Sociology and Anthropology* 27, no. 3 (1995): 58–59.

26. Dangdai zhongguo lishi weiyuanwei, ed., *Dangdai Zhongguo de shenpan gongzuo* (Trial Work in Contemporary China (vol. 1) (Beijing: Dangdai zhongguo chubanshe, 1993), 342–44.

27. Borge Bakken, "Crime, Juvenile Delinquency and Deterrence Policy in China," (1993) 30 *Australian Journal of Chinese Affairs*: 43.

28. For an English version of the three decisions see *The Laws of the People's Republic of China (1983–1986)* (Beijing: Foreign Language Press, 1987).

29. Decision of the "Standing Committee of the National People's Congress Regarding the Severe Punishment of Criminals Who Seriously Endanger Public Security," in *The Laws of the People's Republic of China (1983–1986)*, 32.

30. "Zuigao remin fayuan, zuigao renmin jianchayuan, gong'anbu guanyu panchu wuqituxing, sixing de diyishen putong xingshi anjian guanxia wenti de tongzhi" (Supreme People's Court, Supreme People's Procuratorate and Public Security Bureau Joint Notice on Jurisdictional Issues Concerning Sentencing of Life Imprisonment and the

Death Sentence Cases of First Instance) (August 16, 1983) in *Zhifa shouce: daji xingshi fanzui zhuanji* (Vol. 4) (Law Enforcement Manual: Combating crime), ed. Gonganbu zhengce falu yanjiushi (Beijing: Qunzhong chubanshe, 1984), 15–16.

31. "Zuigao remin fayuan, zuigao renmin jianchayuan, gong'anbu guanyu panchu wuqituxing, sixing de diyishen putong xingshi anjian you zhongji renmin fayuan guanxia de tongzhi," 17–18.

32. Tanner, "State Coercion and the Balance of Awe," 112. The cases of a large number of defendants who were executed were found to be incorrectly handled by the basic courts. Hence, the decision to decentralize decisionmaking powers was reversed four months later, on December 2, returning jurisdiction over capital cases in the first instance to intermediate courts. Another example of the suspension of the courts' new-found procedural propriety occurred on August 19, 1983, when the Ministry of Justice, the Public Security Bureau, the Supreme People's Procuratorate, and the Supreme People's Court issued an urgent joint decision to suspend the release of all prisoners who had served their sentence in reform-through-labor and re-education-through-labor institutions. The stated reason was that the suspension would prevent prisoners who had served their sentences from making trouble (*zirao*) in society on their return from incarceration and would therefore prevent recidivism. The decision took effect immediately and lasted through the first battle to the end of 1983. See "Sifabu, gonganbu, zuigao renmin jiancha-yuan, zuigao renmin fayuan guanyu dui fanren xingman he laojiao qiman de renyuan zanting fanghui shehui de jinji tongzhi" (Ministry of Justice, Ministry of Public Security, Supreme People's Procuratorate and Supreme People's Court Urgent Joint Notice Regarding the Temporary Halting of Return to Society of Inmates Having Served their Full Sentence and Reform through Education Inmates Having Served Their Full Term) (August 18, 1983) in Zhifa shouce: daji xingshi fanzui zhuanji (Vol. 4) (Law Enforcement Manual: Combating crime), ed. Gonganbu zhengce falu yanjiushi (Beijing: Qunzhong chubanshe, 1984), 19.

By December 9, the decision was partly reversed and some low-security prisoners were released. By December 17, the original decision was reversed fully and all prisoners detained in prisons and lockups who had served their full sentences (except a small number of extremely serious offenders) were released. "Gonganbu guanyu kanshousuo guanya de xingshi renyuan jiefang wenti de tongzhi" (Ministry of Public Security Notice on Issues Concerning the Release of Criminals from Watchhouse Detention) (December 17, 1983) in Zhifa shouce: daji xingshi fanzui zhuanji (Vol. 4) (Law Enforcement Manual: Combating crime), ed. Gonganbu zhengce falu yanjiushi (Beijing: Qunzhong chubanshe, 1984), 24. The reasons given in the December decision to release some prisoners who had served their sentences were first, that the first battle has been victorious and second, that Chinese New Year was approaching and it would be a goodwill gesture to release a number of prisoners. The prisoners to be released were: first, prisoners who originated from rural areas; second, prisoners from urban areas who had committed only petty crimes or who had committed fairly serious crimes but whose sentence had previously been reduced; third, all prisoners in re-education through labor institutions. Those not to be released were recidivists and those who would return to urban areas without a residency permit. Prisoners would be released in batches according to their crimes. The first group to be released would be those who had committed crime through negligence, then progressively juveniles, those whose work units kept their position open for them, those who had received a sentence reduction, females, children without siblings, the elderly, the sick, and the handicapped. See "Ministry of Justice, Ministry of Public Security, Supreme People's Procuratorate, Supreme People's Court Joint Notice Concerning the Release of a Portion of Inmates Who Have Fully-Served Their Sentences and Inmates

Released from Reeducation Through Labor Who Have Been Temporarily Retained" (Sifabu, gong'anbu, zuigao renmin jianchayuan, zuigao renmin fayuan guanyu jiang yibufen xingman he jiefang laojiao zanliu renyuan fanghui shehui de tongzhi) (December 9, 1983), in Zhifa shouce: daji xingshi fanzui zhuanji (Vol. 4) (Law Enforcement Manual: Combating crime), ed. Gong'anbu zhengce falu yanjiushi (Beijing: Qunzhong chubanshe, 1984), 21.

33. Andrew J. Nathan, *China's Transition* (New York: Columbia University Press, 1997), 240; and Stanley Lubman, "Dispute Resolution in China after Deng Xiaoping: 'Mao and Mediation' Revisited," *Columbia Journal of Asian Law* 11, no. 2 (Fall 1997): 324.

34. Susan Finder, "The Supreme People's Court of the People's Republic of China," *Journal of Chinese Law* 7, no. 2 (Fall 1993): 149.

35. Finder, "The Supreme People's Court," 149.

36. Liu Xinsheng, ed., *Xuzhou gonganzhi* (Annals of Public Security Work in Xuzhou) (Xuzhou: neibu faxing, 1994), 44.

37. Xining gonganju, ed., *Xining gonganzhi* (Annals of Public Security Work in Xining) (Xining, Qinghai: neibu faxing, 1994), 330.

38. Tanner, "State Coercion and the Balance of Awe," 114.

39. "Summary of Criminal Trial Work," *The Annals*, 30.

40. "Chronicle of Events," *The Annals*, 132.

41. Wu Shanglin, ed., *Miyang xianzhi* (Annals of Miyang County) (Henan: neibu faxing, 1994), 224.

42. Dai Ruilin, ed., *Hebeisheng shenpanzhi* (Annals of Trial Work in Hebei Province) (Shijiazhuang: Hebei renmin chubanshe, 1994), 175.

43. *Tianjin fayuan gongzuo dashiji* (Annals of Tianjin Court Work) (Tianjin: neibu ziliao, 1986), 180.

44. *Tianjin fayuan gongzuo dashiji*, 180.

45. *Tianjin fayuan gongzuo dashiji*, 184.

46. "Chronicle of Events," *The Annals*, 132.

47. Liang Guozhen, ed., *Luoding gonganzhi* (Annals of Public Security Work in Luoding) (Luoding: neibu ziliao, 1997), 289.

48. Dai, *Hebeisheng shenpanzhi*, 175.

49. Qiu Chuangjiao, ed., *Yunnan shenpanzhi* (Kunming: Yunnan renmin chubanshe, 1996), 353.

50. Qiu, *Yunnan shenpanzhi*, 353.

51. "Summary of Criminal Trial Work," *The Annals*, 30.

52. "Summary of Criminal Trial Work," *The Annals*, 30–31.

53. "Summary of Criminal Trial Work," *The Annals*, 30–31.

54. "Summary of Criminal Trial Work," *The Annals*, 30–31.

55. "Summary of Criminal Trial Work," *The Annals*, 30.

56. Ning Yuce, ed., *Qingxu fayuan baogao* (Report on Qingxu Court) (Shanxi: neibu faxing, 1998), 79–81.

57. *Tianjin fayuan gongzuo dashiji*, 178–79.

58. Sichuansheng Jianyangxian gonganzhi lingdaozu, ed., *Sichuansheng Jianyangxian gonganzhi* (Annals of Public Security Work in Jianyang County, Sichuan Province) (Chengdu: neibu ziliao, 1987).

59. Guo, *Jianguo yilai gongan gongzuo dashi yaolan*, 536.

60. Guo, *Jianguo yilai gongan gongzuo dashi yaolan*, 541.

61. Guo, *Jianguo yilai gongan gongzuo dashi yaolan*, 549–50.

62. Guo, *Jianguo yilai gongan gongzuo dashi yaolan*, 553.

63. Guo, *Jianguo yilai gongan gongzuo dashi yaolan*, 564.

64. Guo, *Jianguo yilai gongan gongzuo dashi yaolan*, 564.

65. Guo, *Jianguo yilai gongan gongzuo dashi yaolan*, 568–69.

66. Guo, *Jianguo yilai gongan gongzuo dashi yaolan*, 584.

67. Guo, *Jianguo yilai gongan gongzuo dashi yaolan*, 599–600.

68. Guo, *Jianguo yilai gongan gongzuo dashi yaolan*, 605.

69. Deng Xiaoping, "Talk at a Meeting of the Standing Committee of the Political Bureau of the Central Committee," *Selected Works of Deng Xiaoping Volume III (1982–1992)* (Beijing: Foreign Languages Press, 1994), 155.

70. Guo, *Jianguo yilai gongan gongzuo dashi yaolan*, 618.

71. Cao Feng, *Diwuci gaofeng: Zhongguo wenti baogao* (The Fifth Peak: Reports on China's Problems) Beijing: China Today Publishing House, 1997), 10.

72. The crime rate for 1983 was 6.0 per ten thousand population compared to 8.9 per ten thousand in 1981 and 7.4 per ten thousand in 1982. See statistics on crime rates in Wang Zhongfang, ed., *Zhongguo shehui zhan zonghe zhili lilun yu shijian* (The Theory and Practice of China's Comprehensive Management of Public Order) (Beijing: Qunzhong chubanshe, 1989), 462.

73. Shao Daosheng, *Preliminary Study of China's Juvenile Delinquency*. Beijing: Foreign Language Press, 1992: 161. As noted previously, Borge Bakken describes the panic and fight against juvenile crime, and the moral panic in general, as a "fear of the dangers of modernity." Borge Bakken, "Editor's Introduction," *Chinese Sociology and Anthropology* 27, no. 3 (1995): 5–7.

74. Zhou Zhenxiang and Shao Jingchun, ed., *Xin Zhongguo fazhi jianshe 40 nian yaolan* (Outline of forty years of the construction of the legal system in the new China). Beijing: Qunzhong chubanshe, 1990: 727.

75. Zhou Zhenxiang and Shao Jingchun, ed., *Xin Zhongguo fazhi jianshe 40 nian yaolan* (Outline of forty years of the construction of the legal system in the new China). (Beijing: Qunzhong chubanshe, 1990), 727.

Chapter Six

Chop-Suey Justice

> Prior to the Yanda campaign, crimes such as murder, armed robbery, rape, hooliganism, serious theft, criminal gang activity and serious assault were rampant in Baotou. These crimes were a serious threat to citizens' lives and property and they were also a serious threat to the construction of the "two civilizations." As a result of the Yanda campaign, the number of crimes committed in the above categories decreased each year. From September 1982 to August 1983, the crime rate was 24 per ten thousand individuals in Baotou. This was the highest crime rate recorded in Baotou since liberation. After the first Yanda offensive, the crime rate decreased to 13.8 per ten thousand. After the second offensive, the rate dropped to 9.7 per ten thousand. During the first offensive, offenders under the seven main categories comprised 44.2 percent of total cases. During the second offensive, it was 33 percent and during the third offensive it was 31.9 percent.[1]

The success of the 1983–1986 Yanda campaign in decreasing the crime rate was declared officially as early as November 1983. On November 18, *Chinese Legal System News* (*Zhongguo fazhibao*) published an editorial titled, "We Have Gained Victories in the First Battle and Must Continue to Work Ceaselessly and Unremittingly." The editorial stated that politico-legal organs throughout the country had already tasted the fruits of the initial victory in the first stage of the campaign, with obvious improvements in public order. The editorial urged continued political struggle against criminal elements.[2] In the same issue of *Chinese Legal System News*, a news report stated that the September 2, NPC Decision on the Yanda campaign already had received massive support (*dade renxin*) throughout the country and that the crime rate already had dropped substantially.[3]

From August 1983 to the end of 1986, more than 1,400,000 cases involving 1,721,000 people were tried in the criminal courts nationwide. More than 90 percent of offenders given sentences of life imprisonment or the death penalty came under one of the seven main target categories of the campaign.[4] But even a cursory glance at prison population statistics in the late 1980s and early 1990s instills grave doubts about how much judicial decisionmaking was delivered accurately and "in accordance with the law." Of the 2,366 incarcerated as serious offenders at the Jiangsu No. 4 Prison who had been found guilty and sentenced for offenses between 1983 and 1986, 699 (29.5 percent) had their judgment or sentence amended between 1986 and 1990.[5] A Shanxi No. 3 Prison survey revealed that 90 percent of the entire prison population was convicted during the three years of Yanda from 1983 to 1986. While in prison, a majority of the offenders formally petitioned the courts for clemency or a reversal of verdict. Many, although admitting guilt, believed they had been sentenced too harshly compared to pre-Yanda cases and even to other Yanda cases.[6]

The failure to contain judicial abuses of human rights in the 1980s flies in the face of the authorities' efforts, only a few years earlier, to expiate judicial ineptitude and injustice by rehabilitating victims of the Cultural Revolution. In this chapter, we explore some of the results of "severity and swiftness" for the burgeoning reformist judicial system. The provincial higher courts were given considerable authority in Yanda to set procedural and sentencing policy for the lower courts in their province. In this chapter, discussion of reports from contemporary court records in three provinces provides a useful insight for understanding the contradictory hand dealt to the courts: to be at once bastions of professionalism and tools of social control. Each of the three reports from senior judges in the provinces outlines experiments in "flexible" work practices, many of which resulted in miscarriages of justice. We follow with a brief examination of a court in Shaanxi that, unlike the majority of courts in China, was fortunate enough to be visited by an SPC judge who guided the personnel of the court away from the extremities of "severity and swiftness." We then turn to consider some financial, administrative, and political restraints on courts at the time of Yanda, including the lack, or nonexistence, of courtrooms for the majority of courts across the country. We also pursue a discussion of the incongruities and tensions between the rhetoric and reality of Yanda through an examination of the debates on "flexibility" and "principle."

The main argument underpinning the discussion in this chapter is a claim that I make about the general "state of being" in courts at a crucial juncture in PRC legal history, which is that the rationales and strategies engaged to promote social order and social transformation created a set of competing and shifting tensions in criminal court work. These tensions occurred at the level of operation and rhetoric. In this transition phase of PRC history, courts were confronted with a plethora of operational dilemmas brought on by entrenched structures of officialdom. At the rhetorical level, courts had to deal with the imperative of having to carve out a new public persona of authority based on the ethos of reform, while at the same time preserving the mass-line ethos of crime control that had dominated criminal court work since 1949.

Implementing Severity and Swiftness at the Coalface

Redefining Criminality in Liaoning

In Liaoning province, a key response by courts to the call to arms for Yanda in 1983 took the form of a change in the standards by which criminal behavior was measured. Here we consider three types of crimes—theft, rape, and hooliganism—in which the definition of what constituted a crime was amended during the campaign to uphold the Yanda policy of "severity."

Theft

In the three years of Yanda, 35,630 cases of theft were prosecuted, constituting 26.5 percent of all cases. During Yanda, Liaoning courts decided to lower the standards for what they would recognize as an indictable offense of theft. In 1982, the Liaoning Higher Court issued a decision that thieves stealing money or property valued below two hundred yuan (US $30) would not be prosecuted. The decision also differentiated between common theft and major theft. In the cities, the cut-off amount for a crime to be considered a "serious theft" was 2,200 yuan and in rural areas it was 1,800 yuan. During Yanda, however, the amount was lowered to one thousand yuan. Those involved in multiple thefts but who stole less than two hundred yuan would still be indicted on charges of theft as would those guilty of pick-pocketing offenses under two hundred yuan, which were deemed socially threatening.[7] For cases regarded as major theft, the standard was changed from five thousand yuan or more per crime to include cases of multiple theft in which the accumulated sum was at least five thousand yuan, or cases in which the main perpetrator was the ringleader of an organized gang of thieves. These conditions would constitute "aggravating circumstances" in which the circumstances of the crime were considered especially serious. The September 1983 NPC Decision to amend Article 152 of the Criminal Law raised the highest punishment for theft from ten years' imprisonment to the death penalty.[8]

Rape

During Yanda, 14,833 cases of rape were tried in Liaoning, 18.5 percent of all prosecuted crimes. The Liaoning Higher Court's sentencing rationale for rape cases depended on how serious the court deemed the case to be. For cases deemed not to be extremely serious, the sentence would range from three to ten years imprisonment; for cases deemed to be extremely serious, the sentence would range from ten years' imprisonment to the death penalty. The Liaoning Higher Court defined the circumstance of an "extremely serious" rape case in Yanda as including the following conditions:

- the criminal act was particularly cruel or ruthless;
- one perpetrator committed multiple rapes or a gang rape occurred;

- the victim subsequently committed suicide, developed a mental incapacitation or suffered some other serious outcome;
- the act took place in a public arena or the victim was taken from a public place;
- the victim was raped with a bar or such instrument;
- the rape took place consequent to a break and enter theft in the victim's residence;
- other circumstances outlined in Article 139 of the Criminal Law.

Hooliganism

During Yanda, 12,432 cases of hooliganism were tried in Liaoning, 9 percent of all prosecuted crimes. Although hooligan-related cases accounted for a relatively small share of all prosecuted crimes, these crimes were nevertheless regarded as serious because of the public perception of the threat they presented to the community. The NPC "Decision of the Standing Committee of the National People's Congress Regarding the Severe Punishment of Criminals Who Seriously Endanger Public Security" (September 2, 1983) identified ringleaders or members of hooligan gangs who carried lethal weapons as committing crimes of hooliganism that would attract the death sentence. Article 160 of the Criminal Law defined the original sentencing options for hooligan crime as follows:

> Where an assembled crowd engages in affray, creates disturbances, humiliates women or engages in other hooligan activities that undermine public order, if the circumstances are flagrant, the offenders shall be sentenced to fixed-term imprisonment of not more than seven years, criminal detention or public surveillance.

The Liaoning Higher Court clarified for the lower courts certain definitions of hooligan crime and the sentencing options open to them. First, in relation to Article 160 above, the circumstances described in the law as those who "engage in affrays" would be exemplified as two hooligan gangs fighting each other using weapons, resulting in an outcome that could be deemed to have seriously damaged public order, a result whereby members of one or both gangs were injured or died or an innocent bystander was injured or killed. In these circumstances, criminal responsibility would be with both gangs. Second, in relation to the Article 160 reference to "creating disturbances," the Liaoning Higher Court explained that this referred to individuals who, in a public place, committed the following crimes that resulted in a serious threat to public order: assault and battery without cause or reason, jeering and hooting in a public place, stealing or damaging property, or blocking and disturbing traffic.

The Liaoning Higher Court also specifically defined the meaning of "other hooligan activities" in Article 160: "other" activities could include deceiving a number of females into having sexual intercourse, deceiving one female on multiple occasions, or deceiving a female into having sex which resulted in serious harm to a community or resulted in another serious outcome such as the consequent suicide of the victim. The Court also stipulated that the definition of hooliganism could pertain to persons participating in orgies on numerous occasions who, after police warnings, still refused to discontinue the practice, or groups engaging in group sex and where the act results in an extremely negative impact on society. Another type of hooligan crime, according to the Court, is the act of distributing pornographic film or videos on numerous occasions, and refusing to stop this act despite police warnings.[9]

Miscarriages of Justice in Yunnan

Reflecting on its experience during Yanda, the Yunnan Higher Court recorded in its official court history that the August 1983 decision to give basic level courts across the country the authority to try capital cases resulted in a number of serious problems before the policy was reversed roughly three months later. One problem was that, handing down the authority to try serious crimes to the basic courts, instead of hastening the trial process, actually slowed it down, because the intermediate courts still had to review death penalty sentences imposed by the lower courts before these were sent to the Higher Court for final ratification. More importantly, the Higher Court admitted that the quality of judicial decisionmaking could no longer be guaranteed under this system.[10]

Party committees in some counties decided to abandon the system of people's assessors and open trials, and some even disposed of the procuratorate's function in prosecution proceedings, preferring that the PSB take on the role. Others abandoned the system of public defense, and others abolished the collegiate bench, the key system of judicial decisionmaking.

A number of basic level courts made errors in their decisionmaking. Some defendants who were clearly not guilty were convicted. In other cases, the criminal charges in the indictment were incorrect, for example, manslaughter charges were laid instead of assault charges and so forth. In other cases, minor crimes were punished as serious crimes and serious crimes were given light sentences. The main category of cases featuring these mistakes was hooligan crime. For instance, unmarried couples having consensual sex were charged with hooliganism. People were charged incorrectly with hooligan crime and with "interfering with official duties of a state employee." One example is the case of Wang Xianming, who, on January 2, 1983, took his wife and child to the Kunming Children's Shop to buy some firecrackers for New Year's celebrations. He bought some but then wanted to return them, at which time he became involved in a verbal altercation with the shop assistant who telephoned the police. The police officer asked Wang to accompany him to the local police station but Wang refused to go. He then handcuffed Wang and took him to the station where Wang was held in custody for fifteen days before being released. On September 17 that year, months after Wang had been released, the police reviewed the case and asked the procuratorate to agree to formally charge Wang on charges of interfering with the official duties of a state employee. By the trial date of November 3, the prosecution added two more charges, hooliganism and assault. The Kunming Intermediate Court rejected the assault charges but found him guilty of hooliganism and interfering with the official duties of a state employee and handed down a ten-year prison sentence. Wang did not appeal his conviction or sentence. Wang's wife later petitioned the Supreme People's Court (SPC) in Beijing who then notified the Yunnan Higher Court to investigate the case. The Court found that none of the charges should have been laid in the first place. On March 28, 1984, the Intermediate Court overturned the ruling and Wang was completely exonerated. As a result of this misjudged case, the Yunnan Higher Court decided that, from then on, all misdemeanor cases already dealt with by the police before the start of Yanda could not be prosecuted at a later date.[11]

In its official court history, the Yunnan Higher Court identified five key problems with the implementation of Yanda in Yunnan courts. First, during the campaign, judges failed to focus on procedural justice, concentrating mainly on substantive justice. Second, the official responsibilities of judges during trials were not set out in law (the Judges Law was not implemented until the mid-1990s). Third, the process of evidence verification was extremely slow. The prosecution routinely asked the court to accept cases for trial before sufficient evidence had been obtained, assuming that it would be acceptable to wait until the time of the adjudication to complete evidence. In cases where the court discovered problems or contradictions with evidence, the waiting period for correction or verification was very long. Judges busy accepting new cases would often put aside problematic cases. In one such case, the defense pleaded not guilty of rape by reason of mental illness. In Yunnan province in the 1980s, only one mental health institution—the Chengpo Mental Health Institution, controlled by the PSB—had the authority to determine the mental state of criminal defendants pleading mental illness as a defense against criminal responsibility. The court had to wait in line for months to obtain a formal evaluation of the defendant.[12]

The Yunnan Higher Court also recorded how the trial process could be drawn out even longer if contradictory evidence required verification from forensic labs. For example, in 1984, the Honghe Intermediate Court accepted a rape case involving defendant Ma Dingfu. During the trial when evidence was presented to the court, the defendant argued that the shoes that the prosecution claimed were worn by the perpetrator during the attack were not his. The first determination of evidence was made by a PSB forensic expert, but because the defense argued that the PSB was not an independent arbiter for verifying evidence, the PSB was forced to conduct a second test on the shoes. The defense then argued that the local PSB did not have enough authority to determine the ownership of the shoes and insisted that they be sent to Beijing for testing. The PSB in Beijing determined that the defendant could not have been wearing the shoes during the rape incident and the case was returned to the prosecution for further investigation. This three-stage process of verification took two years.

Fourth, in some cases the three organs of the *gongjianfa* had conflicting opinions on the nature of the criminal charge that should be laid. In these cases, the PSB or prosecution often "asked for instructions" (*qingshi*) from the county, municipal, or provincial politico-legal Party representative. This infringed on the independence of the criminal process as it provided an opportunity for people from the Party to pressure courts to accept a case on their—and by extension the Party's—opinion.

Finally, the lack of judicial expertise caused problems for smoothly implementing the Yanda campaign, as can be clearly demonstrated by the example of Lushui Basic Court. During Yanda, this court had only seventeen employees, including only two judges in the criminal division of the court and one court clerk. One of these two judges had very little formal education and did not have even a basic understanding of mathematics. His judgment notices and case file notes were written illogically, and it was difficult for a reader to interpret even the basic gist of the case content he was describing. The facts in the case notes were routinely contradictory, and he routinely took weeks and sometimes months to read pre-trial case details given to him by the prosecution. He wasted valuable time repeatedly asking the prosecution to clarify basic case details. His basic social knowledge was also far below average.[13]

The Trouble with "Severity" in Ningxia

The Ningxia Higher Court reported in its chronicle of court history that Yanda was thrust upon it with little warning. Therefore, in the first offensive, courts made a number of errors manifested in the following practices:

- three criminal justice officials from the three organs of the *gongjianfa* managing cases together (*sanyuan lianhe ban'an*);
- five heads (heads of the three organs of the *gongjianfa*, plus the head of the bureau of justice and the head of civil affairs administration) jointly determining the criminal charge of cases (*wu zhang lianhe ding'an*);
- three committees—the adjudication committee of the court, the PSB committee on reform through labor and re-education through labor, and the procuratorate indictments committee—jointly deliberating cases and approving convictions (*san wei lianhe taolun he pizhun*).[14]

In some cases, the sentence was determined by various committees even before the trial had begun. In other cases, the three committees jointly decided who would be indicted and tried and who would be sent directly to re-education through labor. The "five heads" and "three committee" practices did not conform to the Criminal Procedure Law and resulted in a number of misjudged or erroneous cases. After the first offensive, these practices were abandoned.[15] In all the committees' Yanda work, the main focus was on dealing out severe punishments. The following cases demonstrate how the policy of "severity" was applied to Yanda-related cases, compared to sentencing policy in non-Yanda times.

Case 1

Homicide—Defendant Ma Zhenya was found guilty of shooting two people in a fit of rage, resulting in the death of one of the victims. The Guyuan Intermediate Court sentenced him to death on September 11, 1985. He appealed to the Ningxia Higher Court but the Court upheld the original sentence and he was executed. The court records explain that, in non-Yanda periods, courts in Ningxia generally do not sentence to death those convicted of murder without forethought in cases related to domestic or neighbor disputes, and courts do not normally hand down a death sentence only because the victim later dies from injuries sustained during the incident.

Case 2

Robbery—Defendants Yang Xianming and Li Cun were found guilty of robberies using a knife between April and August 1983. They were found to have stolen the following amounts of money and property on separate occasions: (1) 15.40 yuan; (2) 2.50 yuan; (3) 3 yuan; (4) three watches; and (5) two bicycles. In the course of one of the robberies, they hit a victim over the head with a brick but the victim did not sustain serious injuries. On September 6, 1983, the Yinchuan Intermediate Court sentenced Yang and Li to death. The Ningxia Higher People's Court explains that generally, in non-Yanda periods, if the violence committed in the course of a robbery is not serious, and if the value of the stolen property is minimal, then the suspect is not usually charged with robbery and the case is not prosecuted.[16]

Case 3

Rape—Defendants Jia Dewu (twenty-two years old), Cheng Hufei (eighteen years old), Li Weihong (seventeen years old), Zhang Zhidong (sixteen years old) and others. With the exception of Jia, who was a peasant, all the defendants were school students. On the evenings of January 12 and March 5, 1986, the defendants assaulted four high school girls. Two were sexually assaulted and two were raped. One of the girls was thirteen years old and the others were older. In an unrelated case, Jia also committed an act of robbery on March 6, 1986, stealing 243 yuan. After the assault cases were reported to police, Jia and Li voluntarily surrendered to police on the advice of their parents. The Guyuan Intermediate Court sentenced Jia and Cheng to death. Li was given a death sentence with a reprieve and Zhang was given thirteen years imprisonment. Jia, Cheng, Li, and Zhang all appealed their sentences but the Ningxia Higher Court upheld the original decision. The Ningxia Higher Court records explain that, in non-Yanda periods, criminals who surrender to police in Ningxia are usually given either lenient treatment (*congkuan*) or have their sentence reduced. Moreover, juveniles who commit crimes, regardless of whether they surrender or not, are given lenient treatment or a reduced sentence or are dealt with through the juvenile detention centers. Specifically in relation to sexual assault and rape, if the circumstances of the crime are not serious or if both victim and perpetrator are juveniles, then the courts can give a lenient or reduced sentence.[17]

Case 4

Hooliganism—Defendants Peng Huagong (twenty-one years), Ma Shaojin (twenty years), Guan Suiping (twenty-one years), and seventeen other defendants were members of a hooligan gang. Under the leadership of Guan, Peng, and Ma, the gang instigated a string of street fights in residential areas from July 1982. The most serious occasion involved over forty gang members from opposing gangs using wooden batons and iron rods. Three bystanders sustained minor injuries. With knife in hand, Guan led the gang to an electronics technical college and beat up two students for no apparent reason, as the victims were not known to the perpetrators. One of the victims was injured, requiring eleven stitches in his head. On another occasion, the gang took a homemade pop-gun to a cinema and assaulted strangers outside the venue for sadistic pleasure. On another occasion, at the Bureau of Food and Beverages and later at the local train station, they again assaulted a stranger for sadistic pleasure. In the most serious incident, the gang damaged property in over thirty residences in the course of a street fight. Over the three-hour period, local residents were too petrified to leave their homes, and the gangs stopped fighting only when the police arrived. This gang also committed acts of theft valued at 250 yuan in cash and 1,560 yuan in goods. On December 3, 1983, the Shizuishan Intermediate Court sentenced Guan to death and Peng and the other ringleaders to term imprisonments. All appealed, but the Higher Court upheld the original sentences.

In non-Yanda periods, members of hooligan gangs or individuals classed as hooligans are not usually given the highest penalty under the law. Individuals who commit minor acts are not considered to be members of a gang, and are dealt with administratively. The Higher Court records note that only ringleaders whose actions seriously endanger public order should be punished severely. "Severity" is usually only applied when the act is carried out in a highly crowded public area where the court determines that the threat to the public is grave. But in the case of Guan and the other defendants, the only occasion in which fighting occurred in a public arena was at the cinema. And importantly, Guan did not start a gang fight in this venue; he assaulted only two people, neither of whom were members of rival gangs.[18]

Case 5

Theft—Defendant Wang Dingli was a truck driver for a drug company. In Spring 1983, he broke into the company premises and stole medicine valued at 20,071 yuan. In April 1986, he committed acts of pick-pocketing on three occasions, stealing 229 yuan in cash, two bank passbooks with 27,561 yuan in the accounts, and ration tickets to the value of twenty-five kg of food. At his trial, it was determined that that he stole the money and goods, but he did not attempt to access the bank accounts, nor did he sell the medicine he stole years earlier. He had spent only the 229 yuan in cash. On October 22, 1986, the Yinchuan Court sentenced him to death with a reprieve. Wang appealed but the Higher Court upheld the original sentence. The Ningxia Court records explain that, in non-Yanda periods, when determining the correctness of the charge, the court focuses on the details of the act of theft, and when determining the severity of the crime, the court mainly takes into account the actual amount stolen. In cases where the amount stolen is small or if the concealed booty is not resold or spent, these crimes are not considered a serious threat to the public order. This type of case is usually handled administratively, with the guilty person given a fine or community service, or the person is prosecuted but given a reduced sentence.[19]

Chop-Suey Justice

The accounts above all indicate that, in retrospect, many judges in the higher courts understood the havoc that campaign-style justice could wreak on an emerging "rule of law" in China. Some senior judges right from the start of the campaign saw the potential for miscarriage of justice, speaking out at the start of Yanda to warn lower courts of the impending problems with "severity and swiftness." The account below of a visit by a Supreme People's Court judge to Yulin Intermediate Court in Shaanxi early in the campaign exemplifies this. This judge presciently referred to the Yanda practices of "flexibility" as "chop-suey" (*yiguozhu*) justice.

Yulin Intermediate Court covers a large regional area in the north of Shaanxi province, with twelve basic courts under its guidance. In the three years of Yanda, the intermediate and basic courts of Yulin region tried 2,620 criminal cases involving 2,350 defendants. Of these, 533 cases (787 defendants) were Yanda cases that came under the seven main categories of serious crime. All 787 defendants were convicted as criminals. Over 10 percent of them received either a death sentence or life imprisonment, a much lower rate than in the rest of the country. In 181 cases the convicted criminal formally petitioned the court for a retrial and of these, the court had only finished reinvestigating twenty-three cases by the time the court history was written in 1995. In seven of these cases, which were tried early in the campaign from August to October 1983, the original criminal charge or criminal sentence was later deemed incorrect and was overturned. Procedural irregularities included these practices: "the three heads of criminal justice managing cases together" (*sanzhang lianhe bangong*), "one criminal justice official representing the three arms of criminal justice" (*yi yuan dai san yuan*), and "one head having supervision over a case from start to finish" (*yi ganzi chadao di*). These methods were all used at the time of the Great Leap Forward. The judges of the Yulin Intermediate Court very early in the campaign decided to change their approach to punishing crime while at the same time ensuring that the Party, the local people's congress, and superior courts maintained their leadership role over Yanda work.[20]

The visit to Yulin by one of China's top court officials early in the Yanda campaign was the main reason for the courts' careful planning and execution of the campaign. On October 29, 1983, a Supreme People's Court judge (anonymous in the court history) visited Yulin from Beijing offering detailed guidance on case handling. The judge heard the Intermediate Court's interim report on Yanda in October, read judgment notices from intermediate and basic court trials, and requested the evidence files on these cases. After carefully studying these files, he convened a meeting to confer with and advise staff at the Intermediate Court. He told court staff that they would need to address three key problems in relation to the quality of case management.

First, all cases entering the system were dealt with from beginning to end by a case-handling team (*zhuan'an zu*) comprising a representative from each organ—the police, the prosecution, and the court. The team was responsible for a case as it was processed through the system from the pre-investigation stage to the approval of arrest, prosecution, trial, and sentencing stages. The SPC judge noted that this practice amounts to the *gongjianfa* acting mutually as stand-in for duties that are, for good reasons, normally performed by only one of the three organs, not all three at once.[21]

The second problem was the practice of "one official having supervision over a case from start to finish" (*yi ganzi chadao di*). This system, the SPC judge reminded court staff, abandoned the practice of separating the authority to investigate, prosecute, and judge a case and was thus an unlawful practice. The third problem was that both major (or serious) crimes and minor (or common) crimes were dealt with in a similar fashion. He advised that this amounted to a type of "chop-suey justice" (*yiguozhu*) that seriously damaged the whole concept of "severe strikes on serious crime." How could courts successfully fight Yanda-related crimes severely and swiftly with any precision if they were to handle all cases in the same manner, he asked. The SPC judge insisted on the need to rectify these problems regardless of the policy from which they derived (that is, whether it came from the Party or not), adding that the most basic obligation of courts is to avoid unjust or wrongly tried cases. Using the analogy of a factory assembly line, he explained that the court's tasks came at the end of the assembly line, not all the way through production. This was supposed to ensure that the courts would be accurate and fair in their judgment. He added, "Our part in Yanda's victory is to be able to guarantee quality [that is, accuracy] in case management. At the very least, you need to guarantee that the facts and evidence are basically clear." The Yulin Intermediate Court wrote the judge's remarks into a document and presented it to the district Party committee, the district heads of the procuratorate, the Public Security Bureau, the Court and Bureau of Justice, and all inferior courts that operated under the guidance of the Intermediate Court. The report stated, "From now on, we will take the 'straight and narrow' procedural path to improve the quality of case management."[22]

Thus far, the court histories outlined above represent the struggle between Yanda politics and the court system and the struggle to determine the role of law in a society in the midst of a profound transition to a market economy. Below, we continue the discussion of "chop-suey" justice in the realm of court finances and administration during the time of Yanda.

Courts with No Courtrooms

Re-establishing the system of "open trials" (public hearings) in 1979 was touted as confirmation of the "strengthening of the legal system." It was to confirm that the socialist legal system in China had come of age and joined other modern societies of the twentieth century in promoting a healthy respect for supervision of the public attending trials as a means of improving accountability in the judiciary. This rhetorical commitment to open and accessible trials was not, however, matched by funding commitments to build actual courtrooms for the majority of courts that had been without a permanent place to conduct trials since the founding of the PRC. In Baotou, the Intermediate Court did not receive funding to build its own standard courtroom until 1986. As indicated in Table 6.1, until 1986, the Baotou Intermediate Court had only one 90 square meter non-standard "courtroom" to conduct trials. Trials were also conducted in offices, auditoriums, and other rented premises.

A report by the Supreme People's Court to the State Council in 1983 indicates clearly that the problems of insufficient funding and dearth of courtroom space were widespread in the early to mid-1980s. The "Report on Urgent Measures Needed to Solve Two Key Problems Affecting the Court System," dated October 31, 1983, noted that, although attempts to reconstruct the legal system had been under way for a number of years, there were still a number of serious impediments to the development of the court system. The report stated that this problem

> has become especially apparent since the beginning of the "Strike Hard" (*Yanda*) crackdown on crime in August 1983, in which local courts throughout

> the country witnessed a 10 to 20-fold increase in caseloads. Since the start of the Yanda campaign, the courts have been placed in a situation where they are pushed to complete criminal cases as quickly as possible, and put the handling of civil and economic cases on hold. The problem of lack of courtrooms and funding is exacerbated by the crime situation and has directly impeded the smooth running of the courts.[23]

Table 6.1. Baotou Intermediate Court: Changes in Number and Size of Courtrooms, 1950–1986[24]

Year	Courtroom	Area (sq. meters)
1950	No courtroom	
1956	One courtroom	90
1972	One courtroom	90
1986	One courtroom	225

Source: "Appendix," *The Annals*, 192.

The report revealed that, of the 3,095 courts in China in 1983, only around seven hundred (approximately 25 percent) had actual courtrooms and of these, only a few had enough space for a public gallery. Courts without their own courtrooms had no alternative but to rent or borrow space from other work units or hold court sessions in office spaces. Some courts were even known to hold two trials simultaneously in one room. Other courts were so behind in their disposal of cases due to lack of courtroom space that they could not complete the cases within the time limit stipulated by law.[25]

The courts' funding problem was equally grave. The 1983 SPC report noted that in 1982, the CCP Central Committee had decreed that six areas of court funding were to be guaranteed: office running costs, judicial administration (including case costs), furniture and equipment, training, technical equipment, and basic construction capital. Local governments were not providing enough funding for courts to cover even basic costs, with the result that courts could not perform basic tasks like conducting investigations and holding public sentencing rallies. This led the SPC to request that the State Council approve funding at the provincial level, not at the local level, declaring that "these problems, on the surface, seem like a simple logistical dilemma but, in fact, they directly impinge on the basic running of courts and hence impinge on the people's democratic dictatorship and on the strengthening of the legal system."[26]

The problem of insufficient funding did not improve substantially and, by 1985, the SPC wrote another report authored jointly with the State Planning Commission. This report pleaded for provincial governments to provide funding to local governments that had not provided for the courts in their budgets. The report stated that at the end of 1984, only one thousand of the existing 3,319 courts across the nation had built courtrooms, and even though one hundred and forty courtrooms were being built and plans were under way to build another two hundred, there were still approximately two thousand courts without courtrooms. As the report claimed:

> These courts are holding trials in office rooms, hallways of office buildings and even out in the open, under trees. In these circumstances, it is difficult to expect the public to take courts seriously. It is difficult to enforce court decisions, it is difficult to promote the law and the legal system and it does not reflect well on the courts' status in the wider community and abroad when foreigners involved in court cases are exposed to these conditions.[27]

This concern was mirrored by CCP General Secretary Hu Yaobang who, on January 10, 1985, issued instructions to the relevant governmental bodies to promptly address the problem. He stated that:

> [t]he court system has been neglected for a long time now by the Party. Its buildings, funding and quality of staff are all lower than in other government systems. This is common knowledge. The strengthening of the legal system is currently being promoted. . . . This problem must be solved.[28]

The 1985 joint SPC and State Planning Commission report emphasized the gravity of the situation regarding the lack of credibility of courts without courtrooms. Actually having a courtroom, the report stated, was the most "basic prerequisite for promoting a system of public trials." It went on to declare that:

> the courtroom is the physical representation of the judicial authority of the state. It is the embodiment of the strengthening of the legal system and the embodiment of the sanctity of the law. . . . While it is important to save as much money as possible in building courtrooms, cost saving must not affect the appearance of the court: the buildings must be stately and tasteful in appearance.[29]

While local governments' lack of funds has been a problem for courts, their use of funding as a lever of control over the courts has exacerbated this problem. Here is a case of whoever pays the piper calls the tune. Local governments sometimes deliberately withhold funds from courts to elicit favors, or mete out punishment for court decisions that have upset the local government. He Weifang's 1992 interview with a judge who was formerly a Party secretary brings home the problems of local government responsibility for court funding and how this can affect the court's duties, dignity, and the integrity of court workers. The judge claimed that local government officials often use their control of funding as a lever to influence court actions, making the courts obligated to do favors for local government when required. He noted that the situation can sometimes be avoided if the people's congress appointed an outsider as court president, that is, someone who has risen through the ranks of the judiciary outside the local area and had not tread on the toes of anyone important in the past. The judge noted that, if a court president is not on good terms with the local Bureau of Finance, then the court's funding, court workers' accommodation, and the finances to build courthouses are not guaranteed. The judge advised that, "If the court's decision on a case goes against the interests of the Bureau of Finance, then the procuratorate next door will get the funding for a new office building, not the court." He explained that, if a court president had risen through the ranks of the local court, it would be very difficult for that person to avoid any court case that had a negative impact on the local Bureau of Finance, and it would therefore be difficult for the person as president to maintain a trouble-free relationship with local government. The judge noted that, in the county in which he was Party secretary, the local court did not have a courthouse because of ill will between the court president and the local Bureau of Finance. When he returned to the area two years later, the judge found that the situation had not changed at all. The judge argues that under this type of system it is impossible to promote an ethos of professionalism and procedural propriety when one's very professional existence depends on the proclivities of local officials.[30]

Judges need accommodation, a regular income, and the basics of life. Yet, in many aspects of court life, judges must confront moral dilemmas. These dilemmas can occur, for example, when a judge faces the everyday problems of applying for a residency permit from the local Public Security Bureau, or dealing with the Bureau of Town Planning when applying to purchase land or housing, or even when applying to have electricity connected. He Weifang argued that while such pressures exist it is extremely difficult for even judges with the best intentions to follow the aspirations of professionalism and rectitude and handle cases "strictly in accordance with the law." This situation compounds the vicious cycle that holds down both the social status of judges and societal expectations toward the judiciary. It places judges and other court workers more and more on the periphery of society. A marginalized judiciary is then increasingly vulnerable to the demands and influences of local government officials, which serves to perpetuate the low social status of the judiciary.[31] In the following, we continue the discussion of "chop-suey" justice in relation to the problem of reconciling two disparate Yanda catchcries.

The "Flexibility" and "Principle" Debate

As discussed above, the short-term decline in crime rates was achieved through a flexible approach toward key aspects of criminal court work. One was judicial procedure using "accelerated" and "simplified" trials under a policy of mutual coordination and mutual cooperation between the public security bureau, procuratorate, and courts. Another was in sentencing serious offenders. The approach of "flexibility" in general and of "severity and swiftness" in particular created tension in the judicial realm. The essence of this tension is the incongruous welding of two of the campaign's political catchcries in the 1980s: *yifa congzhong congkuai*. The catchcry signals that courts were to act in accordance with the law (*yifa*), while at the same time employing "swiftness and severity" (*congzhong congkuai*) as their main lever of success.

In Baotou, court workers had a difficult time coming to terms with combining the idea of *yifa* with that of *congzhong congkuai*. However, after intensive discussion, they were won over and came to the conclusion that acting in accordance with the law was not inconsistent with employing "swiftness and severity." It was recorded that some Baotou court workers originally were suspicious of the policy of *congzhong congkuai*, arguing that the concept of "severity" as a punishment rationale already existed within the Criminal Law to the extent that a particularly wide range of punishments was available for all serious crimes. The fact that this concept already existed in law meant that judges already had ample discretionary powers without adoption of a separate policy of *congzhong congkuai*.[32] Although the Baotou workers eventually became reconciled with the idea, the contention surrounding the issue was not resolved so easily in wider operational and jurisprudential circles. Even the writers of an official text on Chinese legal history, *Zhonghua renmin gongheguo fazhi tongshi* (A comprehensive history of the legal system in the People's Republic of China), note that, at the time of the policy's release, a number of judicial personnel believed that the accelerated procedures deprived the defendant of the right to a defense and infringed on the rights of witnesses and other participants in the trial process.[33] Yet, by far the most serious indictment on the legal culture of the early 1980s was the general decline in government and Party respect for the newfound principles of procedural propriety. Political expectations of the judicial organs to deliver severe punishment put the three organs of criminal justice in a position where "no one dares to punish lightly those who should be punished only lightly."[34] For public security scholars like Dai Yisheng, the flexibility of procedural and sentencing practices during this campaign meant that the principles usually attributed to a "rule of law" (regularity, consistency, and stability) were greatly devalued. Dai, who at the time was head of the research unit of the Public Security Bureau, was referring to the explicit requirements during the campaign that the judicial organs mete out more severe punishment to people who, in normal situations, might not be punished. Dai argued that this had serious consequences for public perception of the "rule of law." Although officially the campaigns were seen as a positive outcome of the "rule of law," in internal circles, there were rumblings of discontent. These were not only because of the enormous strain placed on the judicial organs, but more fundamentally because flexibility in the severity of punishment produced inconsistent court judgment that were seen to harm the development of a "rule of law" and, by association, the credibility of the judicial organs.

The unhappy marriage of the concepts *yifa* and *congzhong congkuai* was a contentious issue right from the first attempts to propagate the new term as a catchcry in 1981. A former division head in the Shanghai Intermediate Court, Yang Shi, recalled how he forfeited his career when he took it upon himself to argue against the logic and benefits of *congzhong congkuai* in the early 1980s. Yang's stance against the policy began after the first time that the term was uttered publicly, in an address given by Peng Zhen at the Shanghai Intermediate Court in mid-1980. According to Yang, Peng Zhen, as head of the Politico-legal Committee of the CCP Central Committee, used the term in a call to "hasten the launch of a drive to attack swiftly and severely . . . *in accordance with the needs of the current circumstances*" (*genju xingshi xuyao*).[35] Judge Yang recalls that the reaction of judicial personnel in Shanghai Intermediate Court at the time was to question the logic of stressing the "needs of the current circumstances" as the pivotal point of judicial action. This was because the whole idea of having the Criminal Law in the first place was so that judicial personnel would not simply act willy-nilly "in accordance with the needs of current circumstances," but in accordance with the law.[36]

Judge Yang argues that the concept of acting "in accordance with the needs of current circumstances" (the core rationale for flexibility) has impacted negatively on criminal court work in four different ways. First, the judicial principle of "mutual coordination" between the three arms—in the form of joint case handling groups—has damaged the judicial principle of "mutual restraint."[37] Second, in some areas, there was confusion over what constituted a "serious crime." It meant that some cases involving offenses such as petty theft that would normally have been tried as petty crimes were tried as serious crimes.[38] Third is the overemphasis on "punishment" at the expense of "education." In some areas, "punishment" was given to juvenile offenders when "education" was the more appropriate mode of handling the case.[39] Fourth is the adverse effect of *congzhong congkuai* on judicial independence. In campaigns where the maximum number of convictions possible was sought, many trial judges experienced pressure from their superiors to "act in accordance with the needs of the current circumstances" under the threat of being labeled "rightist." Yang notes that in some cases superiors used their higher positions to command judges to impose a guilty verdict and a heavy sentence on particular targeted categories of crime before a case was even heard.[40]

Yang brought his doubts about handling cases "in accordance with the needs of the current circumstances" to a forum on jurisprudence in Shanghai a month after Peng's visit. Yang argued that, as the manifestation of a broad policy of economic, social, and political development, the Criminal Law was already based on "the needs of the current circumstances," and hence it was not appropriate to amend the law in response to short-term problems in the social order. Moreover, Yang pointed out that, in formulating the Criminal Law, the range of penalties for crimes against the social order—murder, arson, armed robbery, rape, and other serious crimes—was more than adequately catered for in the existing law, and that in formulating such a wide range of punishments the writers of the Criminal Law had already taken into account every possible new need of the current circumstances.[41]

Yang's arguments against the policy, which he discussed at the forum on judicial work, were published by the CCP Central Committee and distributed to courts nationwide as an example of incorrect thinking that was to be held up as a negative model (*fanmian jiaocai*). Although Peng Zhen and the Party Central Committee rejected Yang's stance, the two main authors of the Criminal Law and Jiang Hua, the President of the Supreme People's Court, supported Yang's claims. Although he was "retired" out of the judicial service, Yang's legacy was that, after he initiated this debate, the phrase "in accordance with the needs of current circumstances" was downplayed in media reports and in internal judicial publications, and was replaced with the phrase "severity and swiftness in accordance with the law."[42]

By far the most serious concern of the negative effects of the "severity and swiftness" policy was fear of indiscriminate use of the death penalty, despite official assurances that cases were being handled "strictly according to the law." In a media report published after the climax of the main battle of Yanda in April 1984, the vice-president of the Supreme Court, Zhu Mingshan, boasted:

> the courts are very cautious in handling death sentences. The records are examined by knowledgeable and experienced judges. In some cases, before a death sentence is approved, the court first listens to the opinions of people of various circles through a forum, or gives printed material to the masses for discussion. Time and time again, it has been emphasized that a person's life is of paramount importance. Once a person is executed, he can never regain his life. Not a single mistake should be made. Otherwise, those responsible must take the blame or even bear criminal responsibility. Because the number of death sentences is strictly limited and trials are carried out strictly according to the law, so far as we know not a single prisoner has been wrongly executed.[43]

It is difficult to reconcile Zhu Mingshan's confidence and optimism in due process when we consider the actions and reactions of Party and criminal justice agencies in the first six months of Yanda. An internally circulated response by the Supreme People's Court to questions sent to the Court from higher people's courts exemplifies the widespread confusion about how far to stretch the "severity and swiftness" policy in trials. The types of questions, paraphrased here, asked by higher courts include:

- Is it possible for the court to hand down a death sentence to a juvenile whose crime is especially heinous?
- Is it possible for the court to disregard Article 154 of the Criminal Law and sentence to death a pregnant woman?

- If it is discovered during trial that the defendant is pregnant, can the court procure a forced abortion so that the death penalty can be carried out on the defendant?
- If a defendant who is diagnosed as mentally ill does not show any signs of mental illness while in custody, is it possible for the defendant to be deemed criminally responsible and thus be executed if found guilty?
- In joint criminal cases where the defendants are given various sentences ranging from term imprisonment to the death sentence, within differing appeal periods ranging from three to ten days, is it possible to make the appeal time uniform, that is, either to change the appeal period for all of the cases to either three days or ten days?
- Is it possible to eliminate the collegiate panel for trials?
- If an offender is sentenced to death in the first instance, and indicates that s/he is not intending to appeal the verdict, can the court execute the offender before the allotted three days for appeal?[44]

The crucial problem of Yanda is not what appears to be indiscriminate punishment on the part of individual judges. It is, of course, at a deeper institutional level, that is, the failure to anticipate, prepare for, and cope with intensive socio-economic change. Internally-circulated evaluations of the failure of the Yanda campaign to make any serious alleviation of the crime problem consider both the inevitability of an increasing crime rate in a rapidly developing economy and the inevitability of the failure of criminal justice agencies to "solve" the crime problem given inadequate training and funding of its members. Despite continued reluctance in official rhetoric to admit to the inevitability of increased crime rates in a rapidly changing society, a number of internally circulated documents published after the 1983–1986 campaign paint a more realistic picture.

For example, in an internally circulated document on the development of strategies to deal with crime in coastal regions, a Public Security Bureau report stressed the need for politico-legal organs to understand the reality and inevitability of the political, economic, and social causes of crime generated by economic reform and the modernization drive.[45] The writer suggests first and foremost that political problems have contributed directly to the increased crime rates. Here, he means that structural incongruities between the rapidly changing economic base and the static socialist superstructure of society have created an intense period of social and political contradiction.[46] On how economic factors relate to the increase in crime, the writer notes that increasing income disparity and the accompanying environment of social inequality contribute to increasing crime rates, a problem, the writer notes, that goes hand-in-hand with the increasing privatization of industry and the rapid increase in inflation. Economic factors, along with rapidly changing attitudes toward wealth and the rapid growth of market consumerism, have led to the rise of a popular social maxim "whoever has money has it all."[47] The writer sees that the lack of educational opportunity and growing unemployment have created a "vicious cycle" where "illiterates (*wenmang*) become legal illiterates (*famang*) and then become hooligans (*liumang*)."[48]

Against this backdrop of the political, economic, and social problems of reform, another Public Security Bureau researcher lashed out against the hopeless inadequacy of the three arms of criminal justice, especially the public security organs, to control crime given the inadequacies of resources and expertise. He asserts stridently that the modernization drive has presented the public security organs with new forms of illegality and criminal constituencies whose professionalism and skills far exceed policing capabilities.

> Under these circumstances, the police and cadres are still required to "bring their initiatives into full play" [*fahui jijixing*]. Asking this is like asking us to push an ox into a jar [*qu niu ru weng*] and is paramount to flying in the face of scientific facts. . . . In the years of Yanda, the public security cadres and police have fought a bloodbath [*yuxue fenzhan*]. Some have been killed, some have been injured, some have laboured, and some have become exhausted [*si de si, shang de shang, lao de lao, lei de lei*]. If you ever wanted our initiatives to be "put into play," well there you have it. But what have our blood, sweat and tears been exchanged for? Whatever it is, it certainly has not been exchanged for "grand times of peace" [*tianxia taiping*]. It's created a situation where there are cries of discontent all round saying, "the more you strike, the more chaotic it gets" [*yue da yue luan*]. . . . The "Strike Hard" campaign in reality, is unstrikeable. We need power, but we don't get any. We need money but we don't get it. We need people but we don't get the numbers.[49]

This critique goes some way in casting a realistic picture of the enormous task confronting those responsible for crime control in China. With overwhelming inadequacies, and the scale of crime concomitant with dramatic, unforeseen socio-economic change, criminal justice agencies had little alternative but to cope by applying the principle of "flexibility."

The Paradox of Reform

Two of the enduring themes of both Chinese and Western scholarship on Chinese law over the last two decades have been the debates over what actually constitutes a rule of law in China and to what extent the Chinese legal system reflects the principles and characteristics of a rule of law.[50] Given the discussion in this and the previous chapter on Yanda, reconciling the rule of law debate with the realities of Yanda is a difficult task. It is, however, important to make sense of how the experience of Yanda sits within the promises of legal reform and the rule of law. The explanation of this that I have chosen to pursue is one that focuses on the paradoxes of the wider reform agenda in China and how these paradoxes are reflected in criminal court work. An explanation of this paradox requires us to revisit the discussion in Chapter One.

In Chapter One, I outlined how the criminal courts in post-1978 China had gained a new purpose and status, resting on the tenet that a regulated, stable, and professionalized bureaucratic apparatus would avoid any future political disaster like the Cultural Revolution and help secure the conditions of social and economic stability necessary for the smooth progress of socialist economic reform. Within this context, there developed a definite expectation that legal reform would provide an institutional and technical solution both to the immediate social problems of crime and the long-term regulation of social and economic order. But the rapid economic and social changes initiated by open door reform were accompanied by an equally expeditious growth in crime rates. Despite the new public commitment to "professionalism" and a socialist rule of law, the response of the judicial organs to the threat of social instability in the early 1980s was to utilize a more authoritarian means of crime control modeled on past political campaigns. Therefore, while the call to a socialist rule of law heralded a new public representation of law within a stable, professional, and increasingly autonomous court environment, this representation coexisted with its ideological antithesis: a representation of law as a coercive "command" style of social control.

We have seen this incongruous duality reflected in the programs and policies described in Baotou and other court records. Politico-legal policies aimed at increasing professionalism and the strict adherence to law outlined in Chapter Two, for example, sit uncomfortably alongside policies and programs aimed at encouraging close coordination between the court and other governmental agencies under the rubric of "mutual coordination" and "comprehensive management of public order," as outlined in Chapters Four, Five, and Six. When we look to Yanda, we find that the morally-charged and emotive law and order campaign policies such as "severity and swiftness" (*congzhong congkuai*) also exist uncomfortably alongside rhetoric such as "trying cases in accordance with the law" (*yifa ban'an*).

These tensions and incongruities of criminal court work are a reflection of a wider tension between two key aims of the Chinese reform agenda: political stability and rapid economic growth. In considering how the tensions of the wider reform rationale, process, and rhetoric are reflected in the tensions of criminal court work, we need to understand this nexus between political stability and economic growth as it was conceived in government and Party circles. The two dual imperatives of national reform provoked continuing tensions within the reform and democratization movement. In essence, the tension between reform and stability has its roots in an assumption by the central authorities that law would be the mainframe of the new rule-governed order and hence would be the source of predictability and stability that would attract foreign investment and lay the groundwork for institutional and infrastructural change. Deng Xiaoping's seminal speech, "Emancipate the Mind, Seek Truth from Facts and Unite as One to

Look to the Future," highlighted the perceived necessity of a predictable and stable process for legal development and justice administration as a means of guiding economic reform and institutionalization of a rule of law.[51] The official call at the Third Plenum of the Eleventh Central Committee to strengthen the socialist legal system became a definitional statement of the national objectives of legal reform, elevating the agenda of legal reform to the centerpiece of economic modernization. Again, in January 1986, Deng reiterated the crucial links between economic development, legal reform, social stability, and Party rule:

> Our original idea was right: in our efforts to realize the modernization programme we must attend to two things and not just one. By this I mean that we must promote economic development and at the same time build a legal system. The Party has its discipline and the state has its law. Why is the principle of upholding the people's democratic dictatorship included in the Four Cardinal Principles? It is because if we practice democracy within the ranks of the people without exercising dictatorship over the saboteurs, we cannot maintain political stability and unity or succeed in the modernization drive. . . . We have been fairly successful in economic development, and the economic situation is gratifying. This is quite an achievement for our country. But if standards of social conduct are deteriorating, what's the use of achieving economic development? Worse, deteriorating social standards will in turn lead to a qualitative change in the economy, eventually producing a society in which embezzlement, theft and bribery run rampant. That's why we cannot do without the Four Cardinal Principles, without dictatorship over the saboteurs. This dictatorship can ensure the smooth progress of the drive for modernization and deal effectively with persons whose actions undermine our construction work.[52]

In the 1980s, at the same time as the push to develop a "material civilization" (*wuzhi wenming*), there was an expectation that law would function as a means of engendering democratic ideals in the wider community and hence improve the spiritual lot of the nation. Legislation and programs to encourage procedural regularity were developed and were linked with the attempt to create a codified set of objective social standards by which legality and illegality could be observed and learned by the wider community. Hence, the "systematization of democracy" in law was envisaged as a social process implemented to develop a sense of observance and respect for law amongst the citizenry. In this way, the function of legal reform was seen to move beyond the imperatives of economic modernization as it placed legislative and procedural changes in a moral context of developing a sound spiritual civilization (*jingshen wenming*). The legal reforms were envisaged as part of the benefits that the wider political economic reform process would bring to the development of a new legitimacy and authority for the post-1978 regime. One aspect of this legitimacy was based on the ideology of the Four Cardinal Principles (the most important principle being the dominance of Party leadership) as a rationale for maintaining political stability. The other was the intention to develop mechanisms of legitimization based on the performance and efficiency of government.[53] This put the politico-legal institutions in the country into a state of what He Baogang describes as a "permanent legitimization crisis."[54] Put simply, the development of the economy through restructuring and privatization and the promotion of democratic political structures and processes were frustrated by the failure of government to first anticipate and then to cope with the massive social changes engendered by reform. Social dislocation caused by unemployment and rapid economic readjustment meant that the democratic reform program met, at each turn, a series of limitations on its development.

The limitations engendered by simultaneous demands of stability and reform had a significant impact on the institutions of social control in the reform era. As Michael Dutton has argued:

> The reaction of the Party and the state when faced with demands for greater levels of democratization, has always been to stress the need for social and political stability as a pre-condition for reform. While stability and reform has been the catch-cry of the Party leadership, it has also been the tension between these two demands which has fuelled the constant shifts from reform to reaction in the political arena. This tension is no less apparent in the domain of social control.[55]

This tension between reform and stability is reflected in criminal court work. It is a tension between the promise of government to ensure greater levels of autonomy and professionalism and the simultaneous requirements of courts to play a coercive role in the domain of social control under the leadership of the Party. This tension links directly to the very limitations of the reform and democratization agenda because the call for social and political stability has repeatedly been expounded as a precursor to reform and democratization. Its relationship to the limitations of reform is born out of a continued refusal by central authorities to admit and accept the inevitability of a degree of social instability in an era of rapid social and economic change.

In short, the courts attempted to develop an authoritative persona of professionalism by portraying their authority to administer justice as residing in their legitimate institutional capacity to judge in a regulated and professional manner in accordance with the newly promulgated criminal codes. At the same time, the courts endeavored to construct an authoritative persona by relying on images of justice as derivative of the moral imperative to punish. Hence, while working to secure one representational form of authority based on the moral and punitive requirements of social order, courts also sought to express their source of authority as a reflection of their legitimate institutional capacity as professionalized administrators of justice.

Conclusion

This chapter has explored a number of arenas which demonstrate the dangers of implementing criminal justice policies such as "severity and swiftness" in local courts that were inadequately equipped—professionally, financially, and politically—to live up to the political expectations of Yanda. The political imperative to punish severely and swiftly meant that court workers had to negotiate organizational and political constraints sourced within and beyond the judiciary, while continuing to attempt to professionalize the work of the courts and develop courts' legitimacy as authoritative bodies in the eyes of the public. The experiences in Yunnan, Liaoning, and Ningxia show the hopeless inadequacy of courts to reach the impossible objective of effecting a "complete turnaround in the state of public order."

In the second part of this chapter we explored a problem that made it even more difficult for courts to succeed in reaching Yanda targets. Local government control over court funding and years of insufficient funding rendered the courts beholden to local governments and incapable of operating efficiently and independently of their financiers. Again, we see tension between the reformist expectation of developing institutional autonomy for the courts and the reality of courts' lack of institutional autonomy over their funding and resources. The "flexibility" and "principle" debate for this discussion indicates that the paradoxes of Yanda lay not only in the sphere of grassroots practice but also at the conceptual level. Judge Yang's efforts to expose the contradiction between delivering "severity and swiftness" "in accordance with the law" reveals the inability of political and criminal justice policymakers to come to terms with the tension between the newly touted socialist "rule of law" and the economic and social stresses and strains of a burgeoning socialist market economy.

In many ways, Yanda is an example of the inability of central authorities to come to terms with the nature and consequences of transforming a planned economy into a market economy. This inability has evolved partly from central authorities' struggle to exercise final control over planning, and execution of a reform agenda that is increasingly open to the possibilities of social instability and unrest. This inability and unwillingness to surrender their control reflects the problem that Barry Hindess has identified where "socialists have never entirely trusted the case for the virtues of the invisible hand."[56] As Chinese criminologist Lei Minyuan put it,

> Adam Smith's "invisible hand" of the economy will continue to deeply affect the superstructure of society, whether or not you want it that way, and whether or not you care to admit it. When it comes down to it, economics is the lever of society. It is the motivating force of history. The economy and crime are inseparable.[57]

As we will see in the following chapter, the failure of authorities to acknowledge rapidly increasing crime rates as an inevitable consequence of the reform program has left the politico-legal organs with a tightly limited choice of response to managing crime. The continued implementation of the Yanda-style campaign in the twenty-first century has failed to make a dint on crime rates and has been successful only as a symbol of the draconian "long-arm" of state power and control.

Notes

1. "Summary of Criminal Trial Work," *The Annals*, 29.
2. Zhou Zhenxiang and Shao Jingchun, eds., *Xin Zhongguo fazhi jianshe 40 nian yaolan* (Outline of Forty Years of the Construction of the Legal System in the New China) (Beijing: Qunzhong chubanshe, 1990), 586.
3. Zhou and Shao, *Xin Zhongguo fazhi jianshe 40 nian yaolan*, 586.
4. Han Yanlong, ed. *Zhonghua renmin gongheguo fazhi tongshi* (A Comprehensive History of the Legal System in the People's Republic of China) (Beijing: Zhonghua zhongyang dangxiao chubanshe, 1998), 870–71.
5. Wang Wenhua, et al., "Yunei zhongxingfan yifa zhongda anjian de yuanyin ji duice," (The Causes and Legal Means of Dealing with Major Criminal Cases in Prisons in Accordance with the Law) in *Xinshiqi fanzui gaizao yanjiu* (Studies on Criminal Reformation in the New Age), eds. Yao Yunhui et al. (Beijing: Qunzhong chubanshe, 1991), 349.
6. Gao Zhixuan, "Dangqian jianguan gaizao gongzuo de xin qingkuang xin bianhua jiqi duice," (Emerging Issues and Measures in the Present Day Work of Prison Management and Rehabilitation) in *Xinshiqi fanzui gaizao yanjiu* (Studies on Criminal Reformation in the New Age), ed. Yao Yunhui et al. (Beijing: Qunzhong chubanshe, 1991), 328.
7. Zhao Rixin, ed., *Liaoning shenpanzhi* (unpublished draft, restricted material), 365.
8. Zhao, *Liaoning shenpanzhi*, 366.
9. Zhao, *Liaoning shenpanzhi*, 366.
10. Qiu Chuangjiao, ed., *Yunnan shenpanzhi* (Kunming: Yunnan renmin chubanshe, 1996), 353.
11. Qiu, *Yunnan shenpanzhi*, 353.
12. Qiu, *Yunnan shenpanzhi*, 356.
13. This situation of the judge's lack of schooling was a serious problem for courts nationwide. See He Weifang, "Tongguo sifa shixian shehui zhengyi," *Zouxiang quanli de shidai*, ed. Xia Yong (Beijing: Zhongguo zhengfa daxue chubanshe, 1995), 237–38.
14. Zou Xianchao, ed., *Ningxia shenpanzhi* (Yinchuan: Ningxia renmin chubanshe, 1998), 206.
15. Zou, *Ningxia shenpanzhi*, 206.
16. Zou, *Ningxia shenpanzhi*, 207.
17. Zou, *Ningxia shenpanzhi*, 208.
18. Zou, *Ningxia shenpanzhi*, 209–10.

19. Zou, *Ningxia shenpanzhi*, 210–11.

20. Bai Hucheng, ed., *Yulin diqu shenpanzhi* (Xi'an: Shaanxi renmin chubanshe, 1995), 129–30.

21. Bai, *Yulin diqu shenpanzhi*, 342.

22. Bai, *Yulin diqu shenpanzhi*, 342.

23. "Zuigao renmin fayuan guanyu quanguo fayuan xitong bixu jiejue de liangge wenti de baogao," (SPC Report on Two Problems Relating to the National Court System that Must be Solved) in *Renmin fayuan guanli gongzuo shouce* (Handbook of People's Court Work Management) ed., Zuigao renmin fayuan guanli gongzuo shouce bianxuanbu (Beijing: Renmin fayuan chubanshe, 1998), 1227–28.

24. The appendix note to this page notes that the courtroom which was built in 1986 was originally a large meeting room and therefore does not fit the standard size and dimension requirements of a courtroom.

25. "Zuigao renmin fayuan guanyu quanguo fayuan xitong bixu jiejue de liangge wenti de baogao," 1228.

26. "Zuigao renmin fayuan guanyu quanguo fayuan xitong bixu jiejue de liangge wenti de baogao," 1229.

27. "Zuigao renmin fayuan guanyu quanguo fayuan xitong bixu jiejue de liangge wenti de baogao," 1224–25.

28. "Zuigao renmin fayuan guanyu quanguo fayuan xitong bixu jiejue de liangge wenti de baogao," 1225.

29. "Zuigao renmin fayuan guanyu quanguo fayuan xitong bixu jiejue de liangge wenti de baogao," 1225.

30. He Weifang, "Tongguo sifa shixian shehui zhengyi," (Achieving Justice through the Criminal Justice System) in *Zouxiang quanli de shidai* (Towards an Age of Rights: A Perspective on Civil Rights Development in China), ed. Xia Yong (Beijing: Zhongguo zhengfa daxue chubanshe, 1995), 259. Some court presidents were in a position where they could effectively play the system. He Weifang recalled a report in the national court newspaper *Renmin Fayuanbao* praising a court president for his resourcefulness and ingenuity in gaining funding for a courthouse. The former county Party secretary was transferred to the Lingbao County Basic Court to take up a post as court president in 1984. In the ensuing decade, he made it a priority to maintain goodwill with the four Party secretaries and three county heads who were posted to the area. The local government gave the court president 1.09 million *yuan* to construct a courthouse, and the town in which the court president was originally Party secretary also provided 1.03 million *yuan* in funding for his court. He, "Tongguo sifa shixian shehui zhengyi," 256.

31. He, "Tongguo sifa shixian shehui zhengyi," 261.

32. "Summary of Criminal Trial Work," *The Annals*, 27.

33. Han Yanlong, ed., *Zhonghua renmin gongheguo fazhi tongshi* (A Comprehensive History of the Legal System in the People's Republic of China) (Beijing: Zhonghua zhongyang dangxiao chubanshe, 1998), 871. One of the arguments was that the wording of one section of the September 2, NPC Decision which began with the phrase, "Those offenders who should be given the death penalty" was considered to have implied a presumption of guilt as it was said to assume punishment and sentencing of an offender before guilt was ascertained. One criticism was that such a statement in the September 2 decision impinged on the court's judicial authority to adjudicate independently (p. 871).

34. Dai Yisheng, "Lianghao de kaiduan, kexi de chengjiu" (Good Beginnings, Gratifying Achievements) in *Yanhai diqu gonggong anquan fazhan zhanyue* (The Developing Strategies for Public Security in Coastal Regions), ed. Wang Zhimin and Zhao Ruigang (Beijing: Qunzhong chubanshe, 1989), 22.

35. Yang Shi and Li Ran, "Yifa congzhong congkuai de laili" (The Origins of "Severity and Swiftness in Accordance with the Law") in ***Zhongguo dangdai faxue zhengmin shilu Veritable Records of the Contentions in Jurisprudence in Contemporary China***, ed. Guo Daohui et al (Hunan: Hunan renmin chubanshe, 1998), 277. (my emphasis)

36. Yang and Li, "Yifa congzhong congkuai de laili," 278.

37. Yang and Li, "Yifa congzhong congkuai de laili," 278.

38. Yang and Li, "Yifa congzhong congkuai de laili," 278. Yang notes that the effect of giving across-the-board mandatory heavy sentences is that it denied the use of the lawful considerations normally employed as mitigating circumstances in sentencing considerations. (This includes considerations of preparation of the crime, criminal attempt and discontinuation of a crime, jointly committed crime, and confession.) (p. 278)

39. Yang and Li, "Yifa congzhong congkuai de laili," 279.

40. Yang and Li, "Yifa congzhong congkuai de laili," 279.

41. Yang and Li, "Yifa congzhong congkuai de laili," 280.

42. Yang and Li, "Yifa congzhong congkuai de laili," 281–82.

43. "Handling Crime Strictly According to Law," *Beijing Review* 27, no. 125 (1984): 20.

44. "Zuigao renmin fayuan guanyu renmin fayuan shenpan yanzhong xingshi fanzui anjianzhong juti yingyong falu de ruogan wenti de dafu" (Reply to Certain Questions Regarding the Specific Application of the Law in Major Criminal Cases in People's Courts) (September 20, 1983) in *Zhifa shouce: daji xingshi fanzui zhuanji* (Vol. 4) (Law Enforcement Manual: Combating Crime), ed. Gonganbu zhengce falu yanjiushi (Beijing: Qunzhong chubanshe, 1984), 45–52.

45. Jing Yingming, "Yanhai diqu gonggong anquan fazhan zhanlue de Beijing guandian he moshi," (Background, Issues and Patterns in the Development of Public Security in Coastal Regions) in *Yanhai diqu gonggong anquan fazhan zhanyue* (The Developing Strategies for Public Security in Coastal Regions), ed. Wang Zhimin and Zhao Ruigang (Beijing: Qunzhong chubanshe, 1989), 99.

46. Jing, "Yanhai diqu gonggong anquan fazhan zhanlue de Beijing guandian he moshi," 99.

47. The writer notes also that the conflicts and disputes among individuals that were previously dealt with in work units had now entered the wider social sphere. The problem was that, at the same time, the authority to solve these problems was not transferred from work units to the police. Also see Zhao Zhenjiang, *Forty years of China's Legal System (Zhongguo fazhi sishi nian)* (Beijing: Beijing daxue chubanshe, 1990), 118, for a similar argument.

48. Jing, "Yanhai diqu gonggong anquan fazhan zhanlue de Beijing guandian he moshi," 103.

49. Rao Yingbao, "Hainandao tequ jingji de gonggong anquan bixu qianghua" (Public Security on Hainan Island Special Economic Zone Must be Strengthened) in *Yanhai diqu gonggong anquan fazhan zhanyue* (The Developing Strategies for Public Security in Coastal Regions), ed. Wang Zhimin and Zhao Ruigang (Beijing: Qunzhong chubanshe, 1989), 232.

50. For a discussion of the rule of law debate in China, see Carlos Wing-Hung Lo, *China's Legal Awakening: Legal Theory and Criminal Justice in Deng's Era* (Hong Kong: Hong Kong University Press, 1995). For a discussion of the issue in Western scholarship see Michael W. Dowdle, "Heretical Laments: China and the Fallacies of 'Rule of Law,'" *Cultural Dynamics* 11, no. 3 (1999): 287–314.

51. Deng Xiaoping, *Selected Works of Deng Xiaoping 1975–1984* (Beijing: Foreign Languages Press, 1984), 157–58.

52. Deng Xiaoping, "Talk at a Meeting of the Standing Committee of the Political Bureau of the Central Committee," *Selected Works of Deng Xiaoping Volume III (1982–1992)* (Beijing: Foreign Languages Press, 1994), 156–57.

53. He Baogang defines regime legitimacy as concerning the foundations of the political system. He argues that the self-legitimization of the Deng regime in the reform era contrasts starkly with the form of ideological legitimization employed in the Maoist era. He Baogang, *The Democratisation of China* (London: Routledge, 1996), 195.

54. He Baogang, *The Democratisation of China*, 196. He argues that "the Chinese developmental state has been caught within a set of contradictory imperatives: if it responds to ideological requirements it undermines the rationality of the market economy; and if it responds to economic rationalism, it undermines the ideological legitimization." (p. 196)

55. Michael R. Dutton, *Policing and Punishment in China: From Patriarchy to the People* (Cambridge: Cambridge University Press, 1992), 325. Dutton further explains the legacy of reform as it relates to the institutions of punishment in the reform era. He says that "Politically and socially, reform appears to offer a means by which the spread of the carceral could be halted. On the other hand, the social instability demanded by economic reform strengthens the validity of calls for an extension of the institutions of social control." (p. 325)

56. Barry Hindess, "Imaginary Suppositions of Democracy," *Economy and Society* 20, no. 2 (1991): 81.

57. Lei Mingyuan, "Lun Yanhai diqu jingji fazhan zhanlue yu gongan gongzuo" (On Economic Development and Public Security Work) in *Yanhai diqu gonggong anquan fazhan zhanyue* (The Developing Strategies for Public Security in Coastal Regions), ed. Wang Zhimin and Zhao Ruigang (Beijing: Qunzhong chubanshe, 1989), 132–33.

Chapter Seven

Courts on the Campaign Path in the Twenty-First Century[1]

This chapter explores the ongoing paradoxical and contrasting requirements of courts to be at once politically sound and also "professional" in their duties. For the last three decades now in China, the systematization and institutionalization of democracy in law has been touted as a social engineering process whereby legal institutions would foster a sense of respect for law amongst the citizenry. These expectations of legal reform have also placed legislative and procedural changes in a moral context of developing a sound socialist spiritual civilization (*shehui zhuyi jingshen wenming*). Part of the courts' process of developing sound spiritual civilization involved a call for judicial staff to transform themselves into professionals, to become models of propriety in carrying out and following the law. The development of a new form of judicial authority in courts has depended on the ability of court workers to make convincing claims to their legitimacy as administrators of justice. Therefore, the courts have attempted to establish and cultivate their belief in their own legitimacy by means of securing particular constitutions of *order* in judicial practice and procedure. An important feature of court processes in the 1980s and 1990s, and even more so today, is not just that judicial procedure is organized within the structures of written working rules but that such rules are an important constituent part of the development of authority in the courts.

In the 1990s, major reforms to the trial system, judicial training, professionalism, and judicial qualifications were detailed in a range of new laws that included the Judges Law (1995) and amendments to the Criminal Procedure Law (CPL) (1996), and an "Outline of a Five-Year Reform of the People's Courts" (1999) drawn up by the SPC in 1999. Changes to the trial system set out in the Criminal Procedure Law and the five-year plan are now well documented in the literature on Chinese law.[2] For example, the revised Criminal Procedure Law now substantially reduces the active role of interrogation by the presiding judge during a trial, allowing questioning and cross-examination also to be handled by the prosecution and defense.[3] These revisions, at least in theory, allow for a more adversarial role for defense and prosecution. A clearer division of decision-making powers between single and collegial panels and the adjudication committee and division chiefs means that judges no longer need to seek approval of a division chief or adjudication committee. The panel itself must render a judgment in a court case, and cases are not automatically given to the adjudication committee to decide. However, the adjudication committee may still advise in difficult or complex cases.[4] The revised CPL also allows for summary trials to deal with minor offences.[5] More recent developments include a new expectation that judges write into their judgment notices their legal reasoning and analysis specific to the case, and judgments in important cases are published in the SPC gazette.[6] The Judges Law (1995) and the "Outline of a Five-Year Reform of the People's Courts" (1999) are the two major sources outlining measures to improve professionalism and the quality of judges. The five-year reform plan addresses four key areas that have impeded judicial independence and professionalism:[7]

> (1) local protectionism that seriously undermined the uniformity of law;
> (2) the overall low professional and moral quality of the Chinese judges, which make them prone to corruption and unfit for impartial administration of justice;
> (3) the bureaucratic management model at odds with judicial independence and efficiency;
> (4) the lack of material provisions . . . necessary for the effective functioning of the courts.[8]

These issues are addressed by seven aspects of the reform plan:

> (1) moves to deepen the trial process and case management system including publishing judicial reasoning in cases;
> (2) reorganization of trial organs, including improvements to the selection of judges and division chiefs, and limitations on the role of the adjudication committee;
> (3) reorganization of the judiciary's internal structures, particularly through clearer differentiation between administrative, judicial, and enforcement roles;
> (4) greater emphasis on the management of personnel, including the selection of judges in higher courts from the ranks of lower courts, strict procedures for the selection of judges from the ranks of law graduates, and removal of unqualified judges;
> (5) improvements to the physical conditions of courts, including courtrooms and facilities;
> (6) improvements to and standardization of the system of supervision of judges; and
> (7) proposals by the SPC to amend the Organic Law of the People's Courts to further protect the rights of judges to independently exercise judicial power.[9]

Despite these changes, the judiciary's relationship with Party and government agencies in China today continues to be organized in such a way as to maximize the successful outcomes of state objectives and to accommodate the smooth implementation of Party policy. Under this structure, courts are still perceived "as part of the bureaucracy rather than as an entity constituted outside of the executive."[10] The powers of adjudication, prosecution, and investigation continue to be exercised under the leadership of the Communist Party. Moreover, the organizational and procedural connections between the police, the procuratorate, and the courts still reflect the arrangements of a political structure in which mutual coordination and cooperation were defining characteristics of their inter-organizational relationship. Given this situation, it is not surprising that, when the two-year Yanda campaign was announced in April 2001, the Yanda formats and strategies discussed in the previous chapters were applied chapter and verse to twenty-first century criminal court work.

As noted above, this chapter examines a paradox in the contrasting requirements of courts to be politically sound while also "professional" in their duties. According to the President of the Supreme People's Court (SPC), to be "professional" during Yanda, judges were expected to be the embodiment of fairness and justice, so courts at all levels were told to handle cases in accordance with the law to protect the integrity and constancy of the law. Each judge must be politically and morally upright, professionally disciplined, and incorruptible. Judges' world outlook, values, and in particular, their sense of morality, are perceived as the foundations of justice.[11] While "judges must work within the law, ensure that a case is ironclad and can stand the test of time, and ensure that the spirit of the law is followed in each case,"[12] they are nevertheless expected to advance the cause of Yanda by trying and executing as many serious criminals as possible. Indeed, the main catchcry of Yanda 2001–2003, the slogan "surely, accurately, and relentlessly" (*wen zhun hen*), brings home this contradiction, encapsulating the Janus-face of court work in China: to act surely means that "courts take the initiative to find facts, address new problems, and work out new solutions to ensure that the success of Yanda is not hampered by poor quality court work"; to act accurately means that "courts must handle cases in accordance with the law, strictly following the Criminal Procedure Law"; and to act relentlessly implies that "courts must attack crime within the limits of the law, destroying the seeds of crime, including the 'protective umbrellas' in government and party posts who harbor criminals."[13] This dual requirement of "attacking" the enemies of the state while protecting the integrity of the courts is explored below through an examination of the rationales, strategies, and events of the first months of Yanda 2001–2003.

Yanda 2001–2003 began the way previous campaigns had begun: a national conference on the state of public order was convened. Key personnel from the three arms of criminal justice, the police, procuratorate, and courts made appearances and were informed by experts and politicians that China's crime rate was unacceptably high and that only a nationwide campaign could effect a turnaround in the situation. As noted in Chapter Three, for the first time in a Yanda campaign, the entire national politburo attended, instantly placing the campaign at the top of state priorities for 2001. President Jiang Zemin, delivering the keynote speech, placed the significance of Yanda in the context of the nation's highest interests: preserving the very future of economic reform and, importantly, the future stability of Communist Party rule in China.[14] The conference confirmed that, although criminal justice agencies, government bodies, and Party committees had already adopted a number of effective anti-crime measures in recent years, the fact remained that the total number of criminal cases was on the increase, in particular, violent crimes, crimes committed by Mafia-style Chinese syndicates, and property offenses. Crime statistics were cited to support the argument that only "striking severe blows" would be sufficient to curb rising crime rates: crimes registered by police had reportedly increased 50 percent over 1999 figures, and over the past twenty years, Mafia-style gang crimes had increased sevenfold, and crimes involving bombings had increased 2.6-fold.[15]

The people's courts' involvement in Yanda 2001–2003 began at a national court work seminar held to discuss implementation of the decisions made at the National Conference on Public Order Work. SPC President Xiao Yang clarified the specifics of the Yanda policies: first, setting down the targets of the campaign; second, announcing the strategy of punishing these targets; and third, outlining the magnitude and format of cooperation that courts would lend to the comprehensive organization and promotion of the campaign.[16] Specifically, the policy of "focusing the attack on particular categories of crime" included the three categories outlined in President Jiang's speech the previous day:

- crimes committed by Mafia-style gangs and other organized criminal groups;
- serious violent crimes including bombings, willful murder, armed robbery, and kidnapping;
- crimes such as burglary, theft, and other offenses that "pose a serious threat" to the sense of security of the masses, as well as crimes of corruption involving government and Party officials who act as "protective umbrellas" of organized crime.

In utilizing the processes of adjudication and using legal deterrents to effect "a complete turnaround in social order within two years," SPC President Xiao Yang explained that the strategy of meting out harsh punishments to serious criminal offenders would entail a policy of "severity and swiftness." Importantly, though, Xiao Yang insisted that the policy of striking severely and swiftly must be tempered with a commitment to adjudicate and make decisions with accuracy. Accuracy, he argued, should take top priority, so that while striking severely and swiftly, courts "must continue to ensure that the quality of court work is not compromised."[17] Professional ethics in the judiciary, he insisted, must be taken seriously. All illegal interference from government bodies must be stopped, and judges must be loyal only to the law, processing cases only in accordance with the legal provisions of judicial procedure and with established professional ethical standards.[18]

Punishment and Professionalism in Yanda

However, in contrast to the SPC president's urging that courts proceed with caution in Yanda, taking accuracy and quality as key criteria for adjudication, President Jiang urged criminal justice organs to launch the campaign with an explosion of publicity and propaganda, to arouse "a great momentum."[19] This expression meant gathering criminals in batches, punishing them severely, and propagating the reality of such punishment through public rallies and on the media. Essentially, this was a propaganda tactic to place the Yanda campaign at the forefront of news coverage. As one official media commentary explained, "[w]ithout a strong momentum, it will be difficult to get the desired results. In the current struggle, we must create an awe-inspiring situation."[20]

The great momentum began on April 11, 2001, simultaneously across the nation with a massive show of state force, including public security bureau arrests and public sentencing rallies. As with previous campaigns, the criminal justice organs in Yanda 2001–2003 employed public rallies as the centerpiece of symbolic politico-legal force. On the same day, in keeping with the "great momentum" theme, joint arrest and sentencing rallies were held throughout the country "to formally start [the] large-scale and momentous 'strike hard' anti-crime struggle."[21] Leading the effort were Beijing criminal justice functionaries, with the first batch of jointly-organized rallies occurring at twenty-one districts across the city. Twenty-one district PSB branches and twenty-one basic people's courts simultaneously convened joint public arrest and sentencing rallies, which were said to have "drawn open the curtain of Yanda" in the capital.[22]

"The curtain of Yanda," reported the *People's Daily*, was "drawn open" in Guangdong province also on April 11, with a "Strike Hard public arrest and sentencing rally" at a large sports stadium in the provincial capital, Guangzhou. In the central China city of Chongqing on the same day, PSB personnel publicly arrested ninety-two members of criminal gangs, hooligans, and other suspects, while in the southern city of Fuzhou, one hundred suspects were arrested at a joint arrest and sentencing rally in which twenty-one convicted criminals were sentenced. Similarly, in the northeast of China in Shenyang, one hundred suspects were publicly arrested, while in the northwest in Xi'an, ten criminals were sentenced to death. In the east, in Zhengzhou, seventeen death sentences were announced at a rally in which 164 suspects were publicly arrested.[23] Again, on the same day, courts across Shanghai convened sentencing rallies to publicly sentence 136 convicted criminals involved in seventy-five separate cases including robbery, kidnapping, and other serious violent crimes. The following day, on

April 12, a joint arrest and sentencing rally was convened in Shenzhen at the municipal sports stadium to publicly sentence forty-five convicted criminals, including a number who received death sentences. Prior to the sentencing, the municipal head of the Shenzhen PSB publicly announced the arrest of thirty suspects.[24] More than one thousand eight hundred criminals were executed in the first three months of Yanda 2001, and many of these offenders spent the last remaining hours of their lives at a public sentencing rally.[25]

The first signs of an emerging tension between the dual requirements of courts—to be politically active while remaining accurate and professional—occurred within days of the April 11 "great momentum" drive. SPC President Xiao Yang began delivering a series of speeches across the nation, warning courts that, while they were to punish offenders severely and swiftly, they were nevertheless not to overstep the mark. The single biggest issue that concerned Xiao Yang was the fine line that courts had to tread between the political imperative of striking hard and their own institutional imperative of professionalism. A circular issued by the SPC on April 13 stressed that while courts must "resolutely mete out severe punishments to criminal offenders," they must do so by "seeking truth from facts."[26] Presenting the argument that punishment should be proportionate to the crime, the circular urged courts not to punish all criminals indiscriminately, but to strike hard only at those serious offenders who endangered the social order, specifically, serious or violent offenders belonging to one of the three targeted categories. Notably, the circular emphasized that four criteria or "checkpoints" (*men*) be met when deciding cases: that the courts must guarantee that the basic facts of a case were clear; that basic evidence was sufficient and reliable; that proper legal procedures were followed in accordance with the Criminal Procedure Law; and that substantive laws were applied correctly to each case. In particular, the circular noted that, "cases related to the death sentence should be made irreversible cases with ironclad evidence."[27]

Within five days of the start of the Yanda rallies, subtle cracks began to appear in the rhetoric of unity. On April 18, in a speech published in the national newspaper *Renmin Ribao* (People's Daily), the Shanghai municipal Party secretary informed courts in Shanghai that the three organs of criminal justice in Shanghai, the PSB, the procuratorate, and the courts, were each to be assigned Yanda tasks. The courts' tasks were to hold simultaneously convened sentencing rallies and to mete out the severest punishment possible under law for *each and every* crime brought before the courts.[28] That idea directly contradicted the April 13 SPC circular, which stressed that courts were *not* to indiscriminately give every criminal on trial the maximum punishment allowable. Only those persons guilty of serious crimes were to be punished severely:

> [P]unishments should be commensurate with the crime. It is also necessary to resolutely carry out the criminal case handling policy of combining severe punishments with leniency. For those who should be punished lightly or should be

> exempted from punishment, lenient judgement should be made according to the laws.[29]

To compound the mixed messages on punishment, the Shanghai Party secretary told the Shanghai Higher People's Court to do its bit for Yanda by approving any death sentences coming before it "as swiftly as possible, in order to ensure that the legal effectiveness and social effectiveness of court work are one and the same."[30] In a clear rebuttal of the Party secretary's speech, on the same day SPC president Xiao Yang issued his own remarks, published by the official Xinhua News Agency, stating that as far as the courts were concerned, court work could only ever be socially effective (*you shehui xiaoguo*) "when the facts of a case are clear and when the evidence is irrefutable."[31] In other words, court work cannot be socially effective in reducing crime unless cases are legally credible.

Clearly, what Party committees were telling courts to do was at odds with the SPC's sentencing policy, and more importantly, this contradiction was being played out in the forum of the national press. On April 18, Xiao Yang's speech to courts in Gansu province, during his inspection tour of courts in western China, was released to the media. Here, as in all his public statements at the time, Xiao Yang again emphasized the four checkpoints required for adjudication in each case.[32] Severity of punishment, the SPC president said, could fall only within the legal scale of sentencing options:

> Those whose crime warrants a severe punishment must be punished severely, and those whose crime warrants the death penalty must be given the sentence, but whether or not a particular case actually warrants capital punishment is a decision that each judge must make based on the law.[33]

Courts, Xiao Yang added, must combine the policies and aims of Yanda with the development of judicial professionalism.

While emphasizing professionalism in decisionmaking, Xiao Yang nevertheless did not fail to include an appropriate measure of the mass-line rhetoric that has accompanied all Yanda campaigns in the last twenty years. Declaring that courts must combine professional legal work with the masses' role in the legal system, he reminded the Chinese judiciary that the masses were represented by the Party, adding that in the Yanda campaign, courts must rely on the leadership of the Party and must take the "mass-line" approach to court work. But interestingly, Xiao Yang's interpretation of "Party leadership" and "mass-line" was decidedly minimalist, rhetorically limiting the Party's involvement in cases to the role of handmaiden to the courts. He stated that, where a difficult or complex question arises when adjudicating a case, courts could rely on the local Party committee "who can 'take the mass line' in asking for the public to help, thus ensuring that the facts and evidence are clear and irrefutable." In other words, the

Party's leadership role is to act as a medium between the masses and the courts, but only for the purpose of gathering information about cases.[34]

Despite Xiao Yang's insistence that the quality of all judicial decisionmaking must "stand the test of time," mass rallies were again hurriedly organized across the nation, with huge batches of cases tried and sentenced in an eight-day period from April 17 to 24. The first major group of criminals indicted and tried between April 7–11 was allowed ten days to appeal. During this period, a large number of criminals whose cases had been tried earlier in the month were sentenced to death. Public arrest rallies, sentencing rallies, and joint arrest and sentencing rallies were widespread across China, as reflected in local and national press reports. On the morning of April 17, 125 suspects were paraded in front of a crowd of over ten thousand at an arrest rally in Xinhua Square in the Inner Mongolia city of Huhhot.[35] The following day in Zhanjiang city, Guangdong province, a public arrest rally was held to arrest suspects and announce reform through education policies, terms of imprisonment, and detention of 471 individuals allegedly involved in murder, assault, armed robbery, theft, drug trafficking, rape, and smuggling cases.[36] Again, on the morning of April 18, cities and districts all across Guangdong province simultaneously convened rallies to publicly "deal with" (*chuli*) 5,485 suspects, arresting 2,769 suspects, remanding 1,294 to criminal detention, sending 935 to "reform through education" facilities, and detaining 487 on public-order misdemeanors or to send to detoxification clinics.[37] In Urumqi, in the northwest of China, the local PSB convened a "Yanda public arrest rally" of sixty suspects in the People's Municipal Square, while at the local Tianshan Department Store, a public rally was convened to announce various terms of "reform through education" imprisonment for one hundred and twenty offenders.[38] A joint public arrest and public sentencing rally was convened on the following day in Nanning, Yunnan province, where the PSB announced reform through education prison terms, the procuratorate approved the arrest of a group of suspects, and the court publicly announced a number of sentences including death and life imprisonment. Nearly twenty thousand members of the public and politico-legal functionaries attended the rally.[39] On April 20, courts across Hainan province simultaneously convened sentencing rallies in nine cities and counties, where one hundred and thirty criminals were sentenced. Eleven of these were sentenced to death and immediately executed.[40] On the same day, sixteen criminals were executed in Beijing.[41] Another twelve who were said to have owed society "a mountain of blood debts" were executed.[42]

On April 22, the Beijing No. 1 Intermediate Court publicly pronounced death sentences on six serious offenders. Before execution, all six were reported to have accepted the judgment of the court and expressed remorse for their crimes.[43] On April 23, in courts across Henan province, 1,168 serious criminal offenders were publicly sentenced.[44] In Sichuan province on the same day, the

Provincial Sports Stadium became the focal point of community attention, with the launch of the province's largest sentencing rally since the start of Yanda, with attendance said to be at full capacity of over ten thousand.[45] Latecomers unable to find seating reportedly lined the streets outside the stadium in "eager anticipation" of the one hundred sentencing pronouncements. As soon as Chengdu Intermediate Court Vice-President Mao Shangui announced that the day's agenda included forty-five death penalty pronouncements, the crowd was reported to have "spontaneously broken out in thunderous applause." Lu Zhuo, head of the Sichuan PSB, told reporters that beginning at precisely 10 p.m. the night before, PSB officers across the province had launched "Operation Hurricane B," capturing many criminals who were then publicly arrested at city-wide rallies organized by the police. In Chengdu city alone, it was announced, over four hundred suspects were to be publicly arrested.[46]

Yanda as Success

By mid to late May 2001, national media coverage of the campaign turned from propagating rallies to propagating Yanda successes. These successes were measured in terms of the number of suspects arrested, the number executed, and the number of firearms and explosives confiscated. In a period of five weeks, from April 4 to May 1, the procuratorate approved the arrests of 99,947 suspects across China.[47] By the end of May, more than one thousand criminals had been executed, and for the three-month period from April to the end of June, the total was at least 1,781 criminal executions, according to Amnesty International reports.[48] According to the Legal System News (*Fazhi Bao*), from early April to late May, during police operations to seize explosives and firearms across the country, the PSB was reported to have confiscated 1,600 tons of explosives, 3.5 million detonators, nearly 50 tons of black powder, 330,000 illegal firearms (mostly homemade guns and rifles), and 1.5 million bullets. Authorities cracked more than 35,000 firearms and explosives cases, arresting 63,000 suspects. More than 5,500 individuals in possession of illegal firearms surrendered voluntarily to police, and 72,000 firearms and 186.6 tons of explosives were voluntarily surrendered.[49]

A notice (*tongzhi*) sent out to all provincial criminal justice agencies from the Party Central Committee's "Comprehensive Management of Public Order Committee" in March 2002 noted that Yanda had achieved noticeable successes to date. In 2001, the number of registered criminal cases in China reached 4.45 million. Although this was an increase from the previous year, the percentage rise was much lower than the percentage rise the previous year. In some provinces, the number of registered criminal cases had even dropped, the notice stated. Throughout the nation, there were approximately 2.4 million cases cracked by police). The clear-up rate for cases rose 20.9 percent from the previous year. In addition, there were 545,000 cases (involving 817,000 suspects) already sent to courts, an increase of 19.5 percent over the previous year, which indicated that the rate of prosecutions was quicker than it had been the previous year. The number of criminals formally indicted for prosecution was the highest since 1949. There were 751,000 finalized cases in the court system, a 16.2 percent increase from the previous year. On December 31, 2001, there were 1.507 million prisoners in China—an increase of over sixty-five thousand (3.8 percent) from the previous year—and 317,000 people undergoing re-education through labor, an increase of 15.7 percent.[50] Over two billion Yanda propaganda pamphlets had been distributed in 2001, and five hundred and eight one thousand Yanda exhibitions and information boards had been put on display. The police received five hundred and twenty-three thousand sources of information from the public, and this information led to the cracking of one hundred and eight-four thousand cases.[51]

The notice reported that, in 2001, the crime incident report rate (*fa'an lu*) was still increasing, therefore the Yanda strategy of attacking crime severely and swiftly had become more difficult. The rise in crime was slower in 2001, but the actual number of cases did not decline. Only in three areas did the number of officially registered criminal cases (*li'an*) decline; all other twenty-eight provinces recorded an increase. This situation had to do in part with the crackdown on falsifying crime statistics, but it was mostly due to real increases in crime. Organized group crime and Mafia-style syndicate crime had increased, and the floating population had also contributed to increases in crime. In some areas, crimes committed by the floating population had increased over 70 percent in one year. Increasing unemployment also made the law and order situation more unstable.[52] Violent crime still posed a serious threat to public security. For example, there were 3,317 registered bombing cases, and although this figure constituted a decrease in the actual number of bombings, the damage caused by the crimes was more serious than had been the case in the previous year: 634 people were killed as a result of bombings, an increase of 21.9 percent. Moreover, bombings increasingly occurred in public arenas, therefore resulting in more victims and seriously affecting the public's sense of security. Bombings increased in areas of high unemployment in Henan, Shanxi, Sichuan, Yunnan, and Gansu provinces.

The following year, the committee's notice reporting on Yanda in 2002 noted that Yanda had secured many positive successes that year.[53] The total number of registered crimes in 2002 was 4.3 million, a 2.8 percent drop from the previous year. The number of victims injured during the course of a crime was 221,000, a drop of 4.2 percent, and the number of bombing cases had also dropped 29.5 percent. There were 765,899 people formally charged (512,540 cases), a drop of 5.6 percent from the previous year, which indicated that fewer people were willing to risk committing crimes during the Yanda campaign period. These successes were short-lived. By 2004, the crime rate had again risen to 4.7 million.

The Problems of Campaign-style Justice Today

The above descriptions of the ferocity of the campaign to "severely and swiftly" deal with serious offenders prompt the question of whether these campaigns actually work to reduce the long-term crime rate. Chinese government reports note that in 1996 more than 1.5 million criminal cases were registered in China. By 1998, the figure rose to 2 million, and in 1999, to 2.2 million. By 2000, there was a 50 percent increase from the 1999 rate.[54] Economic and property-related crimes continued to become more violent, more organized, more reliant on corrupt government and Party officials, and in the use of technology in more sophisticated ways. In particular, the emergence of "Mafia-style" criminal gangs (*heishehui xingzhi de fanzui tuanhuo*) and the "protective umbrellas" (*baohu san*) in government and Party posts who harbor and profit from organized crime has sparked this latest state-sponsored moral panic about crime.[55]

But it is not only the contemporary economic climate, the dramatic rise in official corruption, and the increase in population mobility that impacted on the state's decision to "strike hard" in 2001. An entire sector of society has emerged from the economic reform process much worse off than expected, and through criminal activity, this sector of the dispossessed contributes significantly to the decline in social order through criminal activity. Commentary in *Renmin ribao* (The People's Daily) about this explains the emergence of an entire social underclass of people who know that they will never benefit from the open door reforms who have taken up arms against the general public in a show of force to shock the public into acknowledging that many individuals have fallen through the cracks of economic reform. For example, the notorious bombing by Jin Ruchao of apartment blocks in Shijiazhuang early in 2001, which killed 108 people, was said to have been directed not at a particular individual but against society and humanity in general.[56]

Borge Bakken's 2000 study points to another significant reason for the increasing extent and violence of crime in China. It concerns the brutalizing effect of state violence against criminals.[57] The relationship between increasingly violent crimes and an increasingly violent government response to crime in China is, as one media commentator put it, "interdynamic."[58] One simple example of this relationship is the consequence of amending the 1979 Criminal Law to make crimes such as serious theft a capital offense.[59] The certainty that a death penalty would follow for those tried and convicted of a whole range of property-related crimes during Yanda 1983 to 1986 meant that ever more criminals were ever less willing to leave behind any witnesses.[60]

An increasing number of judicial officers, including higher court judges and provincial public security heads, scholars, and other criminal justice professionals who oppose some or all aspects of Yanda, are voicing opinions publicly. Some are being published in law and criminology journals and in the general press. Let us consider a cross-section of the key arguments against Yanda that emerged during and after the latest campaign.

The most common argument against Yanda is that the campaign overemphasizes the idea that punishment is an efficient mechanism of deterrence and crime control. Scholars at one forum on Yanda in Beijing during the latest campaign argued that Yanda has never realized its desired outcome, which is to provide social stability during a time of rapid social transformation. In practice, they argued, Yanda, has lost its purpose and appropriateness and has therefore become an ever less effective means of combating crime. This is because Yanda was established on the basis of a spurious assumption about its deterrence value. Yet the concept of "deterrence value" has many limitations acknowledged by criminologists and practitioners alike. Hence, the Yanda policy of "getting crime under control" (*e'zhi fanzui*) has little long-term efficacy. It is simply not possible to "get crime under control" completely. The deterrence value of Yanda, these scholars maintain, is affected by the law of diminishing returns, which means that the more Yanda tactics are used the less its deterrence effect on would-be criminals.[61]

Another scholar, Sun Guoyang, contends that Yanda's overemphasis on heavy punishment does not deter a large proportion of people who commit crimes. Many crimes are impulsive rather than premeditated, he argues, and those who commit premeditated acts have already thought about how to avoid punishment, whereas those who commit crimes on a compulsion don't think about the punitive consequences beforehand. Therefore, the scare tactics of Yanda have little or no deterrent effect on this category of criminal. Sun asks why despite all Yanda campaigns criminal justice agencies have been unable to break out of the cycle that crime "is still not completely defeated nor completely preventable?" Sun's response is simple: attacking crime does not eliminate crime; the ebbs and flows of crime rates are connected to changing social contradictions in the wider community, so significant benefits in crime reduction cannot come about simply through the efforts of the criminal justice agencies alone.[62]

Although commentators point out that not all crimes during Yanda should be given a harsh sentence, the old Chinese dictum that "In times of chaos, harsh punishment must be used" (*zhiluan shiyong zhongdian*) remains a prominent part of the law and order psyche in China.[63] Sun Guoyang adds that Yanda therefore becomes the stage on which to act out this dictum. The Yanda catchcry to "expand the force of the attack" (*jiada daji lidu*) is applied indiscriminately across all crimes, even those that are not Yanda targets. A few areas even have a quota system with quotas on the minimum number of cases that must result in the death penalty and the percentage of cases that must receive life imprisonment. Courts use these figures to compare sentencing rates in order to assess their degree of "success" in Yanda.[64]

A number of scholars trace the erroneous assumption of Yanda's efficacy as a crime deterrence mechanism to its roots in the traditional idea that severe punishment can eliminate crime. In the traditional Chinese view, criminal law is used as a sword to be wielded in a fight against crime. Since the law was traditionally conceived as a tool to fight and eliminate crime, other important aspects of the law, such as its function in protecting human rights, did not develop in traditional jurisprudential thinking.[65] Other scholars argue that policymakers should reconsider the main objective of the Yanda campaign, which is "to effect a complete turnaround in public order" (*genben hao zhuan*). The idea of *genben hao zhuan* as the basic marker of Yanda success or failure, they argue, has always been a highly subjective and immeasurable concept.[66] In a similar vein, scholars Su Huiyu and Sun Wanhuai point out that, because the traditional motivation behind punishment was to eliminate crime, the intrinsic value of procedural justice had little importance in China. Criminal law was simply a device to determine punishment to prevent crime. They remind us that the idea that crime prevention through punishment could eliminate crime is not simply an historical footnote to current crime policy in China. Yanda policy has as its very roots the ideal that crime can be eliminated, with minimalist concern for procedural justice.[67] In short, Yanda is the historical product of the traditional thinking that, "In times of chaos, use severe punishment to eliminate crime" (*zhi luan shi zhongdian, yong xing chuxing*).

Many in the criminal justice system doubt Yanda's ability to live up to the hype thickly spread about. Lu Zhuo, provincial head of the PSB in Sichuan, for example, commented on the inevitable failure of Yanda in 2001 to effect a long-term turnabout in crime trends. He asked, "If Yanda was such an effective way to control crime then how do you account for the rapid increase in crime rates following every past Yanda campaign?"[68] Or, as another commentator puts it:

> Yanda is overused. This year [2001], Yanda is not well coordinated. It's "hot" at the top and "cold" down at the bottom. On a national level, leaders embrace Yanda enthusiastically but the masses down below are not really "on the move against crime" as the rhetoric would have it. Yanda is a vicious cycle, it's a treadmill that we can't get off. . . . The more we attack, the busier we get, the harder it is to keep up with the attacks, the harder it is to prevent further crimes occurring.[69]

The second main criticism of Yanda is that far too much emphasis is placed on the task of getting a case to the stage of prosecution and far too little placed on the sentencing rationale for individual cases. Judge Li Yuanhe from the Chongqing Higher People's Court and Judge Yu Tianmin from the Chongqing Intermediate People's Court have offered a number of reasons why. First, the scale of penalties in the criminal law is too wide. Furthermore, little importance is attached to mitigating or aggravating circumstances. They note that the common Yanda practice is that so long as the judge has correctly determined the category of crime under prosecution, it makes little difference to the court whether a convicted criminal receives a few more or a few less years of imprisonment, since all penalties are within the legitimate scope of the criminal law. At appeal, or in petition applications from prisoners, the appellate court usually considers only applications in which the sentencing is manifestly incorrect. The appeal is never upheld if the application is to increase or reduce a sentence by a few years.[70] A second problem, the two judges argue, is that, in practice, courts routinely give the heaviest possible penalty under law. They do so for historical and cultural reasons. Court staff would rather be criticized both within and outside the system for handing down heavy sentences rather than sentences that may be deemed too light, for fear of being accused of not properly implementing Yanda policy with the "severity" it entails.[71]

Similarly, Judge Huang Xiangqing from the Shanghai Intermediate Court argued that when the need for severity is invoked during Yanda, mitigating circumstances are seldom considered in sentencing. Courts usually go directly to the heaviest penalty applicable under the law. For instance, in most robbery cases, if the judge does not give more than eight years, the penalty is generally not considered severe enough, because it is considered to be a crime that "seriously endangers public order." Very few robbery cases are given between three and five years, because judges seldom consider three to five years as a long enough sentence, regardless of the actual circumstances of the robbery. All robbery cases are viewed as "seriously endangering public order," therefore, all robbery cases fall within the scope of the Yanda severity and swiftness policy during campaigns, as Yanda is aimed at crimes that seriously endanger public order. Authorities direct that the severity criterion should be applied only during Yanda.[72] But in reality, as Judge Huang asserted in 2001, "severity" has been applied to the crime of robbery continuously for the last ten years.[73] Huang also noted that some court presidents have reported that the lower courts routinely apply the harshest penalty under the law to all targeted criminal categories, disregarding mitigating circumstances in their sentencing. Other presidents report that some courts treat all criminal cases as Yanda targets, including juvenile cases tried during Yanda. One court president refers to their overexuberance in punishing criminals as "Yanda fever," observing how: "They excitedly join the punishment bandwagon as soon as they hear the battle-cry launching a campaign."[74]

A third criticism is that Yanda strategies and rhetoric are outdated, particularly the idea of "relying on the masses" and "mobilizing the masses." The author Sun Guoyang has explained:

> Yanda employs crime control experiences of the past during the time of the planned economy. It is very much colored by the "rule of man" approach together with the mindset of bureaucratism. During the period of the planned economy, when it came to solving contradictions within the people and between the people and the enemy, the government relied not on law but on the power of the bureaucracy. This power came in two main forms: one was to rely on dictatorship and the other was to rely on a high degree of social pressure. There were no laws to rely on in those days, so the country relied on the bureaucracy to solve crime.[75]

Zhao Yuezeng's view expands on this statement. In 2001, he explained that in Yanda 1983, because China was still a planned economy, "mobilizing the masses" was fairly simple and quite effective. But today's social system is very different from then, having undergone a momentous transformation from a planned to a market economy. Mobilizing and organizing the masses have become a difficult task. He argues that subsequently, before participating in any social action, people nowadays first consider their own interests and weigh up the personal benefits of doing so. People nowadays are more concerned about protecting their own rights and want something in return for their participation in social action. Hence, if the *gongjianfa* wants to mobilize the masses, it has to seek support not only from local Party committees and local government but also from foreign companies and joint ventures, community groups, NGOs, and so forth, to stimulate public involvement. Moreover, these days, people expect to compensated for their time.[76] Zhao explained that the approach to 1983 Yanda was to create a great momentum (*shengshi da*) and in Yanda 2001–2003, the Party wanted to continue with this strategy. In 1983 Yanda, however, the targeted criminals, in particular those involved in street crime, were known to police and were fairly easy to catch. But today, with the increasing complexity of crime, the situation is incomparable with that existing in 1983. The old method of creating a momentum dragged criminals before large audiences to sentence them. Other bogus methods of creating a momentum include chasing after small and insignificant cases simply to appear busy, or worse still, taking inmates from prisons and putting them on display if the real crime suspects are not caught within the "expected" time. Zhao attests that Yanda cannot afford to look like a Kungfu scene from Peking Opera.[77]

Finally, some scholars have argued that the neglect of procedural justice damages the integrity of the law and the legitimacy of courts. One higher court president Zhuang Huining has observed this of the first months of Yanda 2001–2003.

> A few months ago, in many areas, courts were parading handcuffed suspects and convicted criminals in trucks. There have even been reports of public executions. The judge asks rhetorically, "We are going backwards. What type of 'social effects' are they talking about here? I'll tell you what kind, it's the social effect of damaging the 'symbolic authority of the law,' that's the effect these practices are having. These people put on parade end up despising the government and resist rehabilitation in prison. This amounts to manufacturing criminals who will end up taking it out on society."[78]

The criminal justice scholar Wang Wenyuan has contended that the problem with the judiciary in China as a result of Yanda is that social control strategies oscillate so dramatically between soft and hard punishment that the legitimacy of the law is damaged. He has claimed two legal principles are relevant to this problem. One is the principle of "equality before the law," and the other is that "so long as the law remains unchanged, its application must be identical from one day to the next." But "if someone is given a three year sentence one morning and someone else is given four years in the afternoon for the same crime, then the law is devalued."[79] In similar vein, Sun Guoyang has explained how the mercurial nature of Yanda diminishes the integrity of the law.

> It is well known that during Yanda, the law is applied much more severely across the entire gamut of crimes, compared to non-Yanda times. This hot and cold approach diminishes people's confidence in the law. People start to realize that the punishment meted out during Yanda is not the punishment that should be given to the crime. You could be mistaken for thinking that these criminals are the sacrificial lambs of politics and society. This not only damages the integrity of the law, it also affects the social outcomes of Yanda. It is not good for long-term social stability.[80]

One major difference between Yanda 1983 and Yanda 2001 is that the voices of discontent could be heard in public forums such as websites and in major newspapers. The tension within the requirement that Yanda be "civilized" yet brutal in force is underscored in a number of newspaper commentaries that have argued against the draconian displays of state violence and the questionable legality of these practices. One newspaper commentator, for example, organized a forum of experts to discuss the legality of the public arrest rally. The commentator quoted a *Beijing Daily* article published on August 3, 2001, which argued that, while motive behind the public arrest rally was positive (that is, to "create publicity, to frighten criminals, and to educate the masses"), the arrest rally nevertheless infringes on the rights of the individual. The commentator argued, "If a suspect who was selected to take part in an arrest rally line-up was subsequently found not guilty of the offence in court, it could very well constitute a case of infringement of the right to reputation" (*mingyuquan*). The commentator argued that, moreover, the public arrest would inevitably lead to an unfair trial, influencing judicial opinion, causing prejudicial judgment in cases where the public display and humiliation of a suspect ignites public indignation. The pressure on a judge to hand down a guilty verdict, he argued, increases dramatically if public concern is sparked by a public arrest rally.[81]

Other legal commentators have argued that, in many places, courts deliberately detain suspects for the maximum fifteen-day limit in order to accumulate a batch of suspects who can be publicly arrested *en masse*. Some courts arrest the suspect more than once and others tie suspects with rope or make them wear prison uniforms onto the rally stage prior to arrest, leading to a presumption of guilt.[82] While these counterviews and arguments are interesting and add to the complexity of Yanda, they are very unlikely to trigger a change in policy toward degradation ceremonies in anti-crime campaigns in China in the short term.

There are many more reasons why the style of campaigning, now standard in all Yanda offensives, is detrimental to the long-term stability and development of the legal system in China. Some commentators have focused on human rights issues associated with public shaming, and others have argued the futility of the death penalty as a deterrence weapon. But perhaps the most damaging argument against Yanda comes from Yanda heartland, in a statement from Lu Zhuo, the Sichuan provincial PSB head. As he assessed, in the midst of the August 2001 campaign, "Our entire crime prevention program revolves around an idea of 'Comprehensive Management of Public Order,' but this policy is completely void of any real and practical crime prevention measures that actually work."[83]

This comment goes to the heart of the problem for the judiciary. Party officials in China have been promising to professionalize the courts' ranks since the early 1980s. But these promises have been made alongside the Party/state's introduction of a draconian set of "law and order" policies that courts at all levels have been required to follow. The policy of "Comprehensive Management of Public Order," that is, close cooperation among police, procuratorate, and Party, has tied the courts to a course of hard-line anti-crime campaigning and rallying that works in direct contradiction to the image of "professionalism" they are attempting to promote.

Clearly, the insistence by Supreme People's Court President Xiao Yang on "accuracy" and professional ethics reflects an understanding that courts in China will not develop credibility and legitimacy which are essential for their effective operation as sources and arbiters of law on the back of draconian Party-imposed law and order campaigns. The conundrum for the judiciary in China is that most of the top judicial officials understand the need for consistency of action and independence from the Party/state. But they are also required to operate in a political system in which they are obligated by law to serve the political interests of the Communist Party. These officials would argue that judicial authority and legitimacy can only ever develop from a comprehensive change in the behavior and attitudes of judges, government, and Party toward a genuine respect for the law.

Conclusion

Crime in China is perceived as a significant threat to the success of economic reform, and thus to the very legitimacy of the post-Deng and post-Jiang regimes. It is this vital link in the perception that economic reform can only be achieved on the basis of social stability and that crime disrupts social stability that explains the Party/state's preoccupation with crimes against the social and public order.[84] This is not a new issue; it has been explored in the literature on Chinese criminal justice since the 1980s. Borge Bakken, for example, has argued that the hard-line tactics of the 1980s crime policy in China were largely a "defense of moral and cultural values at a time of dramatic economic and social change." The Party/state's hard-line response to juvenile and youth crime was, Bakken says, a central theme of the reform period, directly related to the central question of order in society, "a question that should be seen as parallel to the question of economic growth."[85] Running parallel to the central theme of "law and order" in the reform period has been a call to professionalize the judiciary. The CPL, the Judge's Law, and the introduction of strict educational standards for judges all support a continuing commitment to independent and reliable judicial decision-making. Yet courts have not succeeded in changing their organizational culture from one reliant on the rhetoric and organization of the "mass-line" to one that reflects international standards of judicial professionalism.

Yanda strategies such as "severity and swiftness" will probably continue to be employed as the key political response to serious crime in China well into the foreseeable future. The socialist and the traditional Chinese faith in overt acts of public degradation will probably continue to be publicly touted as a key rationale for campaigning well into the next decade. We may expect that this will remain so, even though for more than two decades now, China has existed in an environment in which the "invisible hand" of the market economy is clearly far more powerful in deciding the fate of social order than any hard-line social-control strategies.

Notes

1. Parts of this chapter were previously published in an article form in the following: Susan Trevaskes, "Courts on the Campaign Path: criminal court work in China's 'Yanda 2001' anti-crime campaign," *Asian Survey* 42, no. 5 (2002): 673–93. Copyright © 2002 by the Institute of East Asian Studies.

2. See Ronald C. Keith and Zhiqiu Li, *Law and Justice in China's New Marketplace* (New York: Palgrave, 2001); Randall Peerenboom, *China's Long March toward Rule of Law* (Cambridge: Cambridge University Press, 2002); Yong Zhang, "Recent Developments in Chinese Criminal Justice," *Asia Pacific Law Review* 8, no. 1 (2000): 77–104; Qianfan Zhang, "The People's Court in Transition: The Prospects of the Chinese

Judicial Reform," *Journal of Contemporary China* 12 (2003): 69–101; Chris X. Lin. "A Quiet Revolution: An Overview of China's Judicial Reform," *Asian-Pacific Law & Policy Journal* 4, no. 2 (2003): 293–314.; Jianfu Chen, *Chinese Law: Towards an Understanding of Chinese Law, its Nature and Development* (The Hague/London/Boston: Kluwer Law International, 1999).

3. Zhang, "Recent Developments in Chinese Criminal Justice," 93; Chen, *Chinese Law*, 215; Peerenboom. *China's Long March*, 286.

4. Zhang, "Recent Developments in Chinese Criminal Justice," 94–95; Chen, *Chinese Law*, 215; Peerenboom. *China's Long March*, 286.

5. Chen, *Chinese Law*, 215.

6. Zhang, "The People's Court in Transition," 89.

7. Zhang, "The People's Court in Transition," 87.

8. Zhang, "The People's Court in Transition," 87.

9. Yuwen Li, "Court Reform in China: Problems, Progress and Prospects," in *Implementation of the Law in the People's Republic of China*, ed. Jianfu Chen et al. (The Hague/London/Boston: Kluwer Law International 2002), 74.

10. Kandishka Jayasuriya, "Corporatism and Judicial Independence Within Statist Legal Institutions in East Asia," in *Law, Capitalism and Power in East Asia: The Rule of Law and Legal Institutions*, ed. Kandishka Jayasuriya (London: Routledge, 1999), 195.

11. "Xiao Yang zhichi yanda douzheng bixu tuchu zhongdian, quebao shixian" (Xiao Yang instructs on the necessity of focusing on particular targets and of stressing realistic outcomes), Xinhua News, April 18, 2001 in *Renminwang* (People's Daily Online), <http://www.people.com.cn/GB/shehui/43/index.html> (website hereafter cited as *RMW43*).

12. "Xiao Yang zhichi yanda douzheng."

13. "Xiao Yang zai Shaanxi kaocha fayuan gongzuo shi yaoqiu 'wen zhun hen' quebao yanda douzheng zhiliang" (Xiao Yang on an inspection tour of court work in Shaanxi exhorts court workers to act "surely, accurately and relentlessly" to ensure the success of Yanda), *Renmin ribao* (*People's Daily*), hereafter *RMRB*, April 21, 2001, 2.

14. "National Public Order Work Conference Held in Beijing," Xinhua News, April 3, 2001, in Foreign Broadcast Information Service (FBIS), *Daily Report*, April 3, 2001, at FBIS-CHI-2001-0403, Article Id.: CPP20010403000169.

15. "China Preparing to Wage New 'Strike Hard' Anti-Crime Campaign," Xinhua News Agency, April 5, 2001, in FBIS, *Daily Report*, April 5, 2001, at FBIS-CHI-2001-0405. Article Id.: CPP20010405000107.

16. "Xiao Yang qiangdiao dui yanzhong xingshi zuifan bixu xingcheng dade xingshi zhengzhili he falu weishili" (Xiao Yang stresses the need to use harsh criminal punishment and legal deterrents against serious criminal offenders), Xinhua News Agency, *RMW43*, April 4, 2001.

17. "Xiao Yang qiangdiao dui yanzhong xingshi zuifan bixu xingcheng dade xingshi zhengzhili he falu weishili." For a detailed official analysis of these targets, see benshubianxiezu ed., *Yanda douzheng yu shehui zhi'an ganbu duben* (Readings on the strike hard campaign and comprehensive management of public order) (Beijing: Zhonggong zhongyang dangxiao chubanshe, 2001).

18. "Xiao Yang qiangdiao dui yanzhong xingshi zuifan bixu xingcheng dade xingshi zhengzhili he falu weishili."

19. "Carrying Out the Struggle to 'Strike Hard' and Put Things in Order, Strengthening Public Order Work," Xinhua News, April 3, 2001, in FBIS, *Daily Report*, April 4, 2001, at FBIS-CHI-2001-0404. Also see "Jiang Zemin criticizes local officials on anticrime campaign," Hong Kong Ming Pao (Internet Version-WWW), April 10, 2001, in

FBIS, *Daily Report*, April 10, 2001, at FBIS-CHI-2001-0410. Article Id.: CPP20010410000063.

20. "Carrying Out the Struggle."

21. "Xinhua Round-up on PRC's 'Strike Hard' Anti-Crime Campaign," Xinhua News, April 11, 2001 in FBIS, *Daily Report*, April 11, 2001, at FBIS-CHI-2001-0411. Article Id.: CPP20010411000106.

22. "Beijingshi yanda zhengzhi zhuangxian douzheng quanmian zhankai," (The Yanda Campaign in Beijing is launched extensively throughout the city) in *RMW43*, April 11, 2001.

23. "Xinhua Round-up on PRC's 'Strike Hard' Anti-crime Campaign," Xinhua, April 11, 2001, in FBIS, *Daily Report*, April 11, 2001, at FBIS-CHI-2001-0411. Article Id.: CPP20010411000106.

24. "Shenzhen xuanpan sishiwuming fanzui fenzi," (Forty-five criminals sentenced in Shenzhen) April 12, 2001, *RMW43*.

25. The figure of over eighteen hundred in three months has been calculated by a number of human rights sources, including Amnesty International. See for example, Craig Smith, "Torture Hurries New Wave of Executions in China," *New York Times*, September 9, 2001, 9.

26. "Zuigao fayuan fachu tongzhi yaoqiu geji fayuan xunsu quanli touru yanda, tuchu zhongdian, dachu shengwei," (SPC Circular urges courts to strike swiftly putting all effort into the start of the Yanda campaign, focusing on campaign targets and on gaining popular support) *Guangming ribao* (Enlightenment Daily) April 14, 2001, 1. For an English description of the circular content, see "PRC Circular Urges all Courts to Strike Hard at Gangs, Explosions, Other Crimes," Xinhua News, April 13, 2001, in FBIS, *Daily Report*, April 13, 2001, at FBIS-CHI-2001-0413. Article Id.: CPP20010413000113. Note that "seeking truth from facts" has been a catchcry in legal circles since the days of Yenan. It is an ancient Chinese saying used first by Mao and then appropriated by Deng Xiaoping.

27. "Zuigao fayuan fachu tongzhi yaoqiu geji fayuan xunsu quanli touru yanda, tuchu zhongdian, dachu shengwei," (SPC Circular urges courts to strike swiftly putting all effort into the start of the Yanda campaign, focusing on campaign targets and on gaining popular support) *Guangmng ribao* (Enlightenment Daily), April 14, 2001, 1.

28. "Yanda zhengzhi douzheng quanmian zhankai," (The Strike Hard campaign begins in earnest) *RMRB*, April 18, 2001, 9.

29. "PRC Circular Urges all Courts to Strike Hard at Gangs, Explosions, Other Crimes," Xinhua News, April 13, 2001, in FBIS, *Daily Report*, April 13, 2001, at FBIS-CHI-2001-0413. Article Id.: CPP20010413000113.

30. "Yanda zhengzhi douzheng quanmian zhankai," 9.

31. "Xiao Yang zhichi yanda douzheng bixu tuchu zhongdian, quebao shixian," (Xiao Yang instructs on the necessity of focusing on particular targets and of stressing realistic outcomes) Xinhua News, in *RMW43*, April 18, 2001.

32. "Xiao Yang zhichi yanda douzheng bixu tuchu zhongdian, quebao shixian."

33. "Xiao Yang zhichi yanda douzheng bixu tuchu zhongdian, quebao shixian."

34. "Xiao Yang zhichi yanda douzheng bixu tuchu zhongdian, quebao shixian."

35. "Gongkai deipu 125 ming fanzui xianyiren," (125 suspects publicly arrested) *Zhongguo qingnianbao* (China Youth Daily), April 18, 2001.

36. "Yanda zai xingdong," (Yanda in Action), April 19, 2001, in *Renminwang*, at <http://www.people.com.cn/GB/shehui/44/index.html> (website hereafter cited as *RMW44*).

37. "Guangdong gedi gongkai chuli 5,000 yifan," (Five thousand suspects publicly arrested across Guangdong province), *Renmin ribao: huanan xinwen* (People's Daily: South China News), April 19, 2001, 1.

38. "Urumqishi Yanda douzheng lakai xumu" (The curtain opens on the Yanda Campaign in Urumqi), *RMW43*, April 20, 2001.

39. "Nanning xuanpan yipi zhongda xingshifan," (Batch of Serious Criminal Offenders Sentenced in Nanning), Xinhua News, in *RMW43*, April 19, 2001.

40. "China's Hainan province executes 11 criminals," China News Agency Report, April 21, 2001, in FBIS, *Daily Report*, FBIS-CHI-2001-0421. Article Id.: CPP20010421000101.

41. "Beijing Executes 16 as part of crime crackdown Campaign," Hong Kong AFP, in FBIS, *Daily Report*, April 20, 2001, at FBIS-CHI-2001-0420. Article Id.: CPP 20010420000105.

42. "Yanzheng yanzhong weihai shehui zhian fanzui: yi pi xuezhaileilei de zuifan fufa" (Severely Punishing Crimes that Cause Serious Social Harm: a batch of criminals with a "mountain of blood debts" are executed) in *RMRB*, April 21, 2001, 2; and "PRC Supreme People's Court Announces 12 Executions in 'Strike Hard' Campaign," Beijing Xinhua in English, FBIS, *Daily Report*, April 20, 2001 at FBIS-CHI-2001-0420. Article Id.: CPP20010420000121.

43. "Beijingshi zhaokai shouci yanda gongpan dahui," (Beijing Launches First Major Yanda Sentencing Rallies) in *RMW43*, April 22, 2001.

44. "Henan gongkai xuanpan 1,168 yanzhong xingshi fanzui fenzi," (1,168 Serious Criminal Offenders publicly sentenced in Henan) in *RMW43*, April 23, 2001.

45. "Sichuan 'kuangbiao' xingdong diyiyi," ("Operation Hurricane" Begins in Sichuan) in *RMW43*, April 21, 2001.

46. "Sichuan 'kuangbiao' xingdong diyiyi."

47. "Teshi tezuo, zhongan zhongchu" (Special matters require special handling, serious cases require serious punishment), *Fuzhou renminwang* (Fuzhou People's Daily Online report), May 6, 2001, cited in *RMW43*, May 6, 2001.

48. "Execution Toll Passes 1,000 in Chinese Crackdowns," in *Sydney Morning Herald*, June 11, 2001, 14; and "1,781 Executed in Three-month frenzy: Amnesty," in *The Age* (Melbourne), July 7, 2001, 24.

49. "Gongan jiquan zhibao jiqiang zhuangxian xingdong chu baojie," (Some early victories for PSB operations in seizing explosives and firearms) *Fazhi bao* (Legal System News), June 13, 2001.

50. "Zhongyang shehui zhian zonghe zhili weiyuanhui guanyu yinfa '2001 quanguo shehui zhian xingshi fenxi baogao' de tongzhi," (Notice Concerning the "2001 National Comprehensive Management of Public Order Crime Report" published by the CPC Comprehensive Management of Public Order Committee, March 8, 2002) in *Zhongguo shehui zhian zonghe zhili nianjian 2001–2002* (The Comprehensive Management of Public Order Yearbook for China 2001–2002) (Beijing: Zhongguo changan chubanshe, 2003), 109.

51. "Zhongyang shehui zhian zonghe zhili weiyuanhui guanyu yinfa '2001 quanguo shehui zhian xingshi fenxi baogao' de tongzhi," 109.

52. "Zhongyang shehui zhian zonghe zhili weiyuanhui guanyu yinfa '2001 quanguo shehui zhian xingshi fenxi baogao' de tongzhi," 109–10.

53. "Zhongyang shehui zhian zonghe zhili weiyuanhui guanyu yinfa '2002 quanguo shehui zhian xingshi fenxi baogao' de tongzhi," (Notice Concerning the "2002 National Comprehensive Management of Public Order Crime Report" published by the CPC Comprehensive Management of Public Order Committee, March 14, 2003), in *Zhongguo shehui zhian zonghe zhili nianjian 2003* (The Comprehensive Management of Public Order Yearbook for China 2003), Beijing: Zhongguo changan chubanshe, 2004, 12.

54. Mao Lei et al., "Duiyu fanzui ruguo queshao zhunquede yuce he chongfen de yufang, name, fanji de daijia jiangshi, shifen ang'gui de," (If accurate crime rate predictions and ample crime prevention measures are not applied in earnest, then the cost of all anti-crime activities will soar) *RMRB*, August 8, 2001, 9.

55. Six main kinds of Chinese Mafia-style gang activities dominate the organized crime scene: violent acts of terrorism including murder and robbery; kidnapping, protection rackets involving "godfather" figures who control whole streets, roads, or villages; criminal acts such as obtaining stolen goods by force; hired hit men; and smuggling rackets working with gangs outside China. The most popular type of gangs in recent years are those who control whole industries in one or more local areas. For a detailed analysis of the Mafia-style gang problem in China, see Zhou Liangtuo, "Lun heishehui xingzhi de zuzhi," (On the Organization of Mafia-style syndicates) in *Heishehui xingzhi fanzui wenti yanjiu* (Research Issues on Mafia-style Organized Crime), ed. Li Zhongxin (Beijing: Zhongguo renmin gongan daxue chubanshe, 2000), 43–51.

56. Mao, "Duiyu fanzui ruguo queshao zhunquede yuce he chongfen de yufang, name, fanji de daijia jiangshi, shifen ang'gui de," 9.

57. For a more detailed analysis of this concept, see Borge Bakken, *The Exemplary Society: Human Improvement, Social Control and the Dangers of Modernity in China* (New York: Oxford University Press, 2000), 394.

58. "Duiyu fanzui ruguo queshao zhunquede yuce he chongfen de yufang, name, fanji de daijia jiangshi, shifen ang'gui de," 9.

59. "Decision of the Standing Committee of the National People's Congress Regarding the Severe Punishment of Criminals who Seriously Endanger Public Security," *The Laws of the People's Republic of China (1983–1986)* (Beijing: Foreign Language Press, 1987), 32.

60. For an examination of this problem see, "Yanda zhongdian mubiao er: yanzhong baoli fanzui de fangfan kongzhi" (Yanda Key Target No. 2: prevention and control of serious violent crime) in *Yanda douzheng yu shehui zhi'an ganbu duben* (Readings on the strike hard campaign and comprehensive management of public order) (Beijing: Zhonggong zhongyang dangxiao chubanshe, 2001).

61. Zhao Xichen, "Yanda zhengzhi douzheng lilun yu shijian yantaohui zongshu," (Summary Report of Views on the Theory and Practice of Yanda) *FaxueLuntan* (Legal Forum) 17, no. 4 (2002): 92–93.

62. Sun Guoyang, "Xingshi yitihua shiyexia'yanda' de lixing sikao" (A Reflection on Implementing an Integrated Vision of Criminal Justice work in Yanda Campaigns) *Jiangsu jinggong xueyuan xuebao* (*Journal of the Jiangsu Police Academy*) 4 (2004): 99.

63. Susan Trevaskes, "Severe and Swift Justice in China," *British Journal of Criminology* 47 no. 1 (2007): 23–41.

64. Sun, "Xingshi yitihua shiyexia'yanda' de lixing sikao," 99.

65. Zhao, "Yanda zhengzhi douzheng lilun yu shijian yantaohui zongshu," 92–93.

66. Zhao, "Yanda zhengzhi douzheng lilun yu shijian yantaohui zongshu," 92–93.

67. Huiyu Su and Wanhuai Sun, "Yanda fangzhen de zingshi faxue sikao," (A Reflection on the Jurisprudential Aspects of Yanda Policy) *Faxue* (*Jurisprudence*) 1 (2001): 27.

68. Mao, "Duiyu fanzui ruguo queshao zhunquede yuce he chongfen de yufang, name, fanji de daijia jiangshi, shifen ang'gui de," 9.

69. "Yanda: zouchu sige wuqu," (Yanda: the four main mistakes) *RMRB*, August 8, 2001, 10.

70. Trevaskes, "Severe and Swift Justice in China."

71. Yuanhe Li and Tianmin Yu, "Yanda xingshi zhengce yu xingfa cailiang," (Yanda criminal justice policy and the range of punishment within the law) *Renmin sifa* (People's Justice) 5 (2003): 40.

72. Trevaskes, "Severe and Swift Justice in China," forthcoming.

73. Xiangqing Huang, "Yanda xingshi zhengce de zhangwo," (Understanding Yanda Criminal Policy) *Zhengzhi yu falu* (Politics and the Law) 7 (2001): 24.

74. Huang, "Yanda xingshi zhengce de zhangwo," 24.

75. Sun, "Xingshi yitihua shiyexia'yanda' de lixing sikao," 99.

76. Yuezeng Zhao, "Jianchi Yanda fangzhen, shenhua yanda zhengzhi douzheng," (Maintain Yanda Policy and Deepen the Impact of the Campaign) *Gongan yanjiu* (Public Security Research) 8 (2001): 42.

77. Zhao, "Jianchi Yanda fangzhen, shenhua yanda zhengzhi douzheng," 42.

78. Huining Zhuang, "Renmin fayuan zai yanda zhengzhizhong tuilian duiwu," (The People's Courts Training of Contingents for Yanda) *Liaowang xinwen zhoukan* (*Outlook News Weekly*) 33 (2001): 31.

79. Wenyuan Wang, "Yanda shiyi" (Clearing up Some Doubts about Yanda), *Shehui* (Society) 5 (2005): 46.

80. Sun, "Xingshi yitihua shiyexia'yanda' de lixing sikao," 99.

81. "Gongpu dahui' hecuozhiyou," *Beijing qingnianbao* (Beijing Youth Daily), August 7, 2001. *RMW46* (August 7, 2001).

82. "Gongpu dahui' hecuozhiyou."

83. Cited in Mao, "Duiyu fanzui ruguo queshao zhunquede yuce he chongfen de yufang, name, fanji de daijia jiangshi, shifen ang'gui de," 9.

84. For more detailed analysis of the reform versus stability conundrum, see Michael R. Dutton, *Policing and Punishment in China: From Patriarchy to the People* (Cambridge/Melbourne: Cambridge University Press, 1992); Harold M Tanner, *Strike Hard! Anti-Crime Campaigns and Chinese Criminal Justice 1979–1989* (Ithaca, New York: East Asia Program Cornell University, 1999); Murray Scot Tanner, "State Coercion and the Balance of Awe: The 1983–1986 'Stern Blows' Anti-Crime Campaign," *The China Journal*, 44 (July 2000): 93–125; Borge Bakken, "Editor's Introduction," *Chinese Sociology and Anthropology* 27, no. 3 (Spring 1995): 3.

85. Borge Bakken, "Editor's Introduction," 3.

Chapter 8

Conclusion: Criminal Court Work Then and Now

The guiding rationale of this book is that to understand the Chinese judicial system today we need to understand its underlay. This book has explored criminal court life at a crucial juncture in PRC history: the transition period from the Cultural Revolution to the period of Deng Xiaoping's open reforms from 1979 to 1986. This is because this period of criminal justice in the 1980s set in concrete both the foundations and approaches to criminal justice administration that continue to inform court work today. This crucial period of transition from Maoist-Communism toward a market economy fueled speculation about the possible development of a rule of law in China. Some scholars of post-Mao Chinese law claim there is no Western-style pluralism to enable development of a Western-style rule of law. In this study, I have identified a type of pluralism that is a defining feature of criminal court work in China and is outside the typecast of rule of law. It is a hybridity of authoritarian politics, mass-line justice, and bureaucratic law, institutionalized through the courts.

After rethinking this distinctive context, my approach in this book was to turn to the courts to see what Chinese courts present about themselves and how they do so. This is why *The Annals* and other chronicles are a crucial part of this study. Using *The Annals* and other sources, this study sought to explore how courts rationalize their practices, ergo, how they communicate their vision of law, justice, and punishment to their social audience in a time of far-reaching economic and social reform. To grasp as fully as possible the mechanics of criminal court work and the rationales underpinning it at a crucial juncture in PRC history, we have considered criminal court work in socio-political and historical contexts. *The Annals* gives a fascinating and detailed entree into the mechanics of courts from the inside out and from the outside in: it gives us an ant's eye view from the ground floor of courts and it gives an eagle's view from above by placing local court work in the wider frame of political, economic, and social change in China. It is a springboard for examining the national scene, with local detail that fills in some of the missing pieces of the larger narrative of contemporary history of Chinese courts. Most importantly, *The Annals* gives us a means for understanding the larger history of law, justice, and order in PRC courts. Because the Baotou document was written for professionals in the legal system, it contains the kind of detail missing in this subject from other officially-sanctioned material published for popular consumption. Yet, as an official history, written by people involved in its making, it projects a particular image of criminal court work. This makes *The Annals* both unique and crucial to an understanding of courts in China: it is both a rich reservoir of details and a quality piece of political rhetoric promoting a new vision for court work in the reform era.

The Annals contains a "who's who" of Baotou court staff describing the career paths of court presidents and vice-presidents from 1950 to 1986. These page-long descriptions of each president's and vice-president's employment background neatly parallel the historical path of courts from the politico-military organization in the 1950s and 1960s to a more modern legal institution in the 1980s. The Baotou court's first court president in the PRC, Judge Wu Qinghe, was a government official and a People's Liberation Army (PLA) political instructor in the early 1940s, and was a section head of a county Bureau of Industry and Commerce. Later, he went on to become a local district head of government before being appointed Head Secretary of the Taxation Office in May 1947, and then General Secretary of a municipal government Finance and Economics Committee and Deputy Mayor of Yangquan City. Wu had only a six-year primary school education. The second court president, Judge An Ping, had only a junior high school education. Before becoming court president in 1954, she had held a succession of Party posts. From May 1948 to June 1949, she was Deputy Secretary of the Municipal Party Committee in Haila'er City, and in 1949 was appointed Section Head of the Inner Mongolia Party Committee Organization Department. She was then appointed Party Secretary of a Municipal Party Committee and, following this, was promoted to the position of Vice-President of the Inner Mongolia Higher People's Court, a position she held from April 1953 to May 1954. She was transferred (or possibly demoted) to Court President of the Baotou Municipal Court from June 1954, and in 1958, after her court career, moved back into the position of Party Secretary at the Baotou Medical College.

The first court president in Baotou since 1950 with a university education was Judge Batucang. He had worked for the Public Security Bureau in the 1950s, and from September 1958 to August 1962, studied in Beijing at the People's University. After another stint in the Public Security Bureau in the early 1970s, he was transferred to Baotou Intermediate Court to the position of Court President from October 1974 and remained so for much of the 1980s. He was the first court president to be elected, not appointed, by the Baotou People's Congress, in November 1978.

At first glance, Batucang's appointment to court president seems emblematic of a new era of court work in China. He was educated. He was a product not of the military but of the criminal justice bureaucracy. His Mongolian ethnicity sent a message that the court's make-up in the post-Mao era should represent the majority of the citizens of Baotou, not the Han minority. Yet very few of Batucang's colleagues in Baotou shared his criminal justice background and his educational qualifications. In 1986, only one of the three vice-presidents of the Intermediate Court had a university education, and of the chief judges of judicial divisions, only one had a university education. This situation with senior cadres is certainly not unique to Baotou. Judge Jiang Hua, former Court President of the Supreme People's Court (SPC), made an assessment of the two hundred personnel in the Sichuan Higher People's Court in 1983. His assessment revealed that, of the fifty-six personnel who had a university education, none in the senior ranks of division chief judge or higher had studied law, and not even the court president or vice-president had a university education.[1] Ten years on, in 1993, only 70 percent of higher court presidents had received a tertiary education, and many had no experience as a judge before becoming court president. Of the 30 percent who did not have a tertiary education, only 73 percent described themselves as being familiar or partly familiar with the law. Two of the court presidents who were not familiar with the law had been transferred from the Party Department of Organization and five were Party secretaries transferred from various municipal and regional Party branches.[2]

The chronic shortage of trained and educated judges was one of the main factors contributing to the judiciary's uphill battle to gain recognition as credible and authoritative administrators of justice. But there were a number of other systemic conditions that mitigated against an environment of professionalism that can be attributed to both the longstanding militaristic culture and the "mass-line" culture of court work. A judge, formerly a county Party secretary, interviewed by the Chinese law scholar He Weifang, best explains the militarized and "mass-line" culture of court work.

> The management style of our courts is a kind of "non-professionalised" style of management. Why is it that the measures to reform the judiciary of late have proved so difficult? It is because law in China is a type of "popularized" [*dazhonghua*] law which is "anti-professional" in nature. On the legislative front, [the logic employed is that] the simpler the law is written, the better it is, thus enabling the common folk to better comprehend the law.[3]

We have see throughout this study that popular justice and mass-line politics remained an important part of criminal court work in the post-1978 period as a key rallying point in anti-crime campaigns, because criminal law in this new era continued to be promoted as "collective social order." Yet the *means* by which justice was supposed to be attained was no longer represented in the "uninstutionalized" and unmediated will of the masses. Instead, it was portrayed as professional, and was increasingly institutionalized in the procedural and bureaucratic processes of criminal court work. Here the issue of court authority is vital. The moral authority of socialist legality continued to be represented as a reflection of the will of the masses as the legitimizing force of punishment. However, in the 1980s, judicial authority was reconstructed under a new vision that inextricably tied the authority of the court and its representation to the project of national institutional and political reform. These issues were the main theme of Chapter One.

Chapters Two and Three carried on this theme of judicial authority and how it is represented in the public practices of courts. In Chapter Two, we examined how courts construct and project their authority through propaganda programs and the symbolic rituals of trials. The focus of Chapter Three was on sentencing rallies. We found in both these chapters that the messages of trials and sentencing rallies are surely about law and crime: how the state develops laws to protect and "civilize" citizens, how the state responds to crime, and how crime does not pay. But these messages are also about the court itself. Trials and sentencing rallies provide an arena for courts to showcase their authority and to project that authority to the community. In the 1980s, as is the case today, trials and rallies depicted the authority of courts deriving from the two sources mentioned above. Authority resided in the courts' professional execution of judicial duties in accordance with the law; in Dengist China, socialist law was represented as an organized, systematized, and scientific reflection of the regulative rules of socialist society. But courts simultaneously continued to project their authority to administer justice as a direct expression of the will of the masses. Adjudication and sentencing give expression to this dual message about the source and expression of court authority, as simultaneously representing the "nature" of socialist law (in the form of legal sanctions and procedures) and reflecting popular will.

In Chapters Four, Five, and Six, we found that the court's newfound image of professionalism and procedural propriety was seriously compromised by the draconian practices of anti-crime campaigns, in particular, the Yanda campaign from 1983 to 1986. Here, we highlighted an incongruity between the image of the court as a showcase of procedural propriety and its image as a bastion of hard-line law and order policies. Analysis of the form, rhetoric, limitations, and tensions of anti-crime campaigns found that, in Baotou, as nationwide, the courts' response to the burgeoning crime problem in the post-1978 period was to continue to use mass-line practices of social control to try to accommodate both of the key main imperatives of national reform: political stability and economic growth. In Baotou, as across China, criminal court work was caught between the promises of economic prosperity and the threat of social instability. This fraught position required the criminal courts to be virtually "all things to all people": an increasingly autonomous and thus a legitimate bastion of "rule of law" values; a simultaneous expression of institutional procedural propriety and a raw expression of state power; and a simultaneous embodiment of the virtues of "socialist spiritual civilization" and a protector of "socialist material civilization."

In Chapter Six, we explored the proposition that the tensions and incongruities of criminal court work described in the preceding chapters reflected a wider tension between two key aims of the Chinese reform agenda: political stability and rapid economic growth. These dual imperatives of national reform provoked ongoing tensions within the reform and democratization movement. It was argued that the tension between reform and stability had its roots in an assumption by the central authorities that law would be the mainframe of the new rule-governed order and hence would be the source of predictability and stability that would attract foreign investment and lay the groundwork for institutional and infrastructural change. One aspect of Party/state legitimacy in the Deng era was based on the ideology of the Four Cardinal Principles (the most important principle being the dominance of Party leadership) as a key rationale for maintaining political stability. The other was the objective to develop mechanisms of legitimization based on the performance and efficiency of government. This put the politico-legal institutions in the country into a state of what He Baogang describes as a "permanent legitimization crisis." The reforms were frustrated by the failure of government first to anticipate and then to cope with the massive social changes engendered by the reform agenda itself. Unemployment, social dislocation, and rapid economic readjustment meant that the democratic reform program met, at each turn, a series of limitations on its development. This tension between reform and stability was, and continues to be, reflected in criminal court work. It manifests as a tension between the commission of government to ensure greater levels of autonomy and professionalism and the simultaneous requirements of courts to play a coercive role in the domain of social control under the leadership of the Party. As argued in Chapter Six, it ties in directly to the very limitations of the reform and democratization agenda in the sense that the call for social and political stability has repeatedly been expounded as a precursor to reform and democratization. In short, the dissonance that this examination has emphasized in so many dimensions of criminal court work in the post-1978 period appears to derive from a fundamental shift in national ideology from pre- to post-1978. The type of society to be created under the reform ideology, through marketization and increasing political liberalism, to "develop" and "transform" Chinese society, incorporates economic, political, and legal principles that are at odds with the conception of Marxist principles that dominated national ideology before reform.

The crunch comes and continues to keep coming with attempts to engineer the ideological shift in what are becoming economic, political, and legal marketplaces in the new Chinese national context. Whatever the reform rhetoric "socialist" tries to convey, whether in "socialist modernization," "socialist market economy," or "socialist rule of law," as rhetoric it inevitably collides with practice while an ideological surrogation labeled "reform" uproots the nation from its socialist past.

Baotou Criminal Court Work Today

What do these findings indicate about the operations and rationales of criminal court work in Baotou and in China today? The problems and incongruities of the 1980s have such continuing resonance in criminal court work, that an observer of criminal court work at the time could well appreciate the discussion of criminal justice issues in newspaper editorials and websites two decades later. As Chapter Seven described, in April 2001, a new and larger-than-ever Yanda campaign was announced. The sequencing of the four stages of campaign implementation was remarkably similar to the Yanda campaign in 1983. In Chapter Seven, we have seen in the 2001–2003 Yanda campaign how powerfully the work of PRC criminal courts speaks to their social audience, and how this power is recognized and used explicitly by the state again and again to achieve state objectives. The "curtain of Yanda" was drawn open in early April with mass arrests which were followed soon after by trials and mass sentencing rallies. Thousands were executed in the first three months. According to the president of the SPC in his annual address to the National People's Congress, ninety-eight million members of the public in China attended pubic trials and public sentencing rallies in 2001. Consistently resorting to the potent language and ritual of criminal law and punishment to speak to the people suggests that placing law on display continues to be the *modus operandi* of delivering justice in China. Yet, as outlined in Chapter Seven, there are increasing murmurs within criminal justice circles complaining of the dead weight of shame punishment, and its negative effect on the development of judicial authority in China.

Baotou continues its role as a model court in China and remains a preferred travel destination for visiting politico-legal dignitaries. The court hosts regular visits from top public security and court officials, including visits in 2003 and 2004 from the President of the Supreme Court, Judge Xiao Yang, and the head of the politburo's Politico-Legal Affairs Committee, Mr. Luo Gan. Given Baotou's continued status as a showcase of procedural propriety, it is perhaps not surprising that, in 2003, the No. 1 Criminal Tribunal was awarded a national medal for its exemplary Yanda practices. In order to secure the success of sentencing rallies held on June 26, 2003, to commemorate International Anti-Drugs Day, the No. 1 Criminal Division adjudicated twenty major cases in twenty days. The three most prominent types of cases were crimes involving the manufacturing of drugs, the trafficking of drugs, and the organization of prostitution rings. A fourth prominent crime in the area at the time was fraud. Zhu Xiaoyun, for example, was convicted of committing major fraud involving bank transfers exceeding 112 million yuan. He was executed in 2003.[4]

In 2005, the number of criminal cases adjudicated in Chinese courts declined for the first time since 2000. In 2005, police registered 4.648 million crimes, a small drop of seventy thousand from the previous year.[5] It is interesting to note that this slight decline in adjudicated cases and registered crimes occurred in a "non-Yanda" year. Despite this drop, the figure of over 4.6 million is still startling: crime in China has increased six-fold since 1979.

Evidence that discontent with Yanda tactics is beginning to seep through into the policy rhetoric is demonstrated in the colorful reformist jargon that the Baotou Court president, reporting on the Court's achievements of the previous year, used in his speech to the Baotou People's Congress on March 27, 2006. He informed the congress that the Court placed particular emphasis on strictly observing the law when deciding on the appropriate punishment by ensuring that the punishment meted out corresponded appropriately to the seriousness of the crime committed. He said that leniency and severity were tools that must be used in unison in order to obtain a balanced level of punishments in the spectrum from light to heavy sanctions. He also boasted that in 2005 the Court followed strictly the guiding principle that "only those crimes that are extremely serious should be given severe punishment." The Court, he noted, placed increasingly greater importance on the rights of the individual. Moreover, in 2005, the Court made great strides in overcoming the pervading "culture of excessive punishment" (*zhongxing zhuyi*), upholding the view that not only is the punishment of divesting an individual of his/her right to life the only serious punishment open to courts; the punishment of depriving a criminal of his/her personal liberty should be regarded as a serious alternative.[6]

In Baotou, despite this rhetoric, the culture of the court's identity as an agent of crime control has not changed fundamentally in the years following the first Yanda campaign in 1986. But there is cause for optimism. The Baotou court structure has indeed evolved impressively over the last twenty years to reflect a far more sophisticated system of judicial administration that reflects the demands placed on the court by an increasingly complex economic and social system. In the 1980s, there were eleven internal divisions and offices in the Intermediate Court. In 2006, the Court had eighteen administrative and judicial divisions whose tasks are listed in the Table 8.1.

Of the total of 235 judicial officers employed at the Baotou Intermediate Court in 2006, 61.3 percent now have a university education and thirty-six individuals come from non-Han ethnic backgrounds. There are sixty-four females on staff and thirty-five judicial officers who are not members of the Communist Party. Batucang is now retired, following a long stint in Beijing as deputy head of the National Minority Committee of the China Association of Publishers. The new court president, Zhang Min, holds a master's degree in law from one of the country's top universities, the People's University in Beijing. There are now five vice-presidents, all of whom hold a bachelor's degree. For the first time since 1949, one of the vice-presidents is not a Party member.[7]

Table 8.1. Tasks of Divisions and Offices of the Baotou Intermediate People's Court, 2006

	Division/Office	Tasks
1.	No. 1 Criminal Case Registration Division	Makes decisions about the readiness for trial of all registered criminal cases sent to the court; files cases into the appropriate judicial division; arranges trial dates; decides on the jurisdiction of cases.
2.	No. 2 Criminal Case Registration Division	Deals with retrials and with petitions from prisoners. Responsible for dealing with correspondence and visits from the public.
3.	No. 1 Criminal Tribunal	Adjudicates the following cases at first and second instance: crimes of endangering national security; crimes of endangering public security; crimes against the person; crimes infringing citizens' democratic rights; crimes disrupting the social order, crimes related to national defense; and guidance work over basic-level courts in relation to cases involving the above crimes.
4.	No. 2 Criminal Tribunal	Adjudicates the following cases at first and second instance: crimes of disrupting the order of the socialist market economy; property crimes; crimes of corruption and bribery; other crimes related to property and finance; and guidance work over basic-level courts in relation to cases involving the above crimes.
5.	No. 1 Civil Tribunal	Adjudicates marriage and family-related disputes.
6.	No. 2 Civil Tribunal	Adjudicates corporate disputes.
7.	No. 3 Civil Tribunal	Adjudicates disputes between individuals and corporations.
8.	No. 4 Civil Tribunal	Adjudicates intellectual property disputes; adjudicates disputes between overseas and Chinese corporate parties.
9.	Administrative Law Tribunal	Adjudicates disputes related to administrative law; and compensation claims against government bodies.
10.	Adjudication Supervision Tribunal	Oversees procedural regularity in all the above divisions; supervises the retrial process; supervises decisions involving the reduction of sentences for prisoners and parole.

Table 8.1 (continued)

11. Bureau of Judicial Enforcement	Responsible for enforcement of all property-related civil decisions.
12. Research and Investigations Office	Researches on all areas of judicial experience. Assists basic-level court judges with questions regarding application of the law.
13. Office of Evidence Verification	Performs forensic and other medical examinations; makes estimations on the value of property; verifies death and issues death certificates following the execution of convicted criminals.
14. Office of Court Police	Responsible for: order in the court and general security of the court building; transporting criminals to prison, executes criminals convicted of capital offences.
15. Politics Section	Responsible for matters relating to human resources, staff development, social functions for retired staff, supervising staff birth control and equity issues.
16. Office of Internal Discipline	Investigates bribery claims against judges and other misconduct claims against staff.
17. Court Management Office	Tasks include secretarial functions, organizing law propaganda events, writing and distributing the court newsletter, supervising the distribution of correspondence from superior courts, organizing case files, overseeing library resources, and any computer and technology related tasks and equipment.
18. Administration Office	Organizes payroll and budgets, oversees the use and maintenance of equipment, oversees the canteen and organizes court drivers.

Source: Official Website of the Baotou Intermediate Court: <http://btzy.chinhacourt.org>, accessed on August 15, 2006.

Despite these significant advances in professionalization of staff and specialization of tasks, in Baotou today, and in courts across the nation, "law on display" continues to dictate the narrative and practice of criminal law, at least in the area of punishing serious crime. Despite considerable efforts on the part of Chinese jurists and legal practitioners who continue to advocate for procedural openness and fairness, the political privileging of law as a performative act on display in anti-crime campaigns and in everyday punitive practices will remain a key means of agenda-setting and propagating key programs of crime control.

It may be little wonder, then, that the narrative of criminal court work in China today, as in the post-1978 period, is a story of courts' struggles to reconcile multiple, inconsistent, and ever-changing agendas, as the nation, its institutions, and its people move further ahead with reform. This is less about national development and more about transformation into a very different, very powerful nation, with a distinctive socialist rule of law.

Notes

1. He Weifang, "Tongguo sifa shixian shehui zhengyi," (Achieving Justice through the Criminal Justice System) in *Zouxiang quanli de shidai* (Towards an Age of Rights: A Perspective on Civil Rights Development in China), ed. Xia Yong (Beijing: Zhongguo zhengfa daxue chubanshe, 1995), 237.
2. He, "Tongguo sifa shixian shehui zhengyi," 238.
3. He, "Tongguo sifa shixian shehui zhengyi," 243.
4. <http:// baotou.gov.cn/btrd/rd-fybg.htm> accessed on August 15, 2006.
5. <http://chinacourt.org/public/detail/202090> accessed on August 15, 2006.
6. <http:// baotou.gov.cn/btrd/rd-fybg.htm> accessed on August 15, 2006.
7. <http://btzy.chinhacourt.org> accessed on August 15, 2006.

Glossary of Chinese Terms

beigao	defense
beigaoren	defendant
bianlun	debate
congzhong congkuai	severity and swiftness
dangzu	leading party group
diaocha	inquiry
falu wenmang (famang)	legal illiterate
fazhi xuanchuan	law propaganda work
fazhi	legal system
fazhi	rule of law
gaoji renmin fayuan	higher people's court
gong'anju	public security bureau (PSB)
gongjianfa	public security, procuratorate, and court
gongkai chu'li dahui	public arrest rally
gongkai deipu dahui	public arrest rally
gongkai shenli	open trial/proceedings
gongpan dahui	mass sentencing rally
gongpu gongpan dahui	joint arrest and sentencing rally
gongshen dahui	mass trial
heishehui xingzhi fanzui	Mafia-style crime
jianchayuan	procuratorate
jiceng renmin fayuan	basic people's court
jizhong bingli	concentrated military strength
jizhong gongpan dahui	simultaneously-convened sentencing rally
jizhong tongyi xingdong	intensive united operation
kongsu dahui	accusation meeting
lianhe ban'an	joint handling of cases
liucuan	itinerant criminal
liumang	hooligan
neibu faxing	restricted circulation document
panjue	judgment

pingfan	to redress
qunzhong dahui	mass rally
renmin fating	people's tribunal
sanzhang lianhe bangong	the three heads of criminal justice handling cases together
shehui zhi'an	public order
shehui zhixu	social order
shehui zhi'an zonghe zhili	comprehensive management of public order
shenpan gongzuo	trial work
shenpan weiyuanhui	judicial committee
shenli	to adjudicate
shenpan	court trial
shenpanyuan	judge
sifa duli	judicial independence
taofan	fugitive
tiqian jieru	intervening in a case before the standard time
tongyi xingdong	united operations
wen, zhun, hen	surely, accurately and relentlessly
wenming shenpan	civilized trial
xingerting	No. 2 criminal division
xingyiting	No. 1 criminal division
xuanchuan che	propaganda truck
xuanchuan gongzuo	propaganda work
yanda zhengzhi douzheng	strike hard and rectification struggle
yanda zhihuibu	yanda command post
yanda	strike hard
yifa ban'an	handling cases in accordance with the law
yifa	in accordance with the law
yizhang dai sanzhang	one head representing all three heads
yuanzhang	court president
zhan	battle
zhanguo	fruits of battle
zhanlue bushu	deployment plan
zhanyi	offensive
zhengfa weiyuanhui	politico-legal affairs committee
zhidao gongzuo	guidance work
zhongji renmin fayuan	intermediate people's court
zhuanxiang douzheng	specialized struggle
zhuanxiang gongpan dahui	special sentencing rally
zongjie jingyan	to summarize experience
zuigao renmin fayuan	Supreme People's Court (SPC)
zuigao renmin jianchayuan	Supreme People's Procuratorate (SPP)
zuzhibu	Organization Department

Selected Bibliography

Selected Materials in English

Bakken, Borge. "Crime, Juvenile Delinquency and Deterrence Policy in China." *Australian Journal of Chinese Affairs* 30 (1993): 29–58.

———. "Editor's Introduction." *Chinese Sociology and Anthropology* 27, no. 3 (Spring 1995): 3–18.

———. *The Exemplary Society: Human Improvement, Social Control and the Dangers of Modernity in China.* New York: Oxford University Press, 2000.

———. "Moral Panics, Crime Rates and Harsh Punishment in China." *The Australian and New Zealand Journal of Criminology* 37 (2004): 67–89.

———, ed. *Crime, Punishment, and Policing in China.* Lanham, MD: Rowman & Littlefield, 2005.

Brigham, John. *The Cult of the Court.* Philadelphia: Temple University Press, 1987.

Brown, Ronald. *Understanding Chinese Courts and Legal Process.* The Hague/Boston: Kluwer Law International, 1997.

Carlen, Pat. *Magistrate's Justice.* London: Martin Robertson and Co., 1976.

Chen Xianglong and Qiu Xinlong. "The Relationship between Crime and Punishment." *Social Sciences in China* Third Issue (September 1988): 180–99.

Chen, Albert H. Y. *An Introduction to the Legal System of the People's Republic of China.* Hong Kong: Butterworths, 1992.

Chen, Jianfu Chen et al., eds. *Implementation of Law in the People's Republic of China.* The Hague/Boston: Kluwer Law International, 2002.

Chen, Jianfu. *Chinese Law: Towards an Understanding of Chinese Law, its Nature and Development.* The Hague/London/Boston: Kluwer Law International, 1999.

Chen, Phillip M. *Law and Justice: The Legal System in China 2000 B.C. to 1960 A.D.* New York/London: Dunnellen Publishing Company, 1973.

Cohen, Jerome. *The Criminal Process in the People's Republic of China 1949–63: An Introduction.* Cambridge, MA: Harvard University Press, 1968.

Cohen, Stanley. *Folk Devils and Moral Panics: The Creation of the Mods and Rockers.* New York: St. Martin's Press, 1980.

Cotterrell, Roger. *Law's Community: Legal Theory in Sociological Perspective.* Oxford: Clarendon Press, 1995.

Criminal Law of the People's Republic of China. Beijing: China Legal System Publishing House, 2000.

Criminal Procedural Law of the People's Republic of China. Beijing: China Legal System Publishing House, 1999.

Damaska, Mirjin. *The Faces of Justice and State Authority: A Comparative Approach to the Legal Process*. New Haven/London: Yale University Press, 1986.

Deng Xiaoping. *Selected Works of Deng Xiaoping 1975–1984*. Beijing: Foreign Languages Press, 1984.

———. *Selected Works of Deng Xiaoping Volume III (1982–1992)*. Beijing: Foreign Languages Press, 1994.

Dowdle, Michael W. "Heretical Laments: China and the Fallacies of 'Rule of Law.'" *Cultural Dynamics* 11, no. 3 (1999): 287–314.

Du Xichuan and Zhang Lingyuan. *Chinese Legal System: A General Survey*. Beijing: New World Press, 1990.

Dutton, Michael R. *Policing and Punishment in China: From Patriarchy to the People*. Cambridge: Cambridge University Press, 1992.

———. *Policing Chinese Politics: A History*. Durham, NC: Duke University Press, 2005.

Ericson, Richard V. "Why Law is Like News." Pp. 195–230 in *Law as Communication*, edited by David Nelken. Aldershot: Dartmouth, 1996.

Ericson, Richard V., Patricia M. Barnanek and Janet B. L. Chan, eds. *Representing Order: Crime, Law, and Justice in the News Media*. Buckingham: Open University Press, 1991.

Finder, Susan. "The Supreme People's Court of the People's Republic of China." *Journal of Chinese Law* 7 (1993): 145–224.

Findlay, Mark. "'Independence' and the Judiciary in the PRC." Pp. 281–99 in *Law, Capitalism and Power in East Asia: The Rule of Law and Legal Institutions*, edited by Kanishka Jayasuriya. London: Routledge, 1999.

Garland, David. *Punishment and Modern Society: A Study in Social Theory*. Chicago: University of Chicago Press and Oxford University Press, 1990.

———. "Punishment and Culture: The Symbolic Dimensions of Criminal Justice." Studies in *Law, Politics and Society* 11 (1991): 191–222.

———. *The Culture of Control: Crime and Social Order in Contemporary Society*. Chicago: University of Chicago Press, 2001.

Garland, David, and Peter Young, eds. *The Power to Punish: Contemporary Penalty and Social Analysis*. New Jersey: Humanities Press, 1983.

Grafstein, Robert. "Legitimacy of Political Institutions." *Polity* 14 (1981): 51–70.

Griffin, Patricia. *The Chinese Communist Treatment of Counterrevolutionaries: 1924–1949*. New York: Princeton University Press, 1976.

He Baogang. *The Democratisation of China*. London: Routledge, 1996.

Henry, Stuart, and Dragon Milovanovic. *Beyond Postmodernism*. London: Sage Publications, 1996.

Hunt, Alan. "Dichotomy and Contradiction in the Sociology of Law." Pp. 74–101 in *Marxism and Law*, edited by Piers Beirne and Richard Quinney. New York: John Wiley & Sons, 1982.

Jayasuriya, Kanishka. "Corporatism and Judicial Independence Within Statist Legal Institutions in East Asia." Pp. 173–204 in *Law, Capitalism and Power in East Asia: The Rule of Law and Legal Institutions*, edited by Kanishka Jayasuriya. London: Routledge, 1999.

Keith, Ronald C. *China's Struggle for the Rule of Law*. London: St. Martin's Press, 1994.

Keith, Ronald C., and Zhiqiu Li, *Law and Justice in China's New Marketplace*. New York: Palgrave, 2001.

———. *New Crime in China: Public Order and Human Rights*. London and New York: Routledge, 2006.

Keller, Perry. "Sources of Order in Chinese Law." *The American Journal of Comparative Law* XLII (1994): 711–59.

Lacey, Nicola, Celia Wells, and Dick Meure, eds. *Reconstructing Criminal Law: Critical Perspectives on Crime and the Criminal Process*. London: Weidenfeld and Nicolson, 1998.

Lin, Chris X. "A Quiet Revolution: An Overview of China's Judicial Reform." *Asian–Pacific Law & Policy Journal* 4, no. 2 (2003): 293–314.

Liu Hua. "Hooliganism." *Chinese Sociology and Anthropology* 27, no. 3 (Spring 1995): 57–63

Lo, Carlos Wing-Hung. *China's Legal Awakening: Legal Theory and Criminal Justice in Deng's Era*. Hong Kong: Hong Kong University Press, 1995.

Lubman, Stanley. "Dispute Resolution in China after Deng Xiaoping: 'Mao and Mediation' Revisited." *Columbia Journal of Asian Law* 11, no. 2 (Fall 1997): 229–391.

———. *Bird in a Cage: Legal Reform in China After Mao*. Stanford, CA. Stanford University Press, 1999.

Manning, Peter. *Police Work: The Social Organization of Policing*. Cambridge, MA: MIT Press, 1977.

Mao Tse-tung. "On the People's Democratic Dictatorship." Pp. 411–24 in *Selected Works of Mao Tse-tung Volume 4*. Peking: Foreign Languages Press, 1973.

———. "On the Correct Handling of Contradictions Among the People." Pp. 384–421 in *Selected Works of Mao Tse-tung Volume 5*. Peking: Foreign Languages Press, 1973.

Mathieson, Thomas. "General Prevention as Communication." Pp. 218–37 in *A Reader on Punishment*, edited by R. A. Duff and David Garland. Oxford: Oxford University Press, 1994.

Munro, Donald. *The Concept of Man in Contemporary China*. Ann Arbour: University of Michigan Press, 1977.

———. "Belief Control: The Psychological and Ethical Foundations." Pp. 14–36 in *Deviance and Social Control in Chinese Society*, edited by Amy Auberacher Wilson, et al. New York: Praeger, 1977.

Nathan, Andrew J. *China's Transition*. New York: Columbia University Press, 1997.

Peerenboom, Randall. *China's Long March Toward Rule of Law*. Cambridge: Cambridge University Press, 2002.

———. "Out of the Pan and into the Fire: Well-Intentioned but Misguided Recommendations to Eliminate All Forms of Administrative Detention in China." *Northwestern University Law Review* 98, no. 3 (2004): 991–1104.

Potter, Pitman. *The Chinese Legal System: Globalization and Local Legal Culture*. London and New York: Routledge, 2001.

Sarat, Austin, and Thomas R. Kearns, eds. *Law in Everyday Life*. Ann Arbour: University of Michigan Press, 1993.

———, eds. *Law in the Domains of Culture*. Ann Arbour: The University of Michigan Press, 1998.

Shao Daosheng. *Preliminary Study of China's Juvenile Delinquency*. Beijing: Foreign Language Press, 1992.

Sibley, Susan. "Making a Place for Cultural Analysis of Law." *Law and Social Inquiry* 17 (1992): 39–62.

———. "Ideology, Power, and Justice." Pp. 272–308 in *Justice and Power in Sociolegal Studies*, edited by Bryant G. Garth and Austin Sarat. Evanston, IL: Northwestern University Press, 1998.

Tanner, Harold M. *Strike Hard!: Anti-Crime Campaigns and Chinese Criminal Justice 1979–1985*. New York: East Asia Program, Cornell University, 1999.

Tanner, Murray Scot. *The Politics of Lawmaking in Post-Mao China: Institutions, Processes and Democratic Prospects*. Oxford: Clarendon Press, 1999.

———. "State Coercion and the Balance of Awe: The 1983–1986 'Stern Blows' Anti-Crime Campaign." *The China Journal* 44 (2000): 93–125.

———. "Campaign-style Policing in China and its Critics." Pp. 171–88 in *Crime, Punishment, and Policing in China*, edited by Borge Bakken. Lanham, MD: Rowman & Littlefield, 2005.

The Laws of the People's Republic of China 1983–1986. Beijing: Foreign Language Press, 1987.

Trevaskes, Susan. "Courts on the Campaign Path: criminal court work in China's 'Yanda 2001' anti-crime campaign." *Asian Survey* 42, no. 5 (2002): 673–93.

———. "People's Justice and Injustice: Courts and the Redressing of Cultural Revolution Cases." *China Information* 16, no. 2 (2002): 1–26.

———. "'Strike Hard 2001': form and strategy in a Chinese anti-crime campaign." *Australian and New Zealand Journal of Criminology* 36, no. 3 (2003): 272–92.

———. "Public Sentencing Rallies in China: the symbolizing of punishment and justice in a socialist state." *Crime, Law and Social Change* 39 (2003): 359–82.

———. "Propaganda Work in Chinese Courts: public trials and sentencing rallies as sites of expressive punishment and public education in the People's Republic of China." *Punishment and Society* 6, no. 1 (2004): 5–21.

———. "Severe and Swift Justice in China," *British Journal of Criminology* 47 no. 1 (2007): 23–41.

Trevaskes, Susan, and Mary Farquhar. "Tigers, Pandas and Bears: the making of wildlife protection law in the PRC." *Asia Pacific Law Review* 11, no. 2 (2003): 135–56.

Winn, Peter A. "Legal Ritual." *Law and Critique* 2 (1991): 207–32.

Zhang, Qianfan. "The People's Court in Transition: The Prospects of the Chinese Judicial Reform." *Journal of Contemporary China* 12 (2003): 69–101.

Zhang, Yong. "Recent Developments in Chinese Criminal Justice." *Asia Pacific Law Review* 8, no. 1 (2000): 77–104.

Selected Materials in Chinese

Bai Hucheng, ed. *Yulin diqu shenpanzhi* (Annals of Court Work in Yulin District). Xi'an: Shaanxi renmin chubanshe, 1995).

Baotou fayuanzhi bianxuan weiyuanhui, ed. *Baotou fayuanzhi* (The Annals of the Baotou People's Courts). Neimenggu: Neimenggu chubanshe, 1990.

Chen Zexian, ed. *Sixing zhongwei guanzhu de jiaodian* (The Death Penalty and its Control: A Global Focus). Beijing: Gongan daxue chubanshe, 2005.

Dai Ruilin, ed. *Hebeisheng shenpanzhi* (Annals of Trial Work in Hebei Province). Shijiazhuang: Hebei renmin chubanshe, 1994.

Dangdai Zhongguo lishi weiyuanhui, ed. *Dangdai Zhongguo de shenpan gongzuo* (Trial Work in Contemporary China). Beijing, Dangdai zhongguo chubanshe, 1993.

Gao Mingxuan, ed. *Xin zhongguo xingfa lifa wenxian ziliao* (Documents on Criminal Legislation in the New China: Volume 1). Beijing: Renmin gongan daxue chubanshe, 1998.

Gonganbu zhengce falu yanjiushi, ed. *Zhifa shouce: daji xingshi fanzui zhuanji* (Vol. 4) (Law Enforcement Manual: Combating crime). Beijing: Qunzhong chubanshe, 1984.

Gonganbu zhengzhi bu, eds. *Yanzhong baoli fanzui anli pingxi* (Critique and Analysis of Violent Criminal Cases). Beijing: Qunzhong chubanshe, 1998.

Guo Daohui, ed. *Dangdai faxue zhengming shilu* (Records of Contentious Issues in Contemporary Jurisprudence). Changsha: Hunan chubanshe, 1998.

Guo Jisheng, ed. *Fayuan guanli gailun* (Outline of Court Management). Beijing: Renmin fayuan chubanshe, 1992.

Guo Xingguo, ed. *Jianguo yilai gongan gongzuo dashi yaolan* (An Outline of the Chronicles of Public Security Work Since Liberation). Beijing: Qunzhong chubanshe, neibu faxing, 2003.

Han Yanlong, ed. *Zhonghua renmin gongheguo fazhi tongshi* (A Comprehensive History of the Legal System in the People's Republic of China). Beijing: Zhonghua zhongyang dangxiao chubanshe, 1998.

He Bingsong, ed. *Heishehui fanzui jiedu* (Explanations of Organized Crime). Beijing: Zhongguo jiancha chubanshe, 2003.

He Weifang. "Tongguo sifa shixian shehui zhengyi." (Achieving Justice through the Criminal Justice System) Pp. 212–87 in *Zouxiang quanli de shidai* (Towards an Age of Rights: A Perspective on Civil Rights Development in China), edited by Xia Yong. Beijing: Zhongguo zhengfa daxue chubanshe, 1995.

Hou Honglin. *Xingshi zhengce de jiazhi fenxi* (An Analysis of Criminal Justice Policy Values) Ph.D. dissertation. Beijing: Zhongguo zhengfa daxue yanjiushengyuan, Zhongguo zhengfa daxue, 2004.

Huang Xiangqing. "Yanda xingshi zhengce de zhangwo." (Understanding Yanda Criminal Policy) *Zhengzhi yu falu* (Politics and the Law) 7 (2001): 23–26.

Kang Shuhua. *Dangdai zhongguo fanzui zhuti* (Key Crimes in Contemporary China). Beijing: Qunzhong chubanshe, 2005.

Lan Quanpo. *Qishi nian falu yaolan* (Outline of Seventy Years of Law). Beijing: Falu chubanshe, 1997.

Li Yuanhe and Tianmin Yu. "Yanda xingshi zhengce yu xingfa cailiang." (Yanda criminal justice policy and the range of punishment within the law) *Renmin sifa* (People's Justice) 5 (2003): 38–40.

Li Zhongxin. *Heishehui xingzhi fanzui wenti yanjiu* (Research Issues on Mafia-style Organized Crime). Beijing: Zhongguo renmin gongan daxue chubanshe, 2000.

Lian Shanggang, ed. *Ban'an guifan* (Standards for Case Management). Beijing: Renmin fayuan chubanshe, 1995.

Liang Guoqing, ed. *Xin Zhongguo sifa jieshi daquan* (Anthology of Judicial Interpretations in the New China). Beijing: Zhongguo jiancha chubanshe, 1994.

Liang Guozhen, ed. *Luoding gonganzhi* (Annals of Public Security Work in Luoding). Luoding: neibu ziliao, 1997.

Lin Hua, ed. *Zhongguo falu jichu* (The Foundations of Chinese Law). Guangzhou: Zhongshan daxue chubanshe, 1992.

Liu Shangyu, ed. *Heishehui fanzui yu duice* (Organized Crime and Police Countermeasures). Beijing: Qunzhong chubanshe, 1997.

Liu Xinsheng, ed. *Xuzhou gonganzhi* (Annals of Public Security Work in Xuzhou). Xuzhou: neibu faxing, 1994.

Ning Yuce, ed. *Qingxu fayuan baogao* (Report on Qingxu Court). Nanchang: neibu faxing, 1998.

Peng Ke, ed. *Xingfaxue zixue kaoshi dagang* (An Outline of Criminology for Self-Study). Beijing: Beijing daxue chubanshe, 1992.

Qian Hui and Bi Jianlin, eds. *Zhongguo renmin gongheguo fazhi dashiji* (Chronicle of Events of the Legal System of the People's Republic of China). Changchun: Jilin renmin chubanshe, 1992.

Qiu Chuangjiao, ed. *Yunnan shenpanzhi* (Annals of Trial Work in Yunnan). Kunming: Yunnan renmin chubanshe, 1996.

Renmin fayuan nianjian bianji weiyuanhui, ed. *Renmin fayuan nianjian 1990* (Yearbook of the People's Courts: 1990). Beijing: Xinhua chubanshe, 1993.

———, eds. *Renmin fayuan nianjian 1991* (Yearbook of the People's Courts: 1991). Beijing: Xinhua chubanshe, 1994.

Shenyang gonganju diaocha yanjiushi (Annals of Shenyang Public Security Bureau Investigation Research). Shenyang: neibu ziliao, 1988.

Sichuansheng jianyangxian gonganzhi lingdaozu, ed. *Sichuansheng Jianyangxian gonganzhi* (Annals of Public Security Work in Jianyang County, Sichuan Province). Chengdu: neibu ziliao, 1987.

Song Zhansheng, ed. *Zhongguo gongan baike quanshu* (Encyclopedia of Public Security in China). Changchun: Jilin renmin chubanshe, 1990.

Su Huiyu and Sun Wanhuai. "Yanda fangzhen de xingshi faxue sikao." (A Reflection on the Jurisprudential Aspects of Yanda Policy) *Faxue* (Jurisprudence) 1 (2001): 26–32.

Sun Guoyang. "Xingshi yitihua shiyexia yanda de lixing sikao." (A Reflection on Implementing an Integrated Vision of Criminal Justice work in Yanda Campaigns) *Jiangsu jinggong xueyuan xuebao* (Journal of the Jiangsu Police Academy) 4 (2004): 997–102.

Tianjin fayuan gongzuo dashiji (Annals of Tianjin Court Work). Tianjin: neibu ziliao, 1986.

Wang Mingliang. *Yanda de lixing pingjia* (A Rationale Appraisal of Yanda). Beijing: Beijing daxue chubanshe, 2004.

Wang Wenyuan. "Yanda shiyi." (Clearing up Some Doubts about Yanda) *Shehui* (Society) 5 (2005): 46.

Wang Zhimin and Zhao Ruigang, eds. *Yanhai diqu gonggong anquan fazhan zhanyue* (Developing Strategies for Public Security in Coastal Regions). Beijing: Qunzhong chubanshe, 1989.

Wang Zhongfang, ed. *Zhongguo shehui zhian zonghe zhili lilun yu shijian* (The Theory and Practice of China's Comprehensive Management of Public Order). Beijing: Qunzhong chubanshe, 1989.

Wu Jianqiang and Cao Yi, eds. *Zhongguo heishehui zuzhi fanzui wenti yanjiu* (Research on Issues Related to Organized Crime in China). Beijing: Gongan daxue chubanshe, 2005.

Wu Lei, ed. *Zhongguo sifa zhidu* (China's Judicial System). Beijing: Renmin daxue chubanshe, 1992.

Wu Shanglin, ed. *Miyang xianzhi* (Annals of Miyang County). Henan: neibu faxing, 1994.

Xingshi susongfa jiaocheng bianxiezu, ed. *Xingshi susongfa jiaocheng* (A Course in Criminal Procedural Law). Beijing: Qunzhong chubanshe, 1991.

Xining gonganju, ed. *Xining gonganzhi* (Annals of Public Security Work in Xining). Qinghai: neibu faxing, 1994.

Yanda douzheng yu shehui zhian ganbu duben (Readings on the Strike Hard Campaign and Comprehensive Management of Public Order). Beijing: Zhonggong zhongyang dangxiao chubanshe, 2001.

Yang Hegao, ed. *Zhongguo falu sixiangshi* (A History of Legal Thought in China). Beijing: Beijing daxue chubanshe, 1991.

Yang Shi and Li Ran. "Yifa congzhong congkuai de laili." (The Origins of "Severity and Swiftness in Accordance with the Law") Pp. 277–84 in *Zhongguo dangdai faxue zhengmin shilu* (Records of Contentious Issues in Contemporary Jurisprudence), edited by Guo Daohui, et al. Changsha: Hunan renmin chubanshe, 1998.

Yao Yunhui, et al., eds. *Xinshiqi fanzui gaizao yanjiu* (Studies on Criminal Rehabilitation in the New Age). Beijing: Qunzhong chubanshe, 1991.

Zhang Peitian and Zhang Hua. *Jinxiandai zhongguo shenpan jiancha zhidu de yanbian* (Changes in the Modern and Contemporary System of Trial and Prosecution in China). Beijing: Zhengfa daxue chubanshe, 2004.

Zhao Bingzhi, ed. *Xingshi fazhi fazhan yanjiu* (Research Reports on Developments in Criminal Law). Beijing: Gongan daxue chubanshe, 2004.

Zhao Xichen. "Yanda zhengzhi douzheng lilun yu shijian yantaohui zongshu." (Summary Report of Views on the Theory and Practice of Yanda) *Faxue Luntan* (Legal Forum) 17, no. 4 (2002): 92–93.

Zhao Ying, ed. *Guizhou shenpanzhi* (Annals of Trial Work in Guizhou). Guiyang: Guizhou renmin chubanshe, 1999. Zhao Rixin, ed. *Liaoning shenpanzhi*. Neibu chugao (Draft document for internal circulation).

Zhao Yuezeng. "Jianchi Yanda fangzhen, shenhua yanda zhengzhi douzheng." (Maintain Yanda Policy and Deepen the Impact of the Campaign) *Gongan yanjiu* (Public Security Research) 8 (2001): 41–43.

Zhao Zhenjiang. *Zhongguo fazhi sishi nian* (Forty years of China's Legal System). Beijing: Beijing daxue chubanshe, 1990.

Zhonggong fujiansheng zhengfa weiyuanhui and Zhonggong fujiansheng zhengce yanjiusuo, eds. *Shehui zhian zonghe zhili zhengce fagui (huibian)* (Laws and Policies Relating to the Comprehensive Management of Public Order). Beijing: Qunzhong chubanshe, 1992.

Zhongguo gongan nianjian bianjibu, eds. *Zhongguo gongan nianjian 2001* (Yearbook of Public Security in China). Beijing: Qunzhong chubanshe, 2001.

Zhongguo shehui zhian zonghe zhili nianjian 1991–1992 (Yearbook of Comprehensive Management of Public Order in China: 1991–1992). Beijing: Falu chubanshe, 1996.

———. *1993–1994* (Yearbook of Comprehensive Management of Public Order in China: 1993–1994). Beijing: Falu chubanshe, 1997.

———. *1995–1996* (Yearbook of Comprehensive Management of Public Order in China: 1995–1996). Beijing: Falu chubanshe, 1998.

———. *1997–1998* (Yearbook of Comprehensive Management of Public Order in China: 1997–1998). Beijing: Chang'an chubanshe, 2000.

———. *1999–2000* (Yearbook of Comprehensive Management of Public Order in China: 1999–2000). Beijing: Chang'an chubanshe, 2002.

———. *2001–2002* (Yearbook of Comprehensive Management of Public Order in China: 2001–2002). Beijing: Chang'an chubanshe, 2003.

———. *2003* (The Comprehensive Management of Public Order Yearbook for China 2003). Beijing: Zhongguo changan chubanshe, 2004.

Zhongguo sifa zhidu ziliao xuanbian bianjizu, ed. *Zhongguo sifa zhidu ziliao xuanbian* (Selected Materials on the Judicial System in China). Beijing: Renmin fayuan chubanshe, 1991.

Zhongyang zhengfawei yanjiushi, ed. *Jianlai jianquan yanda jingchangxing gongzuo tizhi diaoyan wenji* (Reports on the Work System for Establishing the Regularization of Yanda into Everyday Police Work). Beijing: Changan chubanshe, 2004.

Zhou Zhenxiang and Shao Jingchun, eds. *Xin Zhongguo fazhi jianshe 40 nian yaolan* (Outline of Forty years of the Construction of the Legal System in the New China). Beijing: Qunzhong chubanshe, 1990.

Zhu Guozhi, ed. *Shenpan guanli caozuo guifan* (Operational standards for trial management). Jilin: Renmin fayuan chubanshe, 1995.

Zhuang Huining. "Renmin fayuan zai yanda zhengzhizhong tuilian duiwu." (The People's Courts' Training of Contingents for Yanda) *Liaowang xinwen zhoukan* (*Outlook News Weekly*) 33 (2001): 30–31.

Zou Xianchao, ed. *Ningxia shenpanzhi* (Annals of Trial Work in Ningxia). Yinchuan: Ningxia renmin chubanshe, 1998.

Zuigao fayuan xingshi shenpan diyiting, ed. *Xingshi shenpan shouce* (Handbook on Criminal Trials). Beijing: Renmin fayuan chubanshe, 1989.

Zuigao fayuan yanjiushi, ed. *Renmin fayuan wunian gaige gangyao* (Outline of the Five Years Reform Plan for the People's Courts). Beijing: Renmin fayuan chubanshe, 2000.

Zuigao renmin fayuan guanli gongzuo shouce bianxuanbu, ed. *Renmin fayuan guanli gongzuo shouce* (Handbook of People's Court Work Management). Beijing: Renmin fayuan chubanshe, 1998.

Zuigao renmin fayuan renmin fayuan guanli gongzuo shouce bianxiezu, eds. *Renmin fayuan guanli gongzuo shouce* (Handbook of Court Management Work). Beijing: Renmin fayuan chubanshe, 1998.

Zuigao renmin jianchayuan gongsuting and gonganbu xingshi jianchaju, eds. *Yanli daji weihai shehui zhixu fanzui: falu shiyong zhidao* (A Guide to the Application of Laws to Sternly Combat Crimes Endangering Social Order). Beijing: Zhongguo jiancha chubanshe, 2002.

Zuo Weimin and Zhou Changyun. *Bianqian yu gaige fayuan zhidu xiandaihua yanjiu* (Research on the Changes and Reforms in the Modernization of the Court System). Beijing: Falu chubanshe, 2000.

Index

About the Author

Susan Trevaskes is a research fellow in the Griffith Asia Institute, Griffith University, Brisbane, Australia. Her research interests are in the areas of criminal justice, punishment, and courts in China. She has published in a variety of journals including *The British Journal of Criminology*, *Punishment and Society*, *The Australian and New Zealand Journal of Criminology*, *China Information*, and *Asian Survey*, in the areas of contemporary Chinese criminal court history, shame punishment, and campaign-style criminal justice practices in China. As part of her Australian Research Council Fellowship, she is currently working on her second book in the area, an examination of state responses to serious crime in twenty-first-century China.

www.ingramcontent.com/pod-product-compliance
Lightning Source LLC
LaVergne TN
LVHW101446200926
848483LV00001B/68

* 9 7 8 0 7 3 9 1 1 9 8 7 7 *